Built on the Ruins of Empire

Built on the Ruins of Empire

British Military Assistance and

African Independence

Blake Whitaker

UNIVERSITY PRESS OF KANSAS

Published by the University Press of Kansas (Lawrence, Kansas 66045), which was
organized by the Kansas Board of Regents and is operated and funded by Emporia
State University, Fort Hays State University, Kansas State University, Pittsburg State
University, the University of Kansas, and Wichita State University.

Library of Congress Cataloging-in-Publication Data

Names: Whitaker, Blake, author.
Title: Built on the ruins of empire : British military assistance and
  African independence / Blake Whitaker.
Description: Lawrence : University Press of Kansas, 2022. | Series: Modern
  war studies | Includes bibliographical references and index.
Identifiers: LCCN 2021038338
  ISBN 9780700633128 (cloth)
  ISBN 9780700633135 (ebook)
Subjects: LCSH: Africa—History, Military—20th century. | Military
  assistance, British—Africa. | Great Britain—Foreign relations—Africa.
  | Africa—Foreign relations—Great Britain. | Decolonization—Africa—
  History—20th century. | Great Britain—Race relations—History—
  20th century. | Africa—Colonial influence—History—20th century. |
  Africa—History—Autonomy and independence movements.
Classification: LCC DT32.7 .W48 2022 | DDC 355/.0326094109045—dc23
LC record available at https://lccn.loc.gov/2021038338.
British Library Cataloguing-in-Publication Data is available.

Printed in the United States of America

10 9 8 7 6 5 4 3 2 1

For

Avery, Alexander, and Danielle

CONTENTS

ACKNOWLEDGMENTS

As most books are, this one was a long journey with many obstacles along the way. Were it not for the support and advice of so many people, this book would never have been published. I have to thank the faculty of the Texas A&M University Department of History. I learned so much of what I know about being a historian and an author from R. J. Q. Adams. The days that I spent in Kraków with the late Arnold Krammer made me believe that I had the potential to become a historian. Jeff Crane encouraged me to pursue serious scholarship. Generous funding from the Department of History made research trips to the National Library of South Africa and the National Archives at Kew possible.

Throughout the research and writing process, I subjected friends and colleagues to long discussions of the intricacies of military training missions in Africa. Many of these conversations and perspectives led me to a deeper and more nuanced understanding of the subject. I will be forever grateful to Nathaniel Weber, Dan Johnson, Ron Kinser, Mercedes Pingeton, and Nadia Shoeb for challenging me intellectually. I owe a particular debt of gratitude to Aaron Linderman, who has provided encouragement and sound counsel at every juncture in this process. My most passionate advocates have been my family. My mom and dad always pushed me to challenge myself. My wife, Danielle, has reviewed my work, encouraged me to persevere in the face of setbacks and rejection, and insisted that this book was worth pursuing. Without her, I would never have made it this far.

ABBREVIATIONS

AFZ	Air Force of Zimbabwe
ANC	African National Congress
APs	assembly points
BIA	British Indian Army
BMATT	British Military Advisory and Training Team
BSAC	British South Africa Company
BSAP	British South Africa Police
CAF	Central African Federation
CAR	Central African Rifles
CMF	Commonwealth Monitoring Force
CMT	compulsory military training
EAC	East Africa Command
EADC	East African Defence Committee
EALF	East Africa Land Forces
FCO	Foreign and Commonwealth Office
FRELIMO	Frente de Libertação de Moçambique
GOC	general officer commanding
JHC	Joint High Command
JLC	Junior Leader Company
KAR	King's African Rifles
KR	Kenya Regiment
MOD	Ministry of Defence
MPLA	Movimento Popular de Libertação de Angola–Partido do Trabalho
NCO	noncommissioned officer
NPTS	Native Police Training School
NRANC	Northern Rhodesia African National Congress
NRP	Northern Rhodesia Police
NRR	Northern Rhodesia Regiment
OAU	Organisation of African Unity
OSB	Officer Selection Board
R&N Army	Royal and Nyasaland Army
RAR	Rhodesian African Rifles
RENAMO	Resistência Nacional Moçambicana

RF	Rhodesian Front
RhSAS	Rhodesian Special Air Service
RLI	Rhodesian Light Infantry
RMA	Royal Military Academy–Sandhurst
RRAF	Royal Rhodesian Air Force
RSF	Rhodesian Security Forces
SADF	South African Defence Force
SFA	Security Force Auxiliaries
SOFA	status of forces agreement
SSC	Short Service Commission
TA	Territorial Army
TF	Territorial Force
UDI	Unilateral Declaration of Independence
UNIP	United National Independence Party
WO	War Office
ZAF	Zambian Air Force
ZANC	Zambian African National Congress
ZANLA	Zimbabwe African National Liberation Army
ZANU	Zimbabwe African National Union
ZANU-PF	Zimbabwe African National Union–Patriotic Front
ZAPU	Zimbabwe African People's Union
ZIPA	Zimbabwe Peoples' Army
ZIPRA	Zimbabwe Peoples' Revolutionary Army
ZNA	Zimbabwe National Army

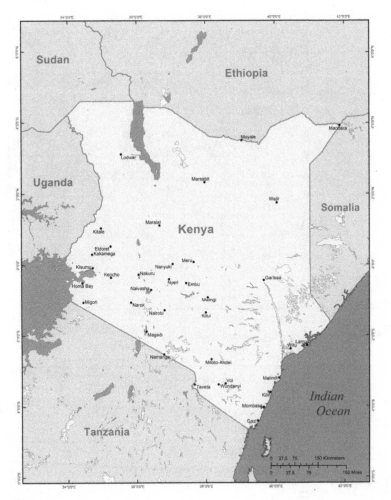

Kenya

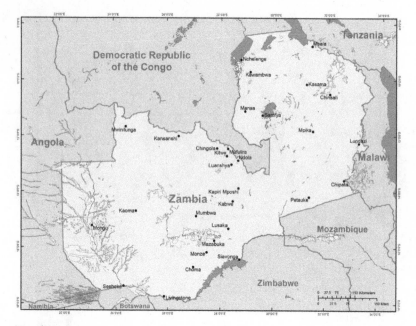

Zambia

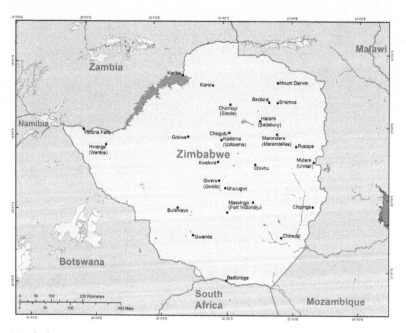

Zimbabwe

Introduction

Modern Zimbabwe made a dramatic debut on the world's stage fifteen years after the Unilateral Declaration of Independence (UDI) by the white settler community in 1965. Tens of thousands of people attended a midnight ceremony, presided over by the Prince of Wales, where the British flag was lowered for the last time, relegating Rhodesia to the annals of history and giving birth to the new nation of Zimbabwe. The end of ninety years of colonial rule in the last British colony in Africa was cause for celebration among African and British leaders alike. President Robert Mugabe's new government held great promise for the future. After all, Mugabe was a highly educated and well-respected leader. The Commonwealth Monitoring Force (known as Operation AGILA) supervised the elections and deemed them free and fair. After the conclusion of Operation AGILA, a British military training team tasked with creating the new Zimbabwe National Army (ZNA) deployed to Zimbabwe.

By February 1981, elements of the newly created ZNA mutinied against the government and were defeated by what had formerly been the Rhodesian Army's First Battalion, Rhodesian African Rifles.[1] Only a few months later, Mugabe's regime began training a new brigade of the Zimbabwean military. Unlike other units of the ZNA, it operated outside of the normal chain of command and reported directly to Mugabe. The unit, trained by the North Korean Army, had the express purpose of suppressing political opposition to the Shona-dominated Zimbabwe African National Union–Patriotic Front (ZANU-PF) government. This notorious unit, simply called the Fifth Brigade, deployed to the ethnic minority homeland of Matabeleland in January 1983 to stamp out political opposition.[2] What followed, Robert Mugabe called the Gukurahundi, "the early rain that washes away the chaff before the spring rain." The Fifth Brigade and other elements of the ZNA killed, raped, and burned their way through Matabeleland until 1988. In the process, they killed at least ten thousand civilians and secured a one-party state for Robert Mugabe and ZANU.[3]

The use of military power in an African state to secure control is not, in itself, unusual. In this case the British government not only was actively involved in training the ZNA but also was attempting to create a professional, Western-style army that remained aloof from domestic politics. The British government's involvement in Africa after the end of colonialism was often defined by the presence of military training teams or military advisers. Additionally, it was often teams of military trainers that went to assist newly independent nations during their first few years of self-government.

The military involvement of British forces in Africa since 1945 took a number of forms. In some places it was rather innocuous, as in the 1960 defense agreement with Nigeria, which allowed Britain overflights as well as military access to ports.[4] In other areas it was a much more pronounced presence, such as the 1964 army mutinies in Kenya, Uganda, and Tanzania in which British forces were called in to restore order.[5] Compared with the involvement of the French in postcolonial Africa, this all seems rather small in scale. The French Army still maintains bases in several African nations, including two large bases in Gabon and Djibouti, and a three-hundred-man force in Senegal at the Center for Military Cooperation. However, British military training teams, while not glamorous and seldom in the public eye, played an extremely important role in creating the military culture of the newly independent African states.

By 1980, the British had trained soldiers in Kenya, Zambia, Uganda, Tanzania, and many other African nations. They had accrued more than twenty years of institutional knowledge, and yet the last British colony to achieve independence is one of the least democratic in Africa. Not only were the British unable to impart a tradition of respecting democratic norms, but the British model of military organization and training had fallen out of use by the 1990s. Additionally, only a few short years after independence the Zimbabwean government had drifted almost completely away from Britain and the West to embrace China, North Korea, and the nonaligned powers as their closest allies.

The foundation on which a military force is built often defines how it will interact with the government and people that it is intended to serve. During the English Civil War of the seventeenth century, Parliament raised an army and filled its ranks with disciplined, professional soldiers who advanced based on merit. The commanders of this "New Model Army" intended that its officers and men would understand what they were fighting for and commit to those ideas. In the modern era, the tenets on which the New Model Army was founded are the same ones that democratic states hope to instill in their soldiers. Additionally, these same tenets of professionalism, separation from politics, and dedication to the principles of the state guide British military training. This is not simply limited to the training given to British soldiers when they enter Her Majesty's Forces, but the training that British military advisers have attempted to perpetuate around the world, particularly in former British colonies.

Armies in Anglophone Africa were formed from the respective colonial regiments of the territory. Each of these colonial regiments maintained a unique culture and history that constitute the foundation of the British regimental system. This was reinforced by the fact that many African colonial soldiers served out their entire careers in the same regiment, if not the same battalion. The development, wartime experiences, and purpose of these colonial military units were extremely influential in the type, size, and character of the newly formed African armies. The nature of the colonial forces and the level of development they had already undergone also influenced the level of involvement of a British training team.

The African liberation wars of the 1950s and 1960s were over long before Zimbabwe became independent, and by 1979 the only remaining colonial relics were Rhodesia, South Africa, and Namibia. In many ways, the situation in Rhodesia was viewed as another battlefront of the global Cold War between communism and the West. Rhodesia was also one of the last bastions of the colonial system that refused to accept the fact that the days of empire had passed. In his memoirs the Rhodesian leader Ian Smith wrote, "It was not surprising that the sons of these pioneers were more British than the British. That is how we were all brought up and taught to live."[6] It was this very attachment to Britishness and the idea of Rhodesian exceptionalism that fed the delusion that the settlers' bid for independence could survive.

The colonial arrangement in Rhodesia depended on government use of coercive powers against the Indigenous population. At the outset of the colonial period, settlers used their technological advantages to overpower African rulers. By the twentieth century, Europeans needed to establish regular military units to perform internal security functions and, secondarily, frontier defense functions. This was not a situation unique to Rhodesia; settlers across the African continent found that while in most cases paramilitary police forces were sufficient, they were not prepared to deal with mass unrest or the threat of military force from other colonial powers.[7]

The scholarship on colonial soldiering and military assistance has grown but it often still focuses on some of the more famous colonial units, namely, the King's African Rifles and the Tirailleurs Senegalais. Studies of the French use of African soldiers are numerous; the interest in French colonial troops could be attributed to the peculiarities of the French system, which involved conscription of Africans. The early French use of African soldiers for imperial service to help conquer other territories was markedly different from the strategies employed by other imperial powers.[8]

The examination of the experiences of African soldiers in anglophone Africa has generally focused on East and West Africa. Additionally, these studies seldom devote any significant time to the transitional period between colonialism and independence. Some of the latest works dealing with the King's African Rifles have done an excellent job of exploring the role of the regiment in the colonial world, but they also explored the reasons that many African men had for serving in the military. While the concept of martial races migrated to Africa from the British Indian Army, it became widely accepted throughout British Africa that only some ethnic groups in a given colony were "warrior peoples."[9] The conditions of colonial military service were always rife with inequality, though for many years African soldiers were unaware of their unequal status because they seldom served in areas where they were exposed to the conditions of service of European rank-and-file soldiers. The experiences of African soldiers during World War II exposed them to the fact that European troops were also required to do fatigue work and were not invincible in combat. These experiences led to a change in the view of service by Africans and were a contributing factor to the East African mutinies that rocked several newly independent nations in 1964.[10]

In South Africa the issue was resolved by the end of the First World War. The Cape Corps was the only armed nonwhite regiment to serve in the conflict, and after it mustered out of service there were no other armed African forces in the South African security establishment until 1973.[11] Nonetheless, there were some significant reasons for oppressed minorities to seek out employment in the military force of the oppressor. Economic conscription was the National Party policy of keeping Africans in such a dire economic position that the reluctance to oppress one's fellow Africans was overcome by granting some measure of economic advantage not otherwise easily available.[12] Similarly, in the colonies that became Kenya, Zambia, and Zimbabwe, military service was a way to support a family in a place the provided few opportunities for black Africans to advance.[13]

While the colonial forces of all African colonies went through some sort of training period and transition with British forces, the colonies that had significant European settler communities most closely reflect the situation in Zimbabwe. The bloody Mau Mau Emergency defined the Kenyan independence struggle that ended in 1963. While the post-1945 era of the British Empire was punctuated by the independence of India in 1947 and the unrest in Palestine and the independence of Israel in 1948, Clement Attlee had other plans for the British colonies in Africa. Although he was very much the anti-imperialist with regard to the Asian empire, Attlee and some in his cabinet regarded the sub-Saharan African colonies as India's replacement in the empire. Additionally, Kenya itself was envisioned as a basing area to forward deploy both troops and resources.[14] After significant discussion in the cabinet and the War Office, however, it was decided that Kenya was just too far away from the Middle East to be a suitable location for a Middle East command headquarters or pre-positioning location.[15]

The War Office was concerned about the postwar cost of imperial defense and did not want to shoulder the burden of garrisoning regular forces all over the empire, particularly in the wake of the massive war debt that Britain faced. Local African troops were utilized for territorial defense, as well as internal security operations. European territorial units could be called up in the event of an emergency. Additionally, the Kenya Police had acquired a significant amount of experience in internal security operations and were, up to a certain point, equipped to handle outbreaks of violence and protest. The Kenya Colony defense establishment was put to the test during the Mau Mau Emergency. The state of emergency and the massive amount of resources that were required to undertake a counterinsurgency operation in Kenya made leaders in Britain question the wisdom of retaining it as a colony. The uprising, which began in mid-1952, required the deployment of regular army units, a call-up of territorial forces, the creation of reserve police forces, and significant Royal Air Force contributions for the next four years. The state of emergency lasted until 1960, yet the stage had been set for independence; by 1963, independence had come to Kenya.[16]

The Africanization program in the East African Land Forces began in earnest in 1960. Well past independence, these forces continued to have white officers seconded from the British Army or on short-term contracts with the host governments until local officers were trained to take their places. The main force in Kenya, the King's African Rifles, was created in 1902; it distinguished itself in both world wars, as well as in the Mau Mau Emergency. The Kenyan battalions of this regiment served as the foundation for the Kenyan Defense Force. The training mission in Kenya was somewhat easier than in other colonies. East African Land Forces had a significant presence in Kenya for many years. There were many training areas available and a large number of British personnel already available to train, mentor, and lead the new African force through the transition to independence.

Even so, the British learned a significant number of lessons from this experience related to selecting trainees, recruitment, officer production, and the importance of organic supporting arms. This was particularly true after the East African army mutinies of 1964. This experience had a significant impact on the way the training mission in Zambia proceeded after the country achieved independence in 1964.

Zambia's path to independence, while not as bloody as Kenya's, was also complicated by a powerful European settler community. Northern Rhodesia became Zambia only a short time after Kenya gained independence, and the establishment of the military in the former colony took many of its cues from the situation in Kenya. The majority of the training and Africanization of the forces in Zambia took place after independence. The large European settler community and its place in the Central African Federation (CAF) delayed the course of independence in Zambia. As it had been in Kenya, the goal of the British was to create a military force that would protect the democratic process and subordinate itself to civilian control.

The early 1950s brought significant political change to the colony. The Northern Rhodesia African National Congress was founded in 1948. At the same time, Roy Welensky, future prime minister of the CAF (along with other settlers), campaigned to secure a federation with the more conservative Southern Rhodesia. The victory of the Conservative Party in Britain in 1951 and the return of Winston Churchill to the prime minister's office reduced the chance that African opinion would be considered when deciding the future of the colony.[17] The creation of a federation in central Africa served a variety of British political interests. Since 1948, the prospect of Afrikaner domination in southern and central Africa had concerned the British government, especially since the National Party in South Africa had drifted closer and closer to republicanism. The Conservative government felt that a CAF with a strong British identity was an excellent counterbalance to the growing power of Pretoria.[18]

The British government was very clear that it would never allow the colony of Northern Rhodesia to merge with the self-governing Southern Rhodesia. The idea of a federation of the two with the addition of Nyasaland, however, was an acceptable compromise.[19] The three territories joined together as the Federation of Rhodesia and Nyasaland in 1953, commonly known as the Central African Federation. All the territorial governments remained intact, with the duties of defense and foreign affairs falling to the federal government in Salisbury.

The Federal Army was made up of forces that had previously composed the Southern Rhodesia Army and those British colonial forces stationed in North Rhodesia and Nyasaland. The CAF was fraught with problems of jurisdiction and financial responsibility. There were three territorial governments, a federal government, and the British government involved in this endeavor; at the simplest of times the lines of communication and authority were confusing. The federal government supported British actions in Suez and always offered up units of the Federal Army and Air Force to be liable for worldwide service in support of British interests.

The willingness of the federal government to be involved in British expeditions around the world encouraged British defense assistance to the CAF military. The air force was modernized and received Canberra bombers, C-47 transports, Vampire fighters, and Hawker Hunter fighter-bombers. The influx of technologically advanced aircraft made the Air Force one of the most modern in Africa. At the same time, the Federal Army grew in size. Previously, the force had been composed primarily of African regulars led by white officers; in 1961, an all-white regular infantry regiment was formed to complement the all-white territorial force.

The independence of Ghana in 1957 and the attitude of Harold Macmillan's government brought change to Africa. During the 1960s, seventeen African colonies achieved independence and a number of others were in the closing stages of independence negotiations. When Macmillan became prime minister in January 1957, he presided over a bruised and bloodied Conservative Party. Decolonization in West Africa was relatively straightforward. Ghana was already set to achieve independence later that year, and the lack of European settlers in the region made the issue comparatively simple. East Africa and Central Africa, with their large settler populations, posed more of a challenge.

While Macmillan believed that dispensing with the empire did not equate to Britain sacrificing its position as a world power, he was not in any hurry to give independence to African colonies. He had witnessed the difficulties that the French had in both Indochina and Algeria and reasoned that fighting insurgencies to maintain colonial possessions cost far too much in terms of both lives and treasure. The prime minister decided to slowly prepare the colonies for independence and attempt to channel the African nationalist movements into the political process rather than suppress them. What complicated the matter even more was the divided nature of the Conservative Party, with its right wing led by the Fifth Marquess of Salisbury, who staunchly supported the settler communities in Africa.[20]

This division led Macmillan to delay action on decolonization until after the general election in 1959 secured his government's position. In 1960, with the election out of the way, Macmillan was able to undertake his grand tour of Africa. The trip took him through both Northern and Southern Rhodesia and ended with his famous "Winds of Change" speech to the South African Parliament in Cape Town.[21] Just before Macmillan's trip to Africa, he formed the Monckton Commission (headed by the lawyer and politician Walter Monckton) to investigate the future of the CAF. When the commission released its findings on 18 October 1960, it was clear that the Central African Federation was finished. The commission recommended that Africans be given equal representation in the Federal Assembly and in the Northern Rhodesia House of Assembly.[22]

Macmillan's plan for both Northern Rhodesia and Nyasaland was to see a quickened pace toward independence; the hope was that the nations would be able to rule themselves.[23] Of course, all of this was predicated on the assumption that these newly created nations would join and be active members of the Commonwealth of Nations. Macmillan envisioned the Commonwealth as a sort of informal empire in which the British government would still be able to exert significant political and economic influence over its former colonial possessions. He also had intended to speed up the process of decolonization in 1960, so as not to be upstaged by the French. In 1958, Charles de Gaulle offered the French territories in Africa autonomy within the French community or full independence. Macmillan did not want to risk falling behind the French in world opinion over decolonization.[24]

Elections were held in 1961 to form majority rule governments in Northern Rhodesia and Nyasaland. On 31 December 1963, the federation was dissolved; Zambia and Malawi became independent nations in 1964. The third member of the federation, Southern Rhodesia (simply called Rhodesia after the collapse of the federation), reverted to its status as a self-governing Crown Colony dominated by the European population. The dissolution of the federation had significant implications for the future of Zambia. Even before the declaration of independence, the division of the resources of the Federal Army and Air Force gutted the Zambian defense establishment. The Victoria Falls Conference in December 1963 was convened to plan the breakup of the federation. The major parties represented were the Conservative-led British government and the Southern Rhodesia government. The African leadership of Northern Rhodesia was barred from the process.

It became clear to the Labour Party and the United Nations that the British intention was to transfer the majority of the federation's army and air force into the hands of the Southern Rhodesian government. Although both Labour and the independent African nations protested, the British government planned to move forward with the division. The issue became so pervasive that the Security Council of the United Nations discussed it. A proposed resolution demanded that Britain not transfer to Southern Rhodesia the aircraft and ground forces as outlined in the Victoria

Falls Conference. In the Security Council, the British government felt as though it had only one option. As a result, it used its veto power for the first time since the Suez Crisis in 1956.[25]

Upon independence, Zambia had only twenty-two hundred soldiers and three transport aircraft. European officers led the entire military; at the time of independence there was only one African officer in the force.[26] The Europeans were either local settlers who had taken commissions in the federal forces who agreed to stay on after independence or British officers who were seconded to the Zambians until African officers could be trained. This arrangement, while similar to the plan used in Kenya, had not even begun until after Zambia had achieved independence. A British officer remained the commander of the Zambia Defense Force until the appointment of Colonel Kingsley Chinkuli in 1970. There were significant issues with the employment of the Kenyan training system in Zambia.

Unlike in Zambia, upon Kenyan independence, the process of Africanization had been going on for several years and had been relatively effective. In the post-1945 years, the regiments of the King's African Rifles employed a system of promoting Africans to the rank of effendi, which gave the East African forces a base of trained and experienced African leaders to promote to commissioned rank. An effendi was a governor's commissioned officer; this was a position similar to the viceroy's commissioned officer in the British Indian Army. While these men were not officers in the same sense as someone holding a queen's commission, they wore officers' uniforms and had a separate mess. The one major restriction was that their authority was limited to African troops. There was no such system in place in Zambia, where the highest rank that an African soldier in the Northern Rhodesia Regiment could attain was warrant officer 1. The Zambian government had almost no choice but to rely on European officers until sufficient Africans were trained. This dependence and the coming tensions with white Rhodesia to the south challenged the development of the Zambian military.

The reliance on Europeans proved problematic only a year after independence. In 1965, Southern Rhodesia came to an impasse with the British government over the implementation of majority rule in the colony. The ultra-right-wing Rhodesian Front Party came to power in Salisbury in the election of 1962, on the wave of discontent generated by European population over the transition to majority rule by the northern members of the federation. By November 1965, the Rhodesian Front decided it could no longer negotiate with the British over the issue of independence. On 11 November 1965, the Rhodesian government's Unilateral Declaration of Independence from Britain.

The events of UDI had serious security implications for Zambia. As a landlocked country, Zambia depended on Rhodesia as a trading partner and for access to the sea. Additionally, the possibility of hostilities between the two nations was not out of the question, and British officers seconded to the Zambia Army were not permitted to lead Zambian soldiers into battle in the event of war against the rebel colony. British defense assistance to Zambia put severe restraints on the freedom of action of the Zambian government during this period of crisis. Kenneth Kaunda and his United National Independence Party were bound by British policy on Rhodesia for as long as they continued to accept British security aid.

The drawbacks of the training system in Zambia became evident during this time. The country as a whole was far too reliant on Europeans, even five years after independence, not only in the area of defense but also with regard to the country's largest industry, copper. In 1969 there were still 43,390 European residents of Zambia, and five years later there were still 4,000 Europeans occupying technical and managerial positions in Zambia's mining industry.[27] After the termination of their training agreement by the United National Independence Party (UNIP) government, the British Joint Services Training Team left Zambia in December 1969. The Zambians were not satisfied with the rate of training by the British team (twelve personnel a year) and contracted with the Italian government to provide training for the Zambian Air Force, as well as seconded officers. By this point, the army contingent of the training team had already departed, leaving behind only European officers until Zambians could be trained. These officers remained in the Zambian Defense Force until 7 January 1971, when the last seventeen officers were summarily dismissed from Zambian service in reaction to British arms sales to the South African government and an increasing need for the UNIP to gain control over all aspects of the government.[28]

In many ways, Rhodesia was different from the other British colonies in Africa. When many historians of British Africa write about the colonies, they generally do not include Rhodesia with countries such as Kenya, Northern Rhodesia, or Nigeria.[29] By the 1880s, Cecil Rhodes had made his first fortune in diamonds, been elected to the Cape Parliament, and launched the De Beers Mining Company. While a student at Oriel College, Oxford, Rhodes was influenced by the inaugural lecture of English art critic John Ruskin. The speech painted a romantic image of the British imperial mission around the world, and it inspired Rhodes to make his life's goal "the extension of British rule throughout the world."[30] Rhodes's part in all of this was focused on the British role in Africa and his dream of extending the realm from the Cape of Good Hope to Cairo.[31]

Rhodes was able to secure the mineral rights to what became Rhodesia for twenty-five years.[32] In 1889, the British South Africa Company (BSAC), controlled by Rhodes, was granted a royal charter upon the amalgamation of the Central Search Association and the Exploring Company, Ltd. The BSAC was given control of Rhodesia and used it as the basis for the settlement of Matabeleland. The Pioneer Corps of the BSAC was formed for the settlement of what became Rhodesia. Company rule continued in the colony until 1923, after which time Rhodesia was a self-governing Crown Colony.[33]

Since its establishment under the chartered company, Rhodesia maintained its own security apparatus, largely without the assistance of soldiers from the British Army. From the time the Pioneer Corps left South Africa until 1954, the British South Africa Police trained as paramilitary police in the style of the Royal Irish Constabulary and charged with the territorial defense of the colony.

During the First World War, the colony raised both European and African regiments. The all-European Rhodesia Regiment was formed in 1914 as an infantry unit. During the course of the war, it saw action in the southern part of West Africa and British East Africa. The regiment was disbanded in 1917, after severe casualties seriously impacted the colony's ability to function without resorting to placing Africans in exclusively European military roles. In order to continue to contribute to the war effort and to prevent German forces from invading the colony, the BSAC raised the Rhodesian Native Regiment. While the officers and most of the noncommissioned officers of this unit were European, the rank and file were African. This was the first employment of armed Africans in military service since the use of African auxiliaries during the First Chimurenga War in 1896–1897. The combat record of the unit was held in high esteem by colonial authorities. Even so, it was disbanded with haste in the opening months of 1919.[34]

During the interwar period, the Rhodesian defense establishment reverted to the previous model, with the British South Africa Police responsible for territorial defense. During this time, African constables were, for the most part, not given weapons training. The exception was the Askari Platoon. This unit mounted the ceremonial guard at Government House and maintained the military nature of the force. It was also responsible for training African constables at the Native Police Training School. The troopers in this unit were the only Africans allowed regularly to carry firearms on duty throughout the interwar period.[35]

After responsible government was granted in 1923, the colony maintained a small staff corps of officers to resurrect the armed forces, were it to be required. When World War II began in 1939, the government again announced its intention that Europeans serve as soldiers and Africans only as laborers. Colonial leaders such as Sir Robert Tredgold thought the Rhodesian contribution to the war would be to allow men from the European community to serve as officers in Her Majesty's Forces. By 1940, however, the colonial administration had decided to resurrect an African regiment.[36] The unit was renamed the Rhodesian African Rifles (RAR), and as in World War I, white officers led the African rank and file. In 1944 the unit saw action in Burma against the Japanese and was applauded for its effectiveness. The RAR was demobilized in 1946 and very quickly was resurrected in 1949 as a regular unit of the Rhodesian Army. Between 1949 and UDI in 1965, the regiment served in Suez, in Malaya, along the Congo border, and Nyasaland. By November 1965, the RAR made up half of the Rhodesian Army's regular infantry establishment.

While UDI gave the Rhodesians de facto independence, UN sanctions and British insistence that it was an internal matter prevented any nation from ever officially recognizing its statehood.[37] Shortly after UDI, African liberation movements began to consider how best to combat the Rhodesian Front government. From 1965 until 1980, both the Zimbabwe African National Union (ZANU) and the Zimbabwe African People's Union (ZAPU) sent liberation fighters into Rhodesia in an attempt to overthrow the regime.[38] The most intense phase of the war occurred from 1973 to 1979. During this period the RAR made up a large portion of the military forces of Rhodesia and deployed constantly to operational areas.

By 1979, the government authorized four RAR battalions, totaling thirty-five hundred soldiers.[39]

By 1979, the Rhodesian Front had held out for as long as it could; the events of the 1970s had increasingly handicapped the Rhodesian Security Force's ability to maintain control over the territory. The security situation in the late 1970s was tense and put increasing amounts of strain on the white community simply to supply enough soldiers to keep the war going. By the end of 1976, the National Service period was extended from a year to eighteen months, and by 1978 those who had completed their National Service and were serving in the Territorial Army were mobilized for active service for 190 days a year.[40] The Rhodesian economy could not survive the strain of war for much longer, and Prime Minister Ian Smith and his Rhodesian Front were forced to seek out a political solution to the conflict.

The British general elections of May 1979 brought Conservative Margaret Thatcher to the prime minister's office. Prior to taking office, Thatcher and the Tories laid plans to recognize the Internal Settlement government of Ian Smith and Bishop Able Muzorewa.[41] However, she was convinced of the folly of this policy by her experienced foreign secretary, Peter Lord Carrington. He knew that the recognition of the Muzorewa government would isolate the British government further from the United States and most African nations. After the Commonwealth Heads of Government Meeting in Lusaka in August 1979, the British attempted to mediate a solution to the Rhodesian problem. By December 1979, an agreement was reached for Rhodesia to return to British control for long enough to hold supervised elections to determine how the majority rule government would take shape. The liberation movements conceded that the settler community would retain twenty seats in Parliament until 1986, and there would be no forcible redistribution of land.[42] A draft constitution was worked out during the conference that called for the liberation forces and the Rhodesians to disband their military forces and merge them to create the Zimbabwe National Army.

In December 1979, the rebel colony returned to British control, and the Commonwealth Monitoring Force (CMF) arrived to supervise the elections and the orderly assembly of the guerrilla forces at designated assembly points. After the elections in February 1980, it was a surprise to the European population that Robert Mugabe was the winner. The CMF departed by March 1980, and the mission of the remaining British forces in the country became the creation of the ZNA. The mission was complex and vast; in addition to demobilizing the large guerrilla armies, the CMF had to retrain for conventional warfare and then integrated into a new force to serve with the men of the former Rhodesian Security Forces. The British goal for the project was the same it had been in Kenya and Zambia: to create a professional military force that would help protect the democratic process in Zimbabwe. Sadly, by January 1983 this mission had already failed with the beginning of the deployment of the notorious Fifth Brigade.

In each of these three cases the transition to independence was complicated by the settler communities. This study is meant to analyze the way that the British government attempted to use military assistance to help favorably imprint their norms on these newly independent nations, hoping this would push these former colonies into the British sphere of influence and making them valued members of the Commonwealth, and if not allies in the Cold War, at least sympathetic to the West. The book's chapters are arranged to follow the development of both British military assistance policy and experience in the rapidly changing world. Furthermore, this study lays out the path of declining British resources and prominence in Africa that only became apparent to British policy makers after the fact.

The role of British military culture comes up frequently in the text; in many ways this culture is a character in its own right. While a somewhat amorphous topic, military culture is what provides the basis for the cohesion of military forces. Military professionals unite around very impersonal procedures and drill that they have learned in training.[43] Training itself provides the touchtone for soldiers to operate together and understand each other.[44]

Since 1945 the British government had used the British regimental system and the officer training at the Royal Military Academy–Sandhurst to inculcate overseas students in British military culture and training.[45] Soldiers in Anglophone Africa became immersed in the regimental system during the colonial period; then, after independence, training in Britain continued to emphasize this same type of social and task cohesion. Regimental culture focused on loyalty, leadership, and both an individual and a collective sense of honor. These same lessons were reinforced in the mess and on the athletic field, where lessons and discipline, both informal and formal, were passed on to new members.[46] This culture and these same values were also exported throughout the Commonwealth. British officers from Sandhurst helped establish a large number of military academies throughout the Anglophone world. They were instrumental in the establishment of military academies in India, Pakistan, Ghana, Nigeria, and Malaysia. By the twenty-first century, the most British example of a mid-twentieth-century officers' mess is likely found in Rawalpindi or New Delhi. While military culture alone might not maintain British influence, it ensured that a form of Britishness persisted long after the end of empire.

The first chapter examines the development of the colonial internal security force in Kenya and its transformation and Africanization after independence into the Kenya Army. It also examines the Kenya Army directly after independence and the lessons learned by the British during the East African mutinies of 1964. Chapter 2 discusses the Zambian separation from the white-dominated Central African Federation and how this process complicated the transition to independence and military self-reliance. The third chapter looks at the establishment and organization of the Rhodesian Security Forces and the liberation armies during the Zimbabwean War for Independence. Chapter 4 deals with the end of the conflict and the British planning process for peace and reconstruction in Zimbabwe. It also covers the way the British saw postconflict Zimbabwe developing and the direction they thought the new military should take. The formation of the British Military Advisory and Training Team, as well as its performance and challenges, is discussed in chapter 5. This chapter also looks at the end result of those training efforts, the rise of the dominance of ZANU-PF, and the beginning of the atrocities in Matabeleland in 1983.

Since 1999, the Movement for Democratic Change, the main opposition party in Zimbabwe, asserted that the Mugabe regime relied upon the military to use increasingly coercive force to maintain power. To ensure military loyalty, the ZNA received large salary increases and a significant stake in major national corporations, guaranteeing that the future of most soldiers would be securely tied to the Mugabe regime. The process of winning the loyalty of the army began with its formation and the British role in trying to create a new army of former enemies. In 2017, after thirty-seven years in power, Mugabe was finally unseated by the very force that had secured his grip on power since 1980.

1

The King's African Rifles, Independence, and Mutiny

The King's African Rifles (KAR) holds an iconic place in the iconography of the British Empire. Images of African soldiers in British uniform adorned imperial propaganda from the early twentieth century until the end of the Second World War. While this regiment is undoubtedly famous for its exploits in battle, its role in the formation of independent Africa is less often acknowledged.[1]

The regiment contained battalions from five separate colonies, and upon independence, these units formed the basis of the national armies in their respective territories. Military culture within these units defined the formation of independent armies. In some cases the uniforms and insignia of the KAR changed only slightly after independence. In the case of Tanganyika, Sixth Battalion KAR's (6KAR) name simply changed to the Tanganyika Rifles (Sixth Battalion the King's African Rifles).[2] The creation of the King's African Rifles was the result of the combination of a number of irregular forces raised by various entities in East Africa. The Foreign Office was in charge of British activities in East Africa and gave the various chartered companies and other semiofficial entities a free hand in levying troops and keeping order. In 1888, Frederick Lugard recruited African irregular troops to combat Muslim slave traders in what would become Nyasaland. When the Central African Protectorate was formed in 1891, an African militia that had been used extensively was formalized and became the Central African Rifles (CAR). This unit, like many in early Anglophone Africa, was strengthened by the use of troops from the British Indian Army—in the case of the CAR, this was the 175-man "Sikh Contingent."[3]

The Origins of Military Service in Kenya

In most cases, African soldiers in the nineteenth century and early twentieth century played almost an exclusively internal security role in the colonies where they were established. Early on, however, the CAR was used in an imperial service capacity. The unit was engaged not only in combating the slave trade but also in the conquest of Somaliland and other African territories.[4] The two other units that combined in 1902 to form the KAR were the Uganda Rifles and the East Africa Rifles.[5] On January 1, 1902, the KAR was officially formed with six locally recruited battalions: two in Central Africa, one in East Africa, two in Uganda, and one in Somaliland.[6]

In 1905, the Colonial Office was given full responsibility for the KAR. Under this arrangement, the individual colonies were responsible for funding and administering each battalion. By 1912, all the Indian contingents of the KAR were withdrawn. These soldiers were paid more than their African counterparts and required a special diet that was more expensive than the young colonies could afford. During the early years many civil officials attempted to disband the KAR due to the costs required to support the unit. Although the War Office prevented the disbanding of the KAR battalions, to ensure there were military forces available in Africa in the event of a large war, they were severely downsized in 1913.

World War I saw a huge expansion of the KAR. While British authorities did not consider African solders suitable for the European theater of operations, they did find them very useful in countering the German threat in Africa. By 1916, specialist units of the KAR were formed; African soldiers served as gunners, sappers, signalers, and many other specialists. This was the first time that African soldiers had the opportunity to leave their service in the British Army with more skills and education than when they enlisted.[7] These African soldiers saw service throughout the campaign against German forces under the command of General Paul von Lettow-Vorbeck. Overall, the African troops performed better than many officers in the British high command had expected. Their performance during the war had challenged many of the racist views that British officers had of African troops, particularly the claim that they were unsuitable as frontline troops.

During the years that followed, the KAR was significantly reduced and control was returned to the Colonial Office. However, there was some concern among the European settler community regarding African troops being the only military organization in the colony. Therefore, in 1937, a part-time Territorial Army (TA) unit was formed, called the Kenya Regiment (KR). This regiment was an all-European unit that was intended to provide both officers and noncommissioned officers (NCOs) to the KAR, in case of another large-scale mobilization in wartime. The regiment was also the holding unit for all eighteen-to-twenty-five-year-old European males who underwent compulsory National Service in Kenya.[8] This territorial unit provided enough assurance to calm the concerns of many in the settler community, who felt safer knowing a white military force was available, should the African force prove ineffective or disloyal. At the time of independence these two units made up the majority of the military establishment of Kenya Colony.

World War II was a period of expansion for the Kenyan military establishment. In 1939, the regiment grew from seven infantry battalions to forty-three, roughly thirteen thousand men. In addition to these infantry units, there were a number of specialist and support units formed to support the newly created East Africa Command (EAC). The EAC's first engagements were not fought until 1941, when the British launched the Ethiopian Offensive against the Italians. The campaign was a great success; Ethiopia was taken in only two months. KAR units were also instrumental in taking Madagascar from Vichy-French forces in 1942.[9]

In 1942, the War Office asked the EAC to send one thousand soldiers to assist South East Asia Command in Burma. The EAC eventually sent fifty-five hundred men to fight in Burma. The KAR performed on a level with many of the other British and Indian units that were in theater and also suffered from morale problems that many of these units experienced. During this harsh campaign, the African soldiers were exposed to the regular British military establishment as well as the British Indian Army. This is significant because the British Indian Army had begun a process of Indianization, the commissioning of Indian officers and putting them in command of Indian troops. After seeing other people of the empire placed in positions of leadership, many Africans began to wonder when their time would come. Additionally, African soldiers saw that European privates in the British Army were required to perform the same labor duties as were expected of African troops. The exposure to the British class system was an eye-opening experience for many African men because, for the first time, there existed a population of white men who were expected to fulfill the same duties.[10]

These experiences were particularly formative for one young Kenyan corporal in the KAR. Waruhiu Itote, a Kikuyu man from Nyeri District, joined the KAR in January 1942 and served in the Burma campaign. During his service he met working-class soldiers from England, African American soldiers from the United States, and intellectuals from India.[11] His experiences in the army and the knowledge he gained in intellectual exchanges with his fellow soldiers crystallized his nationalist ideals.

African servicemen performed well during the war in theaters across the world. While the colonial government of Kenya was often eager to downsize and, if possible, do away with the KAR regiments, there were additional concerns after 1945 that had not been present prior to the war. Africans were exposed to liberties and freedoms they never experienced in the colonial environment. There was a certain level of prestige and status achieved by Africans in military service. Their pay was more than competitive with that of their civilian counterparts, and the living conditions were often better than working on a farm or in a mine. These soldiers also had the opportunity to advance their education while in garrison by taking advantage of classes in English, reading, and mathematics offered by the East African Educational Corps. When these men demobilized at the end of the war, many of them wanted to maintain the social advantages that they had achieved. They sought to achieve middle-class employment and lifestyles when they left military service.[12]

It was not an option for many of these African veterans to return to the prewar social arrangement in Kenya. These men intended to redefine the colonial relationships that were in place; interestingly, many of them felt they could do this from within the construct of the colonial system. It was not only the African soldiers who were cognizant of the changes that would occur at home in the postwar colonial world—the colonial administrations were concerned as well. The Kenyan government was concerned that African veterans would not want to return to their traditional homelands and the labor market that existed prior to the conflict. Additionally, authorities were concerned about war veteran involvement in African labor unions, which they thought would further destabilize the colony.[13] While many military commanders who had served with African soldiers thought that the soldiers' sacrifice should have won them an equal

position in society, others in colonial society did not agree. In addition
to the colonial government's opposition to the reintegration of African
soldiers, the settler community was strongly opposed to any changes af-
fecting the labor market. The war years had been immensely profitable
for white Kenyan farmers, and as a result they enjoyed a heightened level
of power in the colony than previously. During the war, the British government had been unable to devote the same amount of attention to the
colonial administration as it had in the past, and the result was that the
settler community filled the void bolstered by its new economic power.[14]

The rising power of the settler community influenced the government's beliefs that the African veterans were destined for the farm labor
market. Accordingly, the Kenya colonial government made very few arrangements to help demobilized African soldiers reintegrate into society.[15]
Not surprisingly, African veterans were eager to raise themselves up from
their prewar status. They set up investing groups and attempted to translate their military skills into skilled laborer positions. While they resisted
being thrown back into the position that the colonial government had
selected for them, they did not do so in the way that many settlers had
feared. Rather than getting involved in African political movements, African veterans often sought to gain the maximum amount of benefits from
the colonial government. They would often wear their decorations in public and were granted permission by colonial authorities to carry spears in
public as a sign of their martial status, a privilege of having served that had
long been dormant.[16] They attempted to change from within the relationship between Africans and the colonial system; unfortunately, this method
of advocacy did not produce results.

Even though the end of World War II brought a great deal of change
to the British Empire, the conditions in Kenya Colony did not change
as dramatically as many Africans had hoped. While the end of the war
brought independence to the largest colony in the empire, India, African
independence was not even on the minds of Clement Attlee's Labour government in 1945. Additionally the units of the KAR that had served in the
war had truly been used as imperial service troops around the world, from
the fighting in Africa to that in the Middle East and Asia. This changed
the way that British military planners saw African forces in the scheme of
imperial defense. The collapse of the Anglo-Egyptian relationship beginning in 1946 led defense planners to look for other areas in which to base

their Middle Eastern forces.[17] Both Kenya and Southern Rhodesia were excellent candidates to be forward bases for British forces. This reconsideration of the position of Kenya in the British defense plan also led to a reconsideration of the KAR simply reverting to an internal security force.

While the military prospects for Kenya were looking up, the economic situation for Africans was much different. Between 1947 and 1954, the Kenyan economy was growing at a rate of 13 percent a year. At the same time, the technological advances made many African workers redundant. Unemployed farmworkers were increasingly moving into shantytowns in cities like Mombasa and Nairobi while European ex-servicemen were immigrating to Kenya to take advantage of very generous settlement terms. The African population of Kenya Colony had anticipated that the end of the war and the rise of the Labour Party in Britain would bring change, yet all it saw was an increase in the power of the European community, both politically and economically.[18]

Kenya Colony was in an odd position among British holdings in Africa; it was not like any of the West African colonies, which were very much black African colonies. Kenya did not have a large enough settler population to be a dominion like South Africa or Southern Rhodesia. It also never had the level of self-government that either Rhodesia or South Africa had and was in a state of constant negotiation with British authorities in London.[19]

After the loss of British bases in India in 1947, the British government decided it was necessary to build a large military complex in Kenya to support the forward staging of military stores and troops. By the end of 1950, however, the British government had decided to stay on in Egypt.[20] Since British forces were going to remain at the extensive base area already present near the Suez Canal, there was no need to spend the funds to duplicate the effort in Kenya. This turn of events would put the burden of security arrangements back on the colony. Even in the case of a large war, Kenyan forces would not play as significant a role as imperial troops. Rather, these forces were charged with the internal and border security of the colony itself.

At the time, the KAR was organized to conduct conventional operations in the event of another war. The mission of the KAR in 1950 was to be available for operations outside of Kenya, as it had performed in World War II. Yet the British government was searching for ways to economize in the realm of colonial defense. In the past this was accomplished by shifting the cost of these units to the individual colonies, but the increasingly complex nature of warfare made colonial units much more costly to maintain. The colonial governments of East Africa could not possibly shoulder the burden. Even so, the British government knew that African troops were far less expensive to maintain than British Army units, so they decided to put the burden of colonial defense completely on colonial forces, with support functions coming from a small collocated cadre of British officers and NCOs.[21]

Even with this reduction in forces in East Africa, the British government considered the colonial forces themselves too expensive. The East Africa High Commission Defence Committee decided to reduce the size of the KAR battalions rather than reduce them in number.[22] The result was that each KAR battalion was reduced from 728 African soldiers to 656 African soldiers. In addition to the question of size, the members debated who should fund these local forces. The colonial governors wanted the War Office to take complete control, while the War Office continued to insist that the colonies needed to shoulder the burden of their own defense. The compromise was the colonies would raise an all-white TA unit along the lines of those in the United Kingdom. The Kenya Regiment, which existed in wartime from 1939 to 1945, was reborn out of this decision.[23]

The revival of an all-European TA unit in Kenya had a detrimental effect on the forward progress of African soldiers in the colonies. When the KR was first raised prior to the Second World War, it was designed to train white officers and NCOs to lead KAR units when a wartime expansion occurred.[24] During World War II the regiment fulfilled this role and it served mainly as a leadership-training unit. When it was revived, it adopted a standard TA infantry unit organization; however, the goal of forming leaders out of every man was still there.

Shortly after the return of the KR, the Kenya Colony Legislative Assembly passed the Compulsory National Service Ordinance of 1951 and the Compulsory Military Training Ordinance of 1951. These laws required all male European British subjects between the ages of eighteen and twenty-three to undergo five and a half months of basic military training followed by four years of service in the KR as a part-time territorial soldier.[25] Young settlers were liable for service not only in the colony but anywhere in the world. In order to bring the KR up to full fighting strength during the emergency, the basic training period was briefly reduced to ten weeks, and then increased to sixteen weeks in 1956. The regiment annually trained an average of 190 new soldiers. This drastically increased the role of European settlers in the defense of the colony. Prior to the revival of the KR, Europeans had been completely reliant on African soldiers for their defense in peacetime.

With the return of the KR, there really was little need to examine the idea of producing African officers for the KAR due to the fact that there was a leadership reserve available in the KR. In 1948 the British government codified peacetime National Service in the National Service Act of 1948. National Service officers were given the option of spending their two-year term in a colonial unit such as the KAR.[26] With primary, secondary, and emergency sources of white officers available to the KAR in the early 1950s, there was no reason for colonial authorities to consider the idea of commissioning African officers into colonial service. At the time, both military and civilian leaders were under the impression that African colonies would not reach independence for many years. The Attlee government planned to develop Africa and raise the standard of living rather than grant the colonies immediate independence.

The development of the Mau Mau movement was the result largely of the accumulation of long-term grievances over landownership among the Kikuyu community within Kenya Colony. The mechanization of post-1945 Kenyan agriculture led to the disposition of large numbers of Kikuyu squatters who had relied on employment in the White Highlands. Additionally, the end of the war brought more European immigration into the colony. Former British servicemen came to the colony and set up their own farming and business operations, often with the assistance of both the British government and the colonial authorities.[27] This new wave of settlement exacerbated the scarcity of available land for African agriculture. The colonial government helped make sure that land was clear for European development. Between 1946 and 1952, roughly a hundred thousand Kikuyu squatters were removed from their homes and "repatriated" to the Native Reserves.[28] The Kikuyu farmers were limited to the opportunities available in the Native Reserves.

The resistance movement began several years before the mass exodus of Kikuyu from their former homes. As early as 1943, some Kikuyu brought back an old tradition of taking oaths in a time of conflict. Unlike the oaths of the past, however, this oath was administered not only to men but also to women. The meaning of the oath, which was a rite of acceptance into a loose anticolonial resistance organization, was different for every oath-taker. The general meaning was that it was for land and freedom, but what that meant was often vague: to some it meant throwing off the British yoke, but to others it represented simply returning to the homes they were expelled from by the British.[29] Regardless, the oath carried a great deal of cultural significance for the Kikuyu that the settler community often failed to understand. By 1945, the practice of oathing had spread throughout Kikuyuland, and by 1948 it had morphed into what became known as the Mau Mau movement.[30]

The Mau Mau uprising dramatically divided Africans in the colony; the Kikuyu community itself was divided between those who supported Mau Mau and those who simply valued the security and stability in their communities and were often pigeonholed as regime loyalists. Daniel Branch asserted that the Mau Mau episode was less a conflict between the state and the Mau Mau rebels and more of a civil war between members of the Kikuyu ethnic group.[31] "Loyalists" were seldom simply Kikuyu who were supporters of the colonial regime; more often they were Kikuyu who opposed Mau Mau or just wanted to make it through the conflict.

Due to all these issues, the soldiers of the KAR made it through the Mau Mau period rather well. The British government did not consider the Kikuyu to be a martial race and therefore seldom recruited from that population. In 1959 the East Africa Land Forces (EALF) reported that Kikuyu, Embu, and Meru men made up only 3.4 percent of the Kenyan KAR Battalions even though they made up 26.9 percent of the Kenyan male population.[32] As a whole the men of the KAR fought well against the insurgents, with only a handful of cases in which the loyalty of African soldiers was called into question. Major H. N. Clemas of the Twenty-Third KAR gave one example of an African NCO whom he suspected had questionable loyalties; the NCO had lost his pistol on a patrol, and later in the campaign the same pistol was found on a captured Mau Mau insurgent.[33] Clemas also made the point that what Kikuyu soldiers there were in the KAR were never held in high regard before the conflict, so there was no reason to believe that military authorities had any confidence in them to begin with.[34]

The former KAR corporal Waruhiu Itote had been transformed by his experience in World War II and took on a leading role in the uprising. He took the nom de guerre of General China and led a band of insurgents in the forests of Mount Kenya. In his memoir of the conflict he discussed the challenges the insurgents faced in acquiring weapons: "One of our main sources of ready-made guns was the KAR. Although the majority had not taken the oath, many of the Wakambe, Lou, Meru, and Embu men had done so, and within the military camps they operated their own secret committees, supplying us with arms, ammunition, and money."[35] Even so, he goes on to say that this was not the case across the KAR, and that large parts of the regiment were openly hostile to the uprising.[36]

The colonial authorities were concerned about African soldiers' support for nationalist elements. To address this, the EALF reestablished a unit that had been disbanded at the end of World War II, 277 Field Security Squadron, which was made up of African soldiers and led by a British intelligence officer. The unit planted African counterintelligence agents in KAR units to monitor them for subversive activity. In 1957, these duties transferred to Special Branch of the Kenya Police, and 277 Field Security Squadron was disbanded. Even so, these security operations continued until Kenya achieved independence in 1963.[37]

While British officers had a certain measure of trust in their soldiers, the soldiers were not able to complete the task of defeating the Mau Mau on their own. Units of the British Army flew in to assist in anti–Mau Mau operations, as were RAF ground-attack aircraft. The colonial government declared a state of emergency, which expanded the role of the settler community in defense of the colony. As mentioned previously, the KR stymied the prospect of Africans being able to achieve commissioned rank in the near future. The KR continued to expand during the emergency and increasingly provided leaders to small detachments of African soldiers tasked with long-range patrolling in areas of suspected Mau Mau activity. On many occasions men from the KR were simply given rank based on the assignment they were posted in outside the regiment.[38] This also occurred when European men were sent out to lead African troops. European soldiers were not subject to the orders of African NCOs or warrant officers. Therefore, to avoid any uncomfortable situations, European soldiers of the KR were always appointed to officer rank to lead African soldiers.

The KR had units on active service since the beginning of the crisis. The regiment itself was expanded not only for operations but also to run a tracking school for the British battalions operating in Kenya. Even those settlers who did not join the army were pressured to join the Kenya Police Reserve, where they were automatically appointed to the rank of inspector.[39] These experiences renewed interest in military service among Europeans and continued to impede African opportunities to advance in the army into the postcolonial period.

Africanization and the Foundation of the Kenya Army

During the course of the Mau Mau Emergency, the British government considered ways in which to ease the cost of maintaining its empire. The rising costs of military operations in Kenya took their toll. At the height of the conflict, in 1954–1955, the military costs were £14 million per annum.[40] London was looking to grant a greater measure of self-government to Kenya in hopes of reducing the amount of money the metropole had to spend. The example was set in 1954 when the Central African Federation was created out of the two Rhodesias and Nyasaland. Even though a greater degree of independence for the colony was considered, many in the Kenyan government and the EALF did not think the colonies of East Africa would be granted full independence for at least another twenty or thirty years.

The EALF had taken only token measures of Africanization by 1956. That year the command revived the rank of effendi. The British intended to create a rank similar to that of the viceroy's commissioned officers in the British Indian Army without actually giving these soldiers significant officer responsibilities.[41] The original idea was that Africans appointed to this rank would slowly replace the European NCOs who were lent to the KAR for specialist assignments, as well as reduce the number of European junior officers required to lead small tactical units.[42] The African effendis took a six-month course before appointment and were responsible for the administration and training of their units. Trusting African personnel with administrative duties was a new development in the EALF and represented significant progress. Even after African officers were introduced into the EALF, they were not immediately trusted with the same set of administrative tasks as European junior officers. While it seems as though this measure was intended to increase opportunities for Africans, it was more likely done simply to decrease the operating costs of the regiment: an African effendi simply was less costly than a European NCO.

Interestingly, the other arm of the security apparatus in East Africa, the Police Services, was encouraged to promote Africans into higher-ranking positions. A 1955 cabinet report on security in the colonies recommended: "Where practicable, and in carefully selected cases, there should be no hesitation on grounds of principle in operating a colour bar in reverse, to favour rapid promotion of Africans."[43] In 1955, the civil authorities recognized the need for Africans to have the proper experience to manage their own security forces. The cabinet report also addresses the need to fill colonial officer billets with locally recruited officers. There was no hesitation by the British government to extend commissions to Africans or other non-Europeans in areas where there was not a significant settler community. In the West African colonies there were thirty-five Africans officers serving; an additional nineteen West Africans were in training at Sandhurst. Even though the report encouraged and recommended that more West Africans be commissioned every year, it also pointed out that the situation in East Africa was far more complicated and did not recommend any commissioning program or training program to prepare Africans for commissions.[44]

The introduction of the effendi rank is comparable to the establishment of the KAR Junior Leader Company. This unit, established in 1957, combined several East African territorial training schemes that existed at the time. The idea was to consolidate all junior leader training in Kenya for all three East African territories. African boys, generally sons of KAR soldiers, between the ages of fourteen and eighteen were accepted into the program and underwent a training period of four and a half years at the Junior Leader Company. The objective was to "develop the intelligence, education and powers of leadership of suitable African boys with a view to their becoming N.C.O.'s and eventually qualifying for warrant rank."[45] Again similarly to the effendi program, the Junior Leader Company initiative was designed to produce an educated batch of African NCOs who were better able to take the place of more costly European personnel. Interestingly, rather than have these trainees serve in the ranks and then go to a course to become NCOs, as had been the practice, the EALF thought it better to have a dedicated training program for NCO development.

The Kenya Colony report for 1957 states: "It is hoped that one or two suitable candidates for Sandhurst might be found from time to time from the output of the Junior Leaders Company but it is not the aim of the training to produce Sandhurst Candidates."[46] Legally there was nothing preventing an African from becoming an officer, although officer cadets had to meet the educational requirements and pass a selection board in order even to be considered. The educational requirements alone ensured that only a very small pool of Africans could qualify to go before the commissioning board.

Starting in 1958, Kenya Colony sent cadets to the Royal Military Academy–Sandhurst (RMA). However, no Africans were included in groups sent to RMA for training in the first three years. In 1957, the EALF reported that none of the candidates who applied to attend RMA were able to pass the selection board. The following year one European and two Asians went to RMA. Of these three cadets the Asians were required to attend Mons Officer Cadet School prior to being admitted to RMA.

Mons Officer Cadets School was the training institution for National Service officers and Short Service Commissions (SSCs). After the elimination of National Service in 1960, the school trained both SSCs and potential officers who joined the army as university graduates. The course of study at Mons was only six months compared with the two-year course at RMA. Mons closed in 1972 when the course of study at RMA was transitioned into a one-year course for all regular officers.

Kenya Colony sent only Europeans and Asians to RMA until 1963, which is notable because other colonies in East Africa began sending Africans to RMA in 1958.[47] Between 1957 and 1960, nine cadets were sent to Sandhurst from Kenya; of those nine, six were European and three were Asian. During the initial years of localization of the leadership of the forces, Europeans continued to dominate the officer class of the Kenyan forces, which showed few signs of diversifying beyond the Asian community.

Although the Asian community in Kenya made some advances in equality, this should not be seen as a move toward making the forces completely multiracial. In 1958 the Kenya government was only beginning to break the dependence on British Army personnel seconded to the KAR. The goal was to train local Asians instead of Africans as technicians and specialists, and to commission members of the European and Asian community to take over from more expensive British officers. On the cusp of independence, an African warrant officer class 1 was paid £92 a month, whereas a European of the same rank received £600.[48] In 1958 the KAR started its first administration course for African effendis, warrant officers, and NCOs; the course was deemed both successful and necessary.[49] The following year the Kenya government reported that the program was going well and projected that by 1962 African NCOs would be able to replace European other ranks seconded to the KAR.[50]

At that time the colonial secretary, Iain Macleod, recognized that there would be some kind of constitutional change in East Africa, but he was unsure what form it would take. Since taking power back in 1951, Conservative governments had slowed the rate of decolonization in the Empire. In a memorandum he submitted to the Macmillan cabinet in December 1959, Macleod identified four possible scenarios for East Africa in the 1960s: one, the United Kingdom would maintain ultimate power in Kenya and allow the other territories to become self-governing; two, Her Majesty's Government (HMG) would retain control of coastal and port territories in East Africa and allow the rest to become self-governing; three, the territories would be allowed to become self-governing under the auspices of a federal system controlled by the United Kingdom; four, the territories would move toward self-government.[51]

While the option of allowing complete independence was considered, Macleod's various scenarios emphasized Britain retaining some sort of legal and territorial control over most of East Africa and of Kenya Colony in particular. He also advocated making the forces of East Africa more mutually supporting; if Kenya faced internal unrest, local forces from Uganda could reinforce Kenyan authorities, rather than regular British forces. Additionally, Macleod was extremely concerned about local politicians gaining influence over colonial forces in East Africa. This concern coincided with increasing African participation in governing the East African colonies. Macleod believed local politicians would in some way politicize the EALF, which would make it challenging for the governor to use colonial forces to secure British interests.[52] HMG needed to make sure that the EALF were insulated from both constitutional change and the influence of local politicians. Even before British officials were willing to accept that all East African territories were bound for independence within five years, they understood that East African military forces ought to remain divorced from domestic politics. The British government sought to establish an enduring military-to-military relationship with colonies that would soon become independent in order to ensure British influence in the region.

In late 1959 neither the Kenyan colonial government nor the East Africa Commission was making serious preparations for independence. The defense establishment in East Africa thought that self-government was decades away. The Royal East African Navy had a complement of slightly over two hundred men; in 1959 it had no African officers or petty officers, and all African members of the force served as ratings.[53] There were also no plans to train or promote Africans to any leadership positions whatsoever in the small navy.[54] All the changes were focused on reducing costs for both London and the colonial government while ensuring lasting British influence in the region. No one in the colonial defense administration made any plans for how the British government would set up national military forces if East African colonies became independent.

National Consciousness Is a Political Fact

Change came quickly for the EALF in 1960 when British prime minister Harold Macmillan spoke famously in Cape Town about the "wind of change" in Africa. This speech came as a shock to the settler community in Kenya. Many settlers had hoped for some sort of arrangement akin to the federation in central Africa but were confronted by the specter of African majority rule in the near future. The EALF and EAC had no arrangements for the military forces in Africa to transition into African-independent armies. By August 1960, the EAC was scrambling to figure out how to create an independent military force out of these colonial units. One of the major factors in the transition was leadership. Administrative and leadership training among Africans had been kept to a minimum. African effendis were not trained to become the senior leaders of the new army. While they had the necessary military experience—many of them were veterans of Malaya or Mau Mau and sometimes the Second World War—unit administration above the platoon level and quartermaster duties had been firmly in the hands of European officers.

The plan for training Africans for service as commissioned officers in the Kenya Army took shape slowly. The East Africa Commission was unsure how to proceed; it knew that African soldiers would not be able to pass the rigorous screening process for RMA since most lacked the educational qualifications. Initially the Colonial Office looked to newly independent African nations like Ghana as a model for building a national army. It requested information on the recently established Ghana Military Academy and was very curious about the prospect of training Kenyan officers in some sort of Kenyan military academy. The advantage of such a plan was that it would be significantly cheaper than making sure there was space available at Sandhurst for African officers from all over the continent.[55] Even so, the program in Ghana was in its infancy, and most of the serving officers in the Ghanaian Army were sent abroad for training.[56] The 1960 mutiny of the Force Publique in the former Belgian Congo only five days after independence changed the way Kenyan authorities viewed the creation of a national army.

In spite of the Force Publique's horrendous human rights record, European observers considered it a professional military force. While political disputes were taking place among the civilian leadership, the last white commander, General Émile Janssens, refused to promote any Africans to senior rank and intended to make sure that independence changed nothing about the Force Publique. The African NCOs and soldiers felt left out of the independence process, since it appeared nothing would change for them. This discontent led to a violent mutiny in which soldiers murdered their European officers. The mutineers threw professionalism aside, and the force became a threat to the civilian population and the government.[57] Belgian troops and UN peacekeepers from Canada arrived in the Congo and attempted to restore order. Shortly thereafter, the Force Publique was Africanized and renamed the Congolese National Army; it never made the transition from colonial army to national army. Observers noted that an Africanization of the officer corps and a complete subordination to civilian control were the necessary steps in order to ensure that African militaries would support their civilian governments not destabilize them.[58]

The events in the Congo struck fear into the settler communities in Kenya and the Central African Federation. The settlers in Kenya insisted on the creation of a European defense force in addition to the KR as well as the creation of strongpoints stockpiled with weapons and other provisions in case a similar event occurred.[59] The British government helped calm the nerves of Europeans by reinforcing British forces in Kenya with an additional infantry battalion and six hundred Royal Marine Commandos. Yet again the presence of a large and powerful European settler community highlighted how much more complicated decolonization in Kenya was.

At the end of 1960 there were still no African officers in the Kenyan battalions of the KAR. In 1960, Kenya Colony sent four cadets to RMA; three of those were European and one was Asian. Not until 1961 did the Kenyan government and the EAC settled on a plan for creating a Kenya Army led by black Kenyans. Unlike later experiences, the British government did not deem it necessary to send a dedicated training team to Kenya to help establish the army. The establishment would use the resources that were locally available and also send men for training in the United Kingdom. One of the issues that the military authorities saw was that there were not enough spaces at RMA for cadets from African nations to man the new armies in time for independence. The Colonial Office, in partnership with the EAC, developed a two-part plan to produce enough officers for the Kenya Army. The first part was a simple mass solution to the problem at hand: the Kenyan government granted commissions to selected African effendis who had demonstrated sufficient potential to serve as officers in a postindependence army. During this period the EALF would begin searching for suitable Africans to send to Mons Officer Cadet School and RMA. The second part would see these officers begin to return to the KAR and be accompanied by an influx of commissioned effendis to fill vacancies where they existed.[60]

The plan moved very slowly in 1961; by July only six of the roughly seventy effendis were commissioned. By this time, however, two Europeans and two Asians who previously graduated from RMA were also commissioned.[61] Even though constitutional reform in Kenya was moving forward, the rate of Africanization in the military and civil service was extremely slow. In October 1961 the East Africa Defence Committee (EADC) met to discuss the pace of Africanization in all the East African colonies. While both Uganda and Tanganyika had sent African cadets to RMA in the previous year, these men would not graduate for at least two years. Additionally, Kenya Colony had only commissioned a handful of effendis; the rest of the men in the officer training pipeline were Europeans and Asians (at the time of their meeting, five Europeans and one Kenyan Asian were training at RMA). With this slow pace of training and the pace at which African nations were moving toward independence, the EADC endorsed a proposal from Major General Richard Goodwin, general officer commanding (GOC) of the EAC, to grant SSCs to seventy Africans by the middle of 1962. The plan was supposed to provide ten officers to each of the six infantry battalions in the EAC and leave the remaining ten to take up postings in service support units.[62]

In November 1961, Patrick Renison, the head of the EADC and the governor of Kenya, sent a letter to the colonial secretary Reginald Maulding, who had replaced Iain Macleod. The letter set out the goals and costs of the military training program in East Africa with the hope of winning the support of the Colonial Office. Kenyan Africans held Renison in low regard, since many of his public statements did little to reassure them of the progress of decolonization. Nonetheless, his November letter clearly indicated the desires of the EADC. "If when independence comes," he wrote, "a strong officer corps with high professional standards is already firmly established, the East African forces will be that much more resistant to political interference, and that much less vulnerable to any ill-conceived programs of rapid Africanization which could only result in a serious lowering of standards."[63] These tenets would define the way the British executed the training program in Kenya; rather than speedily pushing officer cadets through subpar commissioning programs, their goal was to forge a professional officer corps, created in a very British image. Shortly after this letter was sent to the Colonial Office, Renison was summoned to London and dismissed from his post by colonial secretary Duncan Sandys for growing too close to the settler community in Kenya.[64]

While this ambitious program was starting slowly, the British military took no steps to reduce its presence in East Africa. Since the Suez Crisis and the loss of British influence in Egypt, London considered Kenya to be an important strategic reserve location for both forces and material. Additionally, rather than send a training team to Kenya to take charge of the transition to the formation of a national army, the EAC decided to leave British officers in their billets in the KAR. New African officers would learn through apprenticeship; they would learn by watching European officers. There were 180 officer billets in the entire KAR establishment in East Africa. Colonial officials projected that by the middle of 1962 there would be eighty-four local officers (including Europeans and Asians). Even so, secretary of state for war John Profumo said in his November

1961 report, "It is the intention that during the period of rapid African-isation, British seconded officers will remain at their present strength to train the newly commissioned Africans. . . . By the beginning of 1963, the requirement for British seconded officers, which now stands at 150 for the three East African Territories, should be reduced by half."[65] The reduction of British forces in East Africa was to take place slowly, as both Harold Watkinson, the minister of defense, and Profumo were concerned about the implications of retaining seconded officers after independence.[66] However, Watkinson also did not last until the 1964 general election; he was ousted from the government in a major cabinet reshuffle in July 1962

The British government was trying to force a multiracial army on independent Kenya. Europeans and Asians were the only cadets sent to commissioning courses from civilian life. Even though the government was attempting to Africanize quickly, it considered Africans who were already serving in the army the only available recruiting pool. As Profumo pointed out in his report to Watkinson in January 1962, "Although the G.O.C. East Africa anticipated that suitable material existed in the KAR [for commissioned officers], this hope has not, unfortunately, been realized."[67] This problem became public on 13 December 1961, when an article entitled "Kenya Becomes Aware of Need to Train African Officers" appeared in *The Times*. The article highlighted the example of an attempt to recruit African secondary school graduates. The selection board had identified eleven Africans with the requisite educational credentials; of these eleven, only three showed up for the first interview, and not one of them passed the interview process.[68] The article not only pointed out the problems the Kenya government had in finding Africans to commission but also made the connection between the lack of promotion in the Congo and the mutiny that had occurred there in 1960. The fear was not simply of the prospect of a mutiny but of the potential financial cost of a mutiny. On 29 December, *The Times* published a letter to the editor by Major General William Dimoline, the former GOC of the EAC, who insisted that the events in the Congo served as a reminder of the importance of the training mission in Africa.[69]

The British government was concerned on many levels throughout this period over the economic burden posed by decolonization. The Colonial Office was willing to support decolonization with limited funds, and the Ministry of Defence was willing to provide the personnel. Yet independent nations had to pay for their own armies, and this included the cost of any British officers seconded to them. This cost was substantial as British officers' salaries and allowances were significantly larger than those of any African officer. The main concern of British policy makers, such as Profumo, was what this cost would lead new nations to do. He wrote: "We are apprehensive that because of this they may be tempted to turn elsewhere for their military assistance in this field [officer training]. I am sure that, if necessary, it is worth spending a certain amount of money in preventing this."[70] The prospect of former British colonies leaving the British sphere of influence to receive assistance from nonaligned nations, or worse the Soviet Union, was unthinkable. If the independent Kenyan government decided to look elsewhere for military training and material, it would put the British strategic position in East Africa and the Middle East in jeopardy.

It was not simply the policy makers in London who were concerned about who would become involved in East Africa. As the East African colonies neared independence, the concern over British influence filtered down to the local level. In December 1961, Tanganyika gained independence and was followed by Uganda in October 1962. However, in January 1962 the governor of Uganda, Sir Walter Coutts, voiced his concerns to the GOC of the EAC over the pace of officer production: "Our aim would be to assist the KAR for as long as possible because other countries would be anxious to do so if we were not."[71] While the USSR was not mentioned by name in this passage, colonial officials were constantly suspicious of communist subversion in East Africa. Most events, such as the Mau Mau Emergency, the revolution in Zanzibar, and later the East African mutinies, were initially thought to be caused by communist infiltration. Even though Coutts highlighted the need to get this task done, he was not willing to compromise the mission of British training in East Africa: securing forces that were friendly to Britain and divorced from domestic politics.

A 1962 report by the KAR Course Wing highlighted some of the difficulties British trainers were having in hastening the output of officers and officer cadets. In 1962 the KAR Course Wing held seven different programs, five of which were specifically designed to develop African leadership skills: the Administration Course, Platoon Command, Advanced Platoon Command, Pre–Officer Cadet Training Unit (Pre-OCTU), and

Pre–Sandhurst Cadet Course. The Pre-OCTU course was the first of its kind and began with eleven students, all drawn from the KAR from non-infantry specialties. Of the eleven students, seven passed the course. In the 1962 KAR Course Wing report, students were described as being woefully unprepared for the undertaking: "The standard of students was not high. All being non-inf [noninfantry] personnel, their basic training varied from 6 months down to nil. In no case did this standard approach the standard expected from an inf recruit at the end of 6 months training."[72] The students were seen as being unprepared not only educationally but also militarily. This report certainly was not a ringing endorsement for the commissioning of African officers and creating an independent military force.

Nonetheless, the rate of commissioning had to improve if African officers were to get even the most basic orientation in staff duties in preparation for midlevel and high-level command and staff duty. The Colonial Office decided to grant some effendis SSCs in October 1961; this program was expanded, and all effendis serving in the EALF were granted commissions by the end of 1962. As of July 1962, there were sixteen effendis still serving in the Kenya battalions of the KAR. By December all sixteen were granted SSCs without any additional training. African officers who had been commissioned were not immediately given command positions beyond the platoon level. Those who were not serving as platoon commanders were placed in posts at brigade headquarters to familiarize them with staff duties. Others were placed in a specially created position, company assistant adjutant, to give them experience in the administrative tasks required to run a company.[73]

The main issue for the Colonial Office and the War Office was not simply a lack of funds; there were not enough billets available for both African officers and British officers to be present in the same regiment. The funding of the KAR was based on a table of organization that allocated a specific number of officer posts to each regiment. The British plan for training African officers focused on the experience of shadowing a British officer in a position that the African officer would fill. Since the British Army had no additional billets available in the table of organization, the Colonial Office said that it could only fund the positions allowed by statute. Other regiments avoided this problem with the addition of Emergency Reserve Establishment positions in their tables of organization that allowed the regiment to possess a surplus of officers. Unlike other regiments, the KAR was not allocated any Emergency Reserve Establishment positions when it was established.

A choice had to be made between halting the commissioning of African officers, reducing the number of British officers in the KAR, or finding a way to change the law. Both the EAC and the Colonial Office realized that it was not feasible to slow the pace of commissioning Africans or reduce the number of British officers at that time. They ended up agreeing to have the War Office fund the additional positions for the remainder of the fiscal year, and the provisions for the next fiscal year (1963–1964) were amended to allow the additional officers.[74]

The bureaucratic battle for funds and supply allocations revealed a weakness in the British plan for training the Kenya Army. While a one-on-one trainer-to-trainee relationship was ideal for developing and molding new officers, it was extremely costly for the Colonial Office and took manpower away from the British Army at home. Previously the colonial regiments had not been as much of a burden. By using National Servicemen in the colonies, the regular army did not have to commit significant resources. Yet the last intakes of National Servicemen entered the British Army in November 1960 and left the army in 1962 and 1963. The trainer-to-trainee ratio had to be reduced in the future to make training missions that were both affordable and flexible.

The Kenya Army from the KAR

The Kenyan and the Ugandan colonial governments intended to expand the size of their forces on the eve of independence. While Kenya had three KAR battalions, Uganda possessed only one, and neither force was of acceptable size for an army of an independent nation. In January 1962, Sir Walter Coutts insisted that the training mission had to be successful to maintain British influence: "The present strength of 4KAR is not sufficient to enable Uganda to face the possible threats from Rwanda, Burundi, the Congo and the Sudan with any degree of confidence."[75] The Kenyan administration concluded that a nation of its size required a much larger military force to guarantee its independence. While the local authorities insisted on an expansion of the Kenyan and Ugandan armies, the Colonial Office fundamentally disagreed. Referring to Kenya and Uganda, Lieutenant Colonel W. M. L. Adler of the Colonial Office Defence

Department pointed out, "We know that they are going to have a very difficult task in meeting all their financial commitments and it is therefore clearly in their interests, as well as those of HMG, to keep the cost of the K.A.R. as low as possible."[76] If the KAR was expanded, it was likely that the units that were passed on to the new states would be a ruinous financial responsibility. The expansion of the local forces would have to wait until the onset of independence, when the new nations could make their own missteps.

As Africanization programs moved through 1962, African officers were posted to the majority of the KAR battalions, and at this point the EAC noticed a serious problem in its scheme. Almost all the Africans commissioned up to that point were trained as infantry officers; there were almost no African officers trained in the support or service branches. According to the British Army model, combat support branches include artillery, engineers, intelligence, and signals. The combat services consist of logistics, medical, adjutant general, military police, and electrical and mechanical engineers. All these units require significant periods of specialized training beyond the battle tasks of an infantry officer.

A. Oginga Odinga, a leading member of the Kenya African National Union and member of the National Assembly, was also aware of this issue, which he addressed in the legislative assembly: "We know that in the centre of any organization we have got the planning side, which I understand is always called the 'staff side of the army.' . . . Here we have practically no plan at present for an African to occupy it even when an African will be able to assume that post."[77] He further took the government to task for treating potential applicants poorly:

> The policy, which is at the present pursued, does not encourage the right type of African to serve in the Army because when they go there they are accepted, probably reluctantly, and the treatment which they are given there is most discouraging and which makes many of them get fed up and then even run away from the Army, and in the end we are told that there are no Africans who are qualified to serve in the Army.[78]

In spite of the criticism levied by the African members of the assembly, the government attempted to calm concerns. Although gains were made, however, there was still a huge disparity between the combat and specialty branches.

It proved difficult to find suitable candidates for these specialty branches. Previously, British trainers had looked to the African senior NCOs first, but in these fields seconded British personnel occupied all the senior NCO positions. In his July 1962 memo to the War Office, Sir Richard Goodwin, GOC EAC, made it clear that this needed to be a new priority for the War Office because of the long periods of training and apprenticeship required for these positions.[79] Again, the issue that confronted the EAC was the cost of additional officers. East Africa Command wanted to create eleven new officer positions devoted to service and technical branches.

The new officer positions were not approved until the 1963–1964 fiscal year, which stunted the growth of the service and support component of the Kenya Army. This was not simply a problem in Kenya, for both Uganda and Tanganyika relied on British Army personnel for medical and quartermaster services well into 1964.[80] The War Office was frustrated with the lack of progress on the issue and wanted to revisit the idea of an East African Federation. While the War Office and the EAC had no delusions that they would be able to create a single nation out of the former East African territories, they did want to investigate the possibility of pooling defense resources for the region. The War Office and the Colonial Office would continue to suggest this option to East African governments well into 1965.

Once Uganda achieved independence in October 1962, the only remaining KAR units in the EAC were the three Kenya battalions. By the end of 1962, all the effendis in the KAR had had their appointments converted to commissions. In addition to these new African officers, forty-nine other African soldiers received commissions through either Mons or RMA.[81] By December 1962, compulsory military training for Europeans ended in the colony, and the KR opened up to men of all races for voluntary territorial service.[82] Progress was clearly being made in turning the army over to African officers, but the process was not complete. Major General William Dimoline was GOC EAC from 1946 to 1948 and in his retirement continued to be an advocate for African soldiers. He had published letters to the editor in *The Times* and been outspoken on the need for more African officers since 1955. Despite his enthusiasm, he confessed to Brigadier M. F. Fitzalan-Howard, "I hope that you are right in your estimate that Kenya will retain its European officers for at least ten years otherwise, I am afraid the future of the KAR does not look too good to me. However I may be wrong."[83]

Major General Dimoline's concerns regarding the removal of European officers were not misplaced. As the complement of African officers grew during 1962 and 1963, the government revisited the prospect of expanding the three KAR battalions into an actual army. However, this discussion was put on hold in July 1963 when the EAC identified another stumbling block in the Africanization program. During World War II, the EAC developed its own organic support units to include an ordnance company. In 1956 the ordnance company was disbanded, and British Army units provided these services. In 1963, the 305th Ammunition Depot and the 541st Ordnance Depot supplied ammunition and explosives not only to KAR units but also to British units stationed in Kenya. The issue was not simply that there were no African NCOs to promote to officer ranks but that no Africans at all were trained at any rank to perform or supervise ordnance duties.

Major General Goodwin asked the Ministry of Defence for approval to recruit fifty African soldiers for local training at the ordnance depot. The timing of the request meant that even if these men were recruited immediately, they would not be trained and available until at least mid-1964. However, at the time recruiting safaris were made only once a year, so if the requisite men were not found that year, the entire program would be pushed back. In addition to the fifty other ranks required, the depot also needed four commissioned officers assigned for ordnance training. To completely Africanize ordnance services required sixteen officers, including a lieutenant colonel as the chief of ordnance. This move further strained the already taxed African officer corps. Major General Goodwin had by now accepted the large-scale commitment that British forces had made to a postindependence Kenya when he pointed out, "It can be seen that the Kenya Army Ordnance Units will require seconded officers and NCOs for several years to come."[84]

Once the proposal reached the ministerial level, the perceived needs of the Kenya Army changed. Lieutenant Colonel Adler of the Colonial Office considered it premature to submit the request to the Treasury for only the costs to create one support unit for the Kenya Army. He suggested that the proposal for the entire expansion program be submitted to the Treasury at one time to have a clear understanding of what the final cost would be.[85] At this point in the discussion, officials at the Colonial Office and the War Office admitted they had been too ambitious in their Africanization scheme. Adler made it clear in his letter to the War Office that the creation of supporting units and the expansion of the Kenya Army to a brigade group would be complete by the independence deadline in December 1963. The ordnance issue was yet another reason why Colonial Office officials such as Adler were hoping for a federal defense arrangement in which supporting services could be shared by the three countries.

Major C. D. B. Troughton of the War Office raised the following point to Adler: "Experience in Tanganyika and Uganda has shown that trained African ordnance personnel are an essential part of a newly formed independent army when War Department sources of supply and guidance are removed."[86] He also warned that the longer they put off the decision, the longer seconded personnel would have to remain in Kenya. The cost difference was significant: British personnel cost three and a half times as much as African personnel in the same positions. One of the important things that Major Troughton underscored was that, in spite of their issues aside, it was extremely important for Africans to be in charge of their own affairs sooner rather than later. By 17 October the War Office received an answer: the Colonial Office decided there would be no new supporting services until there was an approved plan for the expansion of the entire Kenya Army.

In order to expand the army and function on the modern battlefield, Kenya needed a variety of new units. The new army needed to be able to confront armor threats, and operate during conventional conflicts. Each infantry battalion needed an additional rifle company as well as an antitank platoon and a reconnaissance platoon. Like the ordnance depot, the EAC had disbanded its organic artillery units shortly after the Second World War. The new Kenya Army also needed an artillery regiment, as well as an armored reconnaissance squadron and a field engineer squadron. All of these combat units also required a robust support organization to include a motor transport company, postal unit, provost unit, stores section, and infantry weapons workshop.[87] Before the Kenya Army would be able to operate without the direct support of British units, it needed all of these support elements. This required the British to commit to a multiyear program to provide support, trainers, and equipment. While on the surface it seemed as though Kenya was the only beneficiary in the arrangement, as long as British forces were required to support the basic functioning of the Kenya Army, they would have to maintain basing rights in Kenya.

Even though the army was composed of only three infantry battalions still partially staffed by British officers, the outlook was not as poor as it seemed. Just prior to independence Major General Goodwin commented, "The crash programme of training African officers, which had been essential, was proving generally successful. There had been some weak spots but on the whole the programme had gone off rather encouragingly."[88] Goodwin's only complaint about African officers was that they were generally weak in the field of administration. Yet he did note the continued training in the area had been encouraging.[89]

By the time of the independence celebrations of 12 December 1963, the Kenya Army was made up of three infantry battalions with no supporting services and was partially staffed by British officers. The KR was disbanded just prior to independence. The history of the regiment and its close relationship with the settler community made it ill-suited to remain a part of the Kenya Army. The total size of the force was 2,500 soldiers, with 165 serving officers, of which 80 were African.[90] Seconded British officers would have to remain in Kenya for the foreseeable future before the army would be able to function on its own.

The Army Is Tested: The East African Mutinies

By the time Kenya reached independence, Tanganyika and Uganda had been independent since December 1961 and October 1962, respectively. At the time these two nations reached independence, the Africanization program was just starting. In Uganda, only fourteen of the sixty-four officers in the army were African. In Tanganyika, Africans filled only six of sixty-four officer billets. In both cases the percentages were far below the 48.5 percent rate that Kenya achieved upon independence. By January 1964, the situation in several East African armies was tense. Police and civil servants received priority in government funding for pay rate increases, and many rank-and-file soldiers felt they were losing the privileged position they had enjoyed.

In addition to complaints regarding pay, many soldiers, particularly in Tanganyika, felt that little had changed for them since independence. The army seemed exactly the same: the officers were mostly British, the uniforms were the same, and one regiment even retained part of its British name, First Tanganyika Rifles (Sixth King's African Rifles). In addition to these issues, African other ranks were frustrated by the lack of promotions they had assumed would come with independence. Many junior NCOs, lance corporals, and corporals felt that the officer ranks should have been opened to Africans upon independence. As in the other colonies, one of the major issues was that Tanganyika was still sending all its officer cadets to Britain for training, and many of the soldiers who were serving in the Tanganyika Rifles did not have the requisite educational qualifications for officer training.

Of the three African colonies, Tanganyika was the least prepared for independence. The new government, led by Julius Nyerere, deeply distrusted the army and had debated the merits of simply disbanding it and replacing it with a paramilitary police force.[91] While the government decided against disbandment, the army was severely limited upon independence. The military establishment in Tanganyika was extremely expensive for the small nation. Nyerere allowed the British to keep so much influence after independence so they would continue to provide funds to offset the costs of the army. Due to the distrust between the government and the army, and the shortage of available funds, Africanization of the army proceeded at a much slower pace in Tanganyika than elsewhere. In the early 1960s, the nation sent only two cadets a year to Sandhurst. In January 1964, there were still only twenty-two African officers in the Tanganyika Rifles.[92]

Britain, however, was not the only source of assistance for Nyerere's government. Oscar Kambona, the minister for foreign affairs, recommended numerous candidates to the officer selection board for commissioning in the TR. However, the board, half of which was composed of British officers, continued to refuse his candidates on the grounds that they were not qualified. Kambona therefore sent sixty men to Israel to undergo officer training. When these men returned to Tanganyika, Kambona insisted they be commissioned into the army. Some, but not all, of the Israeli-trained officers were accepted into the army.[93] This created a divide between those officers trained in Israel and those trained in Britain. The Israeli-trained men had been through a shorter training course, were ignorant of British military traditions, and hence were viewed as unprofessional. The rank and file were also hostile to the Israeli-trained officers, insisting that long-serving NCOs deserved commissions more than these "new men."[94] Dissatisfaction with pay, promotions, and the continued presence of British officers was the foundation of discontent that led to the breakdown of military discipline in the Tanganyika Rifles.

The mutiny itself did not actually start because of any event inside Tanganyika. Violence flared up in nearby Zanzibar on New Year's Day in 1964. Zanzibar achieved independence separately from Tanganyika as a monarchy under the sultan. Within weeks of achieving independence, Arab political parties and the sultan passed legislation banning opposition political parties, censored the press, and politicized the police. A group of six hundred lightly armed Africans rose up on 12 January 1964 and took control of the government by force. Nyerere decided to send one hundred members of the paramilitary Police Field Force to assist in containing the rioting that followed the successful revolution.

The disenchanted soldiers of the Tanganyika Rifles saw how this small, lightly armed force took over the Zanzibar government relatively easily and used it as a model for action in Tanganyika. This realization combined with the absence of the Police Field Force meant there would be little opposition to a potential mutiny. This combination of factors proved far too tempting for the soldiers of the TR, and on 19 January they mutinied.[95]

The First Tanganyika Rifles at Colito Barracks outside Dar es Salaam seized the weapons in the armory and turned on their officers, both British and African. The British officers along with their families were taken to the Dar es Salaam airport and put on a plane to Nairobi. The soldiers seized key locations in the capital, including the State House. Nyerere was not in Dar es Salaam at the time and remained in hiding to avoid capture by the mutineers. The curious part of this mutiny is that it was not actually a coup; it was a military version of a strike. A dispatch from the British High Commission noted: "It is conceivable that the mutinous troops took a simple syndicalist view of their position in the army, believing that, as regards to the right to strike for higher pay and accelerated Africanisation of higher positions, they were in much the same position as civil employees (except that the troops had no trade union of their own)."[96]

Once the troops were guaranteed a pay raise by the government, many of them went back to their barracks. Even so, some of the hard-core mutineers, mainly clerks and education instructors, maintained the mutiny. Out of a desire to restore control of the army and government, Nyerere asked the British for military assistance to put down the mutiny on 24 January. The British government dispatched the aircraft carrier HMS *Centaur* and the Royal Marine 45 Commando. On the morning of 25 January, the marines used the helicopters aboard the ship to conduct an air assault mission on Colito Barracks. They attempted to use a loudspeaker system to call the troops to surrender, but the Africans refused. The marines fired a rocket into the guardhouse, and after a short firefight and the death of two African soldiers, the mutinous soldiers surrendered to the marines. After the main force was arrested at the barracks, the Royal Marine 45 Commando seized control of the airport and government buildings in Dar es Salaam.[97] By the late afternoon the mutiny had been put down, order was restored, and the men of Royal Marine 45 Commando patrolled the streets of Dar es Salaam.

Before the mutiny was contained, news of the soldiers' strike reached troops in the Ugandan and Kenyan armies, themselves also dissatisfied with their pay situation. Prior to the mutiny, government ministers in Uganda had assured the soldiers they would receive a pay raise, yet only enough funds were set aside to give raises to senior NCOs. The men of the Uganda Rifles were inspired by the realization that the soldiers simply had to strike to bring about a pay raise. On 23 January, 150 men of the Uganda Rifles stationed at Jinja simply sat down and refused to obey the orders of their officers. Jinja Barracks was the depot for the First Battalion of the Uganda Rifles, making it the largest concentration of armed strength in Uganda at the time.

The British officers in charge of the battalion had feared such a move and made sure that the armory was secure. This meant that aside from the camp sentries most of the mutinous soldiers were unarmed. The minister of home affairs, Felix Onama, arrived at the camp intending to negotiate with the soldiers, only to be imprisoned by them. While held in the guardhouse, Onama was forced to agree to a pay raise from USh 105 to USh 265 a month. Only then was the minister allowed to leave the camp. Executive prime minister of Uganda Milton Obote had no intention of allowing the mutiny of his army to reach the level of chaos in Tanganyika. To prevent further disorder and to reassert control of the situation, on 23 January he requested assistance from the British government to put down the mutiny.[98] Two companies of the Staffordshire Regiment (1STAFF) and a company of the Scots Guards flew from Kenya and arrived at 10:45 p.m.

that same night. While these troops secured the airport and other government buildings in Kampala, Obote's government certified the pay raises that the soldiers were promised to avoid making the crisis worse.

Even though the situation had not returned to normal, Obote announced to the nation that calm was restored. However, by 27 January the men of First Uganda Rifles (1UR) still refused to obey the orders of their officers. Prime Minister Obote asked 1STAFF to take control of Jinja Barracks. Under cover of darkness the British soldiers infiltrated the barracks and took control without firing a shot.[99] In an attempt to prevent future discontent in the army, Obote promoted a promising young officer, Major Idi Amin, to lieutenant colonel and appointed him deputy commander of the army. After the barracks was taken back, the ringleaders of the mutiny were imprisoned and dismissed from the army.

While the events in Uganda were far less violent than those in Tanganyika, they were not necessarily more easily contained. The East African armies still utilized the same radio network that they had during the colonial period, so throughout the uprisings soldiers in each territory received news of the initial success of each strike. The authorities in Kenya were also closely monitoring the events in both Uganda and Tanganyika. President Jomo Kenyatta took the loyalty of the army extremely seriously and was determined not to allow the same thing to happen in Kenya as had happened elsewhere in East Africa. By 1964, the EAC had changed its name to British Land Forces–Kenya and had a new GOC, Major General Ian Freeland, who concurrently was commander of the Kenya Army. President Kenyatta empowered Freeland to do what was necessary to ensure the stability and loyalty of the army.

For his part, Kenyatta made a number of public statements to try to pacify the soldiers before anything happened. Kenyatta publicly expressed his confidence in the Kenya Army and released a statement on his plans to accelerate the rate of the army's Africanization. Additionally, he promised to form a committee to look into the conditions of service in the army.[100] Despite these well-laid plans to keep the army happy Kenyatta was still concerned it would revolt.

The Kenya Police Special Branch, which had been collecting intelligence for some time on the state of political feelings in the army, provided Freeland with information that there was significant discontent in the Eleventh Kenya Rifles (11KR). The discontent, paired with the comparative success in the two other EA territories in achieving pay raises, was expected to lead to trouble. Freeland warned the British battalion commander of 11KR, Lieutenant Colonel G. W. Stead, that there was a good possibility of unrest from within his unit and that he should remove the weapons and ammunition from camp. Stead was handicapped, however, because his battalion was on alert for possible deployment to Tanganyika and in that case would require its weapons.

In an attempt to address the concerns of the soldiers, Stead met with his men and announced they would receive a 15 percent pay increase back-dated to December 1963. Unfortunately, this did little to calm them, since there had also been a recent increase in taxes that offset this raise in pay. By the end of the evening of 24 January, the men of 11KR broke into their own armory and took up arms against their officers, British and African alike. Almost all the conspirators were corporals and below. As a precautionary measure, Freeland dispatched a troop from Third Royal Horse Artillery (3RHA) to a position just outside of Lanet Barracks where 11KR was stationed. The British officers of 11KR called for support from 3RHA. The British were able to seize control of the armory while under fire from the mutineers. Rather than put down the revolt using overwhelming fire-power, the African officers of 11KR were sent into the barracks to attempt to reason with the mutinying soldiers. The move was unsuccessful, and 3RHA called back to its higher headquarters for guidance.

Kenyatta refused to allow the soldiers' revolt to go on for any longer and instructed Freeland to take the camp by force.[101] A battalion of Gordon Highlanders was trucked into Lanet equipped with armored cars. At 10:00 a.m. on 25 January, after the mutineers refused to surrender, the British troops went in behind the armored cars. The African soldiers, who knew they would not be able to put up any sort of defense against armored vehicles, gave up rather than die.[102] In his report posted right after the mutiny was put down, Freeland noted that the political influence of ministers in the other armies contributed to the outbreak of the mutiny: "In Tanganyika and Uganda it became commonplace for politicians to enter the barracks and talk unofficially to the Askaris, often without the knowledge of their officers, this must not be allowed to happen in Kenya."[103]

The aftermath of the mutiny varied in each nation. Both Uganda and Tanganyika turned away from British defense assistance after the events of January 1964, seeing continued British involvement in their military forces as the impetus for the mutinies in the first place.[104] Tanganyika merged with Zanzibar to form Tanzania and disbanded the entire army, replacing it with the new Tanzanian Peoples Defence Force. The new army was completely political, recruited almost exclusively from the Tanganyika African National Union (TANU) youth wing.[105] Nyerere decided that loyalty to the TANU and loyalty to the government were the same thing; eventually, members of the army were required to be members of the TANU. By tying together party loyalty and national loyalty, Nyerere cemented his place in power for the next two decades. Clearly, in Tanzania the military did not live up to the British hope for a force that would help exert British influence.

Uganda did not entirely disband its army, but Obote did see to it that the ringleaders of the mutiny were prosecuted. British assistance in Uganda was minimized, while the Obote government conspired with Idi Amin to look elsewhere for military assistance. Obote also gave great power to the army and Amin after the mutinies. In 1966, Obote used Amin and the army to consolidate his power by destroying the internal kingdoms in Uganda. Amin himself led the assault on the Kabaka of Buganda's palace. The seizure of power in 1966 led Uganda down a road of increasing political involvement by the military. In 1968, the British defense attaché in Uganda made a trip to the Uganda Army headquarters, where he saw a sign that read, "No Politicians beyond This Point."[106] In 1971, Idi Amin used his power as the commander of the army to seize power in Uganda and embark on his eight-year reign of terror in the country.

Kenya was remarkably different in its reaction to the mutinies. The Kenyatta government embraced British defense assistance after 1964. While it did intend to increase the number of African officers, it was also grateful for the opportunity to build relationships with the British Army. In 1965, Kenyatta sent a company of soldiers to Britain to undergo parachute training, something much envied among African forces.[107]

The training of African officers in Britain continued at an increased pace; in 1964 alone, sixty-two Kenyan officers commissioned from Mons or RMA. Another seventy-six trained in Britain between 1965 and 1967. In 1966, Brigadier Joseph Ndolo, a former colonial soldier, became the first Kenyan appointed commander of the army. At the same time Colonel Jackson Mulinge was the deputy army commander.[108] By 1967, there were no longer any seconded British officers serving in line units in the Kenya

Army.[109] In 1969, Brigadier Ndolo took over from Major General R. B. Penfold as the chief of the Defence Staff in Kenya, the last major command position in the Kenya Army occupied by a British officer.[110]

The mutiny also made Kenyatta even more concerned about the army's ethnic makeup. He was deeply troubled by the low percentage of Kikuyus in the army. Prior to independence, the Kamba, Kalenjin, and Samburu ethnic groups predominated in the KAR. At independence, the officer corps was almost exclusively European, Asian, or Kamba.[111] To shore up any possible threats from other interest groups, Kenyatta launched a Kikuyuization program. By 1966, 23 percent of the officer corps was Kikuyu, and only a year later there were as many Kikuyu officers as there were Kamba.[112]

Conclusion

Despite all the problems that faced British planners and Kenyan authorities during the Africanization process, the program was comparatively successful. The delay in Kenyan independence provided the government with the necessary buffer to utilize British resources to Africanize the army as much as possible. Kenya had the highest rate of Africanization of any army in British Africa up to that point. At independence, 48.5 percent of the officer corps was African; the next highest rate was that of Uganda, with 21.9 percent.[113] This is remarkable considering the size of the Kenya Army, which at 2,500 soldiers was much larger than the other East African forces.

The British Army, in concert with African officers, identified the problem areas of establishing a new army. Support services and technical training plagued the British throughout the transition process. It took almost a decade for British training technicians to leave Kenya and for the army to provide its own logistical support and medical services. Additionally, the navy and air force were established from nothing and were both extremely technical services. The British also learned that the cost of maintaining influence in new nations was extremely high. Parliamentary debates in Kenya frequently revolved around looking elsewhere for military assistance.[114] It was only the relationships built by British forces with important power brokers such as Kenyatta that kept Britain as the sole supplier of military training.

Training through mentorship was an extremely costly and time-intensive process, yet it helped maintain a continuum of culture and discipline impressed upon officer cadets at RMA and Mons. This is not to say that all British officers assigned to the KAR were consummate professionals, but they were able to identify with their new Kenyan officers because of a common training experience in Britain. Like alumni of the same prestigious university, British officers working with African officers knew the challenges they endured at Sandhurst and the Infantry Battle Course. This common military culture helped British and Kenyan soldiers establish important personal and professional relationships. These relationships served as informal conduits to reinforce British influence in Kenya.

The curriculum at Sandhurst and Mons both challenged and indoctrinated the officer cadets. At a minimum, cadets who went to Mons spent a year training to become an officer; at a maximum, those who went to Sandhurst trained for two and a half years. During this time they were exposed to the camaraderie, pride, and uniformity of the British professional officer corps. Additionally, British trainers were often able to weed out those African officer cadets who did not meet the standard or were overly political. When Kenyan officers returned home, they often emulated the officer culture that they had experienced during training in Britain. This professionalism was showcased in 1964 during the containment of the mutinies when Kenyan officers attempted to quell the discontent among their soldiers. Additionally, the military did not become politicized like the other forces in East Africa, mainly due to the efforts of Kenyan and British officers to keep politicians and political activists out of military cantonments. The two major military coup efforts that have occurred in Kenya since independence were unlike those in other parts of Africa. In many places the higher echelons of the officer corps conspired to replace the civilian government with a military one. In Kenya the uprising in 1964 and the attempted coup in 1982 were both led by low-ranking enlisted men. On both occasions army officers leading forces loyal to the government put down the rebellion.

While democracy in Kenya was far from perfect, the goal of the British training establishment was to create a military force that did not interfere in politics. The British have also used the military connection between the two countries to maintain a level of influence in Kenya. After the 1964 mutinies, the Kenyan government eagerly increased the amount of military assistance requested from Britain. The defense agreement of 1964 provided for a continued British military presence in Kenya for the rest of the decade. There were of course provisions for continued officer training schemes in Britain as well as provisions for the British government to supply equipment to the Kenyans. However, the most striking part of the agreement was the assurance that until 1971 Britain would assist Kenya in maintaining both internal and external security. Kenyatta wanted to make sure that the British would help prevent a coup in Kenya, and the British wanted to ensure someone did not replace him who favored the Warsaw Pact.[115] In exchange, the British received permission to fly military aircraft through Kenya airspace, the use of naval facilities and Kenyan training areas, and a secure signals intelligence facility. Even though the internal defense agreement lapsed in 1971, the Kenya Army remained close to the British military. It was not until the late 1970s that the Kenyans started buying some equipment from other sources, namely, the United States. Under Daniel arap Moi, the Kenyan government continued its relationship with the British government on defense issues, while trying to diversify investment in the country.[116] While the Moi government cooperated with the British and US governments in the Persian Gulf War by allowing Western navies to use Kenyan ports, he also was attempting to build relations with China. This was in part due to the criticism he received from Western governments over the undemocratic nature of his regime.[117] The coolness with Britain persisted throughout the 1990s, but the countries grew closer after the end of the Moi regime in 2002. In the twenty-first century the British-Kenyan defense relationship has expanded. The rise of terrorist groups in Somalia and elsewhere in East African has pushed successive Kenyan governments to work with the British to provide military training.[118] The British presence remains: the British Army Training Unit–Kenya is a permanent unit outside Nairobi that helps run a training center in Kenya for British troops that cycles through six infantry battalions and an engineer squadron every year.

The Zambia Army and the Consequences of Poor Policy

In 2014, Guy Scott assumed office as the acting president of Zambia. He was the first white president of an African nation since F. W. de Klerk left office in South Africa in 1994. While this was a puzzling turn of affairs that piqued the interest of international media for a few days, it was also an echo of settler colonialism in southern Africa. Northern Rhodesia emerged from the same exploratory hunger that established Southern Rhodesia. Originally divided into two separate territories, it was unified as Northern Rhodesia in 1911 under the auspices of the British South Africa Company. Company rule in Northern Rhodesia lasted until 1923, when it passed to the administration of the Colonial Office as a protectorate. Miners discovered large mineral deposits in Northern Rhodesia early in its settlement. Known for its rich copper mines in what became known as the Copperbelt, Northern Rhodesia initially was not settled as a "white man's" colony, but as the copper industry grew, a small and influential group of migrants settled in the area. This European community constantly advocated the union of the two Rhodesias and finally realized its dream as the Central African Federation (CAF). The union of these two colonies had long-lasting effects on the security establishment in what became Zambia. Although it was administered by the Colonial Office, the settler community formed a small legislative council. In 1954, shortly after the formation of the CAF, the settler community population was sixty thousand compared with the African population of two million.[1]

The Zambia Army originated from the Northern Rhodesia Regiment, which began as a constabulary of Indian soldiers hired in the 1890s. This small, irregular force gave way with the enlistment of local Africans into the Northern Rhodesia Police (NRP) in 1911. The force, which did not have a centralized system of training or standardization, had a small unit of European policemen who patrolled the settler areas.[2]

During World War I, the NRP fought in the East Africa campaign; after the war, a portion of the NRP broke off to form the Northern Rhodesia Regiment (NRR). From 1933 until 1937, officers of the NRR came from the local settler community, something remarkably different from most other colonial forces. In 1937, the Colonial Office decided to model the NRR on the King's African Rifles (KAR), and from that point until the federation period officers were seconded to the force from the British Army. The regiment primarily recruited from the Ngoni people of the northeastern part of the colony. Like the KAR, the NRR expanded during World War II, growing in size and adding support units. Four of its eight battalions saw active service in East Africa, Madagascar, and Burma.[3]

After the end of the war the NRR reverted to a one-battalion regiment. Shortly after the war the NRR saw action again, this time in Palestine.[4] The establishment of the CAF in October 1953 was a dramatic change for the NRR. Since 1923, the settler populations of both Rhodesias advocated merging the two colonies. The CAF was not a straightforward merger of these territories, as each of the member states retained control of almost all its own governance, ceding only defense and foreign affairs to the federal government.[5] This system was complicated by the fact that neither Northern Rhodesia nor Nyasaland gave up its status as a protectorate and still reported to the Colonial Office in London.

The creation of the CAF brought about the establishment of the Federation of Rhodesia and Nyasaland Army. As the largest of the three colonies, Southern Rhodesia contributed the majority of the forces to the new army. Since 1923 the colony had retained a small military staff corps that during World War II expanded into a small army. After World War II, the Rhodesian African Rifles (RAR) and the Royal Rhodesian Regiment (territorial) were retained along with the support branches. Two battalions of the KAR were stationed in what became federal territories, the First Battalion in Nyasaland, and the Second Battalion in Northern Rhodesia, both of which became part of the new army.[6]

The Federal Period

The federal government supported British imperial ventures and frequently offered up units for Commonwealth missions and defense.

Elements of the RAR and the NRR both saw active service in Malaya during the 1954 emergency. During the Malayan deployment, soldiers of the NRR distinguished themselves against the communist insurgents: one African soldier earned the Military Medal and another the Distinguished Conduct Medal.

The amalgamation of the three territorial forces occurred after the passage of the Federal Defense Act of 1954. The act also formed the Ministry of Defence (MOD) and established the statutory authority to govern the defense forces. Prior to this reorganization, the military forces in Northern Rhodesia and Nyasaland fell under the authority of the British Army East Africa Command.[7]

The first step in creating a centralized command structure under the new federation was the establishment of a defense headquarters. The location of the federation capital in Southern Rhodesia confirmed the suspicions of many Africans that the CAF was a move closer to complete settler power. The defense headquarters was established in Salisbury in 1954 as Central Africa Command. The MOD was formed 1956, the same year that the Southern Rhodesian Air Force was renamed the Royal Rhodesian Air Force.

Even as the federal defense apparatus grew, some policy makers in London questioned the validity of the CAF. Lord Home, Prime Minister Anthony Eden's secretary for Commonwealth relations, expressed the cabinet's concerns, arguing that with all of CAF's restrictions, it did not qualify for full dominion status. However, he also conceded that Newfoundland received dominion status even though the United Kingdom controlled all external affairs. Home feared that this precedent could be used to force the British government to grant the CAF even greater freedoms. Eden worried that if the CAF did not get independent status, it would drift even closer to South Africa, further eroding British influence in the region. Perhaps, if the CAF did not feel accepted as a full member of the British community, "they might go their own way—cf. American Colonies."[8] While the comment was made in jest at the time, in less than a decade the federation was dead and Southern Rhodesia declared its independence.

In the midst of such confused politics, the small Federal Army struggled to establish itself and create a balanced and capable force. The influence of Southern Rhodesia on the military establishment was clear. When the forces combined, Southern Rhodesia's compulsory military training

(CMT) program extended throughout the CAF to whites, Asians, and mixed-race males between the ages of eighteen and forty. These men were liable to undergo four and a half months of basic training, followed by four years of service in the Territorial Force, which was called upon to serve alongside the regular forces in internal security operations.[9]

While CMT service in Kenya was confined to the Kenya Regiment, territorial soldiers in the CAF formed a large part of the supporting services of the Rhodesia and Nyasaland Army (R&N Army). The basic training period consisted of three phases: basic soldiering (including weapons training, field craft, and small unit tactics), internal security, and, finally, field problems. All CMT servicemen went through the first phase of training.[10] African infantry training had a syllabus similar to that of the CMT but was extended to six months to accommodate additional English courses. All soldiers in the R&N Army, both black and white, received internal security training, as well as conventional war training. One of the problems that often plagued this small force was that its training cycles were interrupted by call-ups to support civilian authorities in internal security matters. While this provided excellent experience in internal security operations, the ability of the R&N Army to conduct conventional operations suffered.

The R&N Army had three specified missions: aid to civil authorities, internal security, and limited or conventional warfare. As in other colonial examples, two-thirds of the duties of the military centered on maintaining control of the African population. The major units of the army remained the same until 1960: 1NRR, 1KAR, 2KAR, 1RAR, and the Territorial Force, which primarily consisted of the Royal Rhodesian Regiment. When the CAF was formed in 1953, the statute required that the constitutional arrangement be reviewed by the end of the decade. The Monckton Commission, which performed the review, recommended that there be progress toward majority African rule in Northern Rhodesia. The commission concluded that the federation could only survive if all of the territories agreed to participate, which left the door open for any of the territories to secede.[11]

The release of the report in 1959 and the mutiny of the Force Publique in the Congo, which shared a border with the federation, sent shock waves through the European community. A member of the Federal Assembly, Winston Field of Mwera, Southern Rhodesia, quickly brought up the matter of defense policy. Initially, Field made the point that the N&R Army was woefully underfunded and underequipped, citing the report on defense from 1959, which stated, "Whilst our existing weapons are satisfactory for internal purposes, they are obsolescent in the international sense."[12] Field worried that foreign intervention in Africa, particularly from communist forces, would easily outgun the N&R Army. He went on to call for an expansion of the Federal Army to deal with growing communist threats. He advocated establishing a new all-European infantry regiment, which the Federal Assembly authorized. James Graham, the Seventh Duke of Montrose, expressed the settler's fears: "We no longer find when we read of chaos in the newspaper that it is in Korea or Cuba or even Kenya. It is right here at our frontiers."[13] In addition to a new infantry battalion, the federation created an armored car unit and its own special forces unit. All these formations were composed solely of European soldiers.

The new European units were established over the course of 1961. The infantry battalion, the Rhodesian Light Infantry, was the first regular European infantry force in the history of any of the three territories. The new armored car unit, the Rhodesian Armored Car Regiment (also known as the Selous Scouts), carried on the regimental heritage of a Southern Rhodesian unit raised during World War II.[14] Finally, the special operations capability of the federation was "C" Squadron, Rhodesian SAS Regiment (RhSAS), which was first raised during the Malaya Emergency and recruited exclusively from Southern Rhodesia.[15] In addition to these regular units, new Territorial Force units were added to the order of battle, including artillery batteries.[16]

The government launched a recruiting campaign in 1960; a significant portion of this effort focused outside of the federation, in the United Kingdom and South Africa. In 1960, only 752 of the 4,433 regular force's "other ranks" were European, with most of these soldiers in support and specialist roles. By the end of 1962, there was a 78 percent increase in numbers of Europeans in the regular force. The total number of Europeans in the force in 1960 was 1,054, which included officers. The total number of Europeans in the force by the end of 1961 was 1,878.[17] With this expansion of forces the total number of Territorial Force soldiers and regular Europeans outnumbered African soldiers for the first time; Europeans also occupied all of the integral specialty services and supporting arms.

Even though the CAF was looking a bit broken after the Mockton Commission report, European personnel were instrumental to the functioning of the force. While African soldiers in other colonies saw more leadership opportunities open up for them, those who served in the CAF were still limited to the same colonial arrangement.

Interestingly, the same year that the R&N Army began its large-scale European recruiting campaign, the Federal Assembly removed the statutory bar to commissioning Africans.[18] Mr. M. M. Hove of Gwai, Southern Rhodesia, made it clear that in the wake of the Force Publique mutiny the federation would appear both illegitimate and racist if there continued to be only white officers in the army.[19] During that session of the assembly, the legal barrier against commissioning Africans was removed. However, this did not mean that any African men were invited to serve as officers in the army.

The expansion of the army had ripple effects, as did its participation in internal security operations during this period. In 1961, despite a large influx of new officers, the R&N Army reported a shortfall of fifty-two regular officers. While the recruiting of Europeans proceeded quite well, the recruiting of Africans suffered for the first time in years. Up to this point, the army had always met African recruiting goals for the regular force. In 1961, 100 African soldiers left the army, while only 5 African men volunteered for service.[20] Even though recruiting improved army-wide in 1962, it was not enough to make up the shortfall in African enlistments; there was wastage of 448 while 660 new soldiers joined, leaving a shortfall of 148.[21] This was in part due to the few opportunities for advancement for African soldiers in the R&N Army. Even in 1960, prior to large-scale European recruitment, out of the 3,681 African other ranks, only 13 held the rank of warrant officer 1; of the 752 European other ranks, there were 35 who held this rank.[22]

The only development in these last years of the federation that was a positive step for African servicemen was the establishment of a Junior Leaders Unit in Salisbury in 1962. The unit was established for the sons of African soldiers who would join the army as junior soldiers and were educated up to the General Certificate of Education level. The stated goal of the unit was to identify possible African candidates for admission to the Royal Military Academy, Sandhurst, though in the end none were afforded that opportunity. The unit was based near Salisbury, the most restrictive part of the federation for Africans. Instead of going to RMA, all the junior soldiers went into the army as privates.[23] The Junior Leaders Unit was a short-lived experiment, and by the end of 1962 large fissures were forming in the CAF. By the end of 1963, the federation was only a memory.

The End of the Federation

The reevaluation of the constitution in 1959 and the results of the Mockton Commission made it clear that the federation could not continue on its stated course. While many in the British government saw the CAF as a way to counter the rising power of the Afrikaners in South Africa, most Africans saw it as a way for Southern Rhodesian settlers to dominate the region. Macmillan's policy to accelerate decolonization had a dramatic impact on the CAF. The 1961 CAF constitution removed many of the oversight functions that London had previously exercised over the federation. In return, the franchise was to be extended to a wider portion of the African population in alignment with the recommendations of the Mockton Commission.

These policy changes were paired with increasing pro-independence activities by Zambian nationalists. African political parties grew in both Northern Rhodesia and Nyasaland during the federation era and by the 1960s were serious players in federation politics. Prior to the formation of the CAF, the African nationalist movements had not been able to achieve mass appeal to the African public. The first six years of the federation experiment and the strict enforcement of the color bar led to increased enthusiasm for the movements among the African public.[24] The Northern Rhodesia African National Congress (NRANC), formed in 1948, attacked the federation political system. The NRANC originally attempted to work within the system with the hope that Africans could achieve parity in politics.

In 1957, however, a new wave of militancy took over within the NRANC, in part as a reaction to the British failure in Suez. In exchange for the support the federation offered to the British in the Suez operation, the British government gave federal authorities a free hand in dealing with African aspirations. That same year Alan Lennox-Boyd, then secretary of state for the colonies, told Africans that the federation "is good for you . . . and you must accept it."[25] The NRANC concluded that it could no longer look to Britain as an honest broker in its struggle with the federal government and felt there was no chance of achieving independence by working from within the political system. Divisions also grew within NRANC as Kenneth Kaunda, a rising star in the NRANC in the late 1950s, began to disagree with Harry Nkumbula, one of the other major party leaders, over the best strategy to reach independence. As a result, Kaunda broke away from the NRANC and formed the Zambian African National Congress (ZANC) in 1958.

Kaunda and the ZANC stepped up their protests and opposition to the federal government. His speeches became increasingly militant, encouraging Africans to "begin to hate everything white which had two legs."[26] However, Kaunda himself never advocated violence and intended to stop short of any sort of violent revolution. By February 1959, the settler government was tired of ZANC agitation: Kaunda was arrested, and ZANC banned. At the same time, Dr. Hastings Banda, the leader of the Nyasaland African Congress, was arrested and his organization was banned. For these nationalist leaders, imprisonment was a rite of passage that they hoped would lead to political legitimacy in independence. In response to the ban on activities of the ZANC, its members formed the United National Independence Party (UNIP) in August 1959. When Kaunda was released from prison in January 1960, he was elected president of the UNIP.

The 1959 general election in Britain gave the Conservative Party a one-hundred-seat majority in the Commons. The victory was accompanied by a ministerial shake-up that brought Iain Macleod to the office of secretary of state for the colonies. Macleod was slightly more sympathetic to the ambitions of Africans within the CAF than his predecessors had been. After a series of failed review conferences on the state of the federation, he announced a change in the constitution of Northern Rhodesia, which would divide the territorial assembly into fifteen seats each for Africans, Europeans, and members mutually agreed upon by both communities. The UNIP and the main settler group, the United Federal Party, were unsure of the arrangement. Yet, in June 1960 Macleod released details of the franchise qualifications that limited the possibility of an African majority government. This news was greeted by widespread disorder in Northern Rhodesia. In the Copperbelt, twenty-seven Africans died and three thousand were arrested in the riots that followed. The British government recognized that the only way that African ambitions could be contained was through large-scale force. Rather than take the CAF down this path, the franchise details were revised for the 1962 elections, which provided the basis for the transfer of power to the African majority.[27]

By 1962 it was clear that the territories of the CAF were moving in separate directions. Nyasaland and Northern Rhodesia were on the fast track to independence while Southern Rhodesia was even more entrenched in the idea of independence on its own terms. The United Federal Party fell apart, and another more radical party took its place. In early 1962 a young Rhodesian farmer and former Royal Air Force pilot named Ian Smith formed a small party called the Rhodesia Reform Party. Smith and a wealthy rancher from Southern Rhodesia, Douglas "Boss" Lilford, began negotiations with Winston Field and what remained of his small Dominion Party; the three men agreed to join forces to form a new political party, the Rhodesian Front (RF).[28] The RF was founded on the principles of preserving settler power in the territories, both financially and politically; it did not contest the last federal elections, since they acknowledged that the CAF was coming to an end. Instead, the RF concentrated all its efforts on the 1962 elections for the Southern Rhodesia Assembly. In a dramatic and unexpected turn of events, the RF won thirty-five of the sixty-four seats in the assembly, placing the RF firmly in power in Southern Rhodesia.

By May 1962 it was clear that Nyasaland would secede from the federation. In March 1963, delegations from all the territories traveled to London to discuss the future of the region. The British cabinet decided on 28 March that Northern Rhodesia could secede, and the federation would dissolve. In June all the governments concerned met at the Victoria Falls Hotel to divide up the assets of the soon to be defunct federation.[29] The division of assets shaped the security situation in the region for decades. At the time of the dissolution of the federation, it possessed one of the largest and most advanced air forces in Africa. In the post-1960 military buildup, the RRAF had acquired an impressive fleet of around sixty combat aircraft, including modern jets and helicopters.[30] In addition to the robust airpower capability, the army had built itself up to a two-brigade organization, with armored forces and airborne capability. The only larger military force in the region was the South Africa Defense Force.[31]

Dividing the Assets

The earlier expansion of the R&N Army and the RRAF made the division of the forces among the territories more difficult. In addition to all the forces that had not existed in 1953, the British were left with the task of ensuring that each territory received enough of the federation's forces to form complete defense forces of their own. For African units, this was relatively simple. They remained in the territories they were recruited in. However, 1KAR and 2KAR posed a bit of a problem. Both of the KAR battalions were raised and stationed in Nyasaland, yet the British government did not wish to encourage the small Nyasa government to retain a two-battalion army that it could not afford.[32] The MOD proposed that 2KAR go to Northern Rhodesia and form the second battalion of the NRR.

Prior to the Victoria Falls Conference, Sir Roy Welensky communicated to the British government in a top-secret cable the defense implications of the end of the federation. Welensky and the settler community saw Angola, Mozambique, and the federation as a line of defense against communist influence in southern Africa. Welensky and the federal authorities made it clear that if the northern territories became independent, they would become a base of operations for dissident elements to infiltrate Southern Rhodesia.[33] He also communicated to the British government that if the federation fell apart, Southern Rhodesia would require the same military and air services that the federation had utilized. Additionally, this would require a closer relationship between the Rhodesians and South Africa, both politically and militarily.[34]

The MOD in London thought that Southern Rhodesia would attempt to retain as much of the force as possible. The Southern Rhodesians were keen on retaining the entirety of the RRAF with all its modern equipment. In addition to the forces, the MOD suspected that the Rhodesians would simply try to take over the federation MOD and forces Headquarters that were already in Salisbury.[35] The British government was concerned about how the distribution of forces and talent would end up. Of particular concern was the prospect of white flight from the northern territories if and when the federation was dissolved. There were no African officers in the R&N Army, so if European officers and NCOs in the north chose instead to serve in Southern Rhodesia, there would be serious manpower problems. Yet the most important goal that the British set for themselves in Northern Rhodesia was the same goal they set in Kenya; "We should like to cast the armed forces of Northern Rhodesia and Nyasaland in as British a mold as possible in the short period left before independence."[36]

While the main concern of the British government was the distribution of the European personnel in the new defense arrangement, the British also had questions about African soldiers. The unit that they considered the cause for trepidation was 2KAR. Although in April 1963 the unit was stationed in NR, it was recruited exclusively from Nyasaland. Under the federal arrangement this was not an issue, but once Nyasaland withdrew from the federation, the British government was not confident that 2KAR would be able to recruit enough new soldiers. Additionally, Dr. Banda had made it clear that he did want to retain the two battalions to form the basis of the new Malawian Army. He even offered the British the use of 2KAR as part of the Commonwealth defense scheme.[37] The British government had no intention of accepting the offer; the likelihood of the troops remaining reliably trained and ready for deployment outside the country after independence was quite slim.[38]

The federal government wanted to punish Nyasaland for leaving. Initially the federal government claimed that Nyasaland had no claim on any of the R&N Army since the forces belonged to the federal government, which even wanted to go so far as to disband both KAR battalions.[39] The British government convinced the federal government that since the War Office had handed over fully manned and equipped units to it in 1954, it was obligated to do the same with regard to the KAR battalions. The Nyasaland government was eventually dissuaded from retaining 2KAR in its order of battle due to the cost of the additional battalion. The British government helped this along by refusing additional financial and personnel assistance to support a second battalion in the Nyasaland Army.

The main squabble over forces ended up being between the two Rhodesias. While the disposition of the units of the army was settled with relative ease, the partition of the RRAF was particularly contentious. The Victoria Falls Conference ended up having no African input. An all-European committee outside of the conference itself decided the actual disposition of the forces. The Central Africa Office simply reported that after the dismantling of the federation the situation would revert to the pre-1953 arrangement, Southern Rhodesia would control its own forces, and until independence the British government would retain operational control of the forces in the north.[40]

There were objections to this both in Britain and in Northern Rhodesia. The Labour Party insisted that it was a mistake to allow Southern Rhodesia to be so well armed, considering its opposition to racial equality.[41] Jasper Savanhu, the member of Federal Parliament from Angwa/Sabi, attempted to pass a motion condemning the actions of the Defense Working Committee. He claimed that the committee was "either misled or hoodwinked by the clever manipulations of the settler elements . . . which now seem to have agreed to the permanency of a European-dominated Government in Southern Rhodesia."[42] His assertion was accurate: the working committee consisted of officials from the Southern Rhodesia government, the British government, and a select group of officials from the northern territories invited by the British.[43] The European members of the Federal Assembly put forth a variety of reasons for the form the division of resources took, most if not all of them weak. However, the objections of Labour, local Africans, and the UN fell on deaf ears, and the partition of the forces occurred along the lines set up by the settler-dominated working committee.

In his speech on the division of the defense forces, Mr. Savanhu argued that most of the Europeans in the northern territories intended to flee south after the dissolution of the federation. While this seemed like an ideal arrangement for African nationalists, it was a nightmare scenario for the British government. The entire civil and military administrative organization in the northern territories was composed of Europeans of the settler communities, many of whom were experienced civil servants. If they left without training African replacements, the colony would likely descend rapidly into administrative chaos.

The British government had neither the available manpower nor the resources to replace all the officers in the northern regiments with seconded British officers. The MOD hoped that it would be able to entice enough officers from the Federal Army to stay on in Northern Rhodesia after the disillusionment to train and create an independent force. Officers and European other ranks in the federal forces were given six possible options for the future of their military careers: sign on to serve in the proposed Southern Rhodesia Army; retire or be discharged; apply to serve on a Short Service Commission (SSC) in the Northern Rhodesia Army; apply to serve in the Northern Rhodesian Army on a two-year (extendable)

British Army SSC; apply to serve in the Nyasaland Army on a two-year (extendable) British Army SSC; or join the British Army with a permanent regular army commission, on the condition that the first two years after transferring be spent on secondment to the forces of either of the northern territories.[44]

While the British government knew that it could not absorb all the officers of the R&N Army, it strove to keep as many federal officers as possible in the northern territories after independence. Members of the Southern Rhodesia Army who opted to serve on secondment in the northern territories were offered additional pay.[45] Even though the British offered the chance for some to take up a regular army commission in the British Army, the prospects of acceptance were slim. The average age of officers in the R&N Army was somewhat older than in the British Army, and there were very few opportunities for older men. Most officers in the Federal Army were infantry officers, and there were only twenty-one openings in the British Army for infantry officers over the age of twenty-five.[46]

Even though settlers had limited career prospects in the British Army, both the British government and the African members of the Northern Rhodesia government wanted to make it clear that there was a future for Europeans in the country. In fact, the British government made sure to highlight the opportunities available in the Northern Rhodesian Army. The MOD and the federal authorities made it clear in their advice to federal officers that the Northern Rhodesian Army was going to expand to brigade strength with the requisite support units.[47] The MOD knew that there were simply not enough available junior officers in the British Army to fill the slots. Additionally, there was no prospect of quickly promoting WO and NCOs as had been done in Kenya. In July 1963 the R&N Army had identified only three Africans who had the potential and the requisite educational requirements for commissioning in the forces.[48] Northern Rhodesia needed European officers for the foreseeable future not only to train the army but also to hold it together.

Since the sympathies of the majority of the senior officers in the R&N Army were with Southern Rhodesia, the MOD decided that a British officer would be placed in command of the Northern Rhodesia Army.[49] As early as July 1963, it was understood that a British officer would retain the command until at least 1970. Major General George Lea was the first officer selected for the assignment. Lea's long service and vast experience in both conventional and special operations, including commanding a battalion of paratroopers during World War II, made him an excellent choice to train a new army from the remnants of the R&N Army. Above all else, the British authorities wanted to keep a lasting defense relationship between Northern Rhodesia and Britain. The MOD recognized that it would be very tempting for the new African government of Northern Rhodesia to look elsewhere for assistance; it was Lea's job to prevent this.[50]

Independence

The Federation of Rhodesia and Nyasaland was dissolved on 31 December 1963, bringing an end to settler domination in the two northern territories. Nyasaland achieved self-governing status, and achieved independence in July 1964 as Malawi, under the leadership of Dr. Banda. Similarly, in January 1964, Northern Rhodesia was slated to hold new elections and scheduled to become independent in October 1964. Prior to the elections there was a period of violence between the youth wings of the major African parties, with both sides claiming they were targeting Africans who they believed had supported the Europeans.[51] The elections themselves went relatively smoothly, aside from settler claims that they were marginalized. The UNIP swept to power, and on 23 January Prime Minister Kenneth Kaunda announced an all-African UNIP cabinet. The UNIP and Kaunda agreed that the military needed to reflect the racial makeup of the country. In the end Kaunda said he wanted a multiracial officer corps that included Europeans, Africans, and Asians and insisted that the military be insulated from political interference.[52]

As elections were being held in what from this point became Zambia, mutinies broke out in the armies of East Africa. When the mutinies began, Major General Lea reported to the Central Africa Office that they would only have an "unsettling effect" in Zambia if they were handled in such a way that showed "that mutiny pays we may, repeat, may be in trouble here in the future."[53] While the virus spread throughout East Africa, the mood was calm in Northern Rhodesia. Special Branch reported some feelings of sympathy for the mutineers in the lower ranks, particularly concerning the continued presence of British officers, but the NCOs were reportedly disgusted with the behavior of the East African troops.[54]

There was no evidence of any drop in loyalty or reliability of the Northern Rhodesia forces after the East African incidents. A planned pay raise that took effect in June 1964 prevented immediate complaints over pay. However, the Central African Office made it clear that it could not rule out the possibility of future unrest. It pointed out three scenarios that might have an impact on the loyalty and stability of the military: if Kaunda were overthrown by a more extremist leader; if Kaunda were forced to reward UNIP officials with positions in the army; and if the UNIP was successful in disbanding the Police Mobile Unit.[55] Any one of these situations had the potential to throw off the balance of power in the country. For example, the Police Mobile Unit handled most of the internal security duties in Northern Rhodesia. If it were disbanded, the military would have a monopoly on the use of force in the country.

On 31 January the governor of Northern Rhodesia, Sir Evelyn Hone, discussed the situation in East Africa with Kaunda. The prime minster understood that British action in the region occurred only at the request of the local governments, not out of a desire to reestablish control. Kaunda also assured Hone that he wanted the military to be an apolitical force and subscribed to the idea of promotion only by merit. Along these same lines, Hone wanted to make sure that Kaunda understood that due to financial constraints the British military was able to produce only a limited number of African officers every year. Due to the small number of places allocated at RMA for international students, it was difficult for any one country to be given more than two or three places. Any attempt to speed up the rate of production would almost assuredly dilute the quality of training and preparation that the officer cadets received.[56]

While there were soldiers in Northern Rhodesia who sympathized with their comrades in East Africa, being disconnected from the culture of the KAR since 1953 created ideological distance between the units. The regiments in Northern Rhodesia did not experience the period of increased African responsibility as those in the KAR had. When the East African regiments revived the effendi rank and gave some Africans responsibility for the command of platoons, soldiers in Northern Rhodesia saw an increase in the number of officers from the settler community. The incidents in East Africa reinforced the belief among British officers and policy makers that the Zambia Army needed to be aloof from domestic politics if it was going to succeed.

The War Office asked the governor of Northern Rhodesia and Major General Lea to consider accelerating the rate of Africanization, whether mass commissioning of warrant officers was feasible, and if a crash cadet program there or even in Britain was necessary. Looking back at their experience in Kenya, the British government thought that commissioning a large batch of the most senior African warrant officers might work; African warrant officers and NCOs in Northern Rhodesia were not groomed for advancement. Lea warned that mass promotion of warrant officers would give commissions to many illiterate soldiers.[57] There was simply not a suitable group available as there had been in Kenya within the army to begin a large-scale direct commissioning program.

Major General Lea's intention was to commission thirty-five Northern Rhodesian officers by 1966. These new officers were supposed to be representative of the demographic makeup of the nation at a ratio of five Africans to one non-African. However, when Kaunda's government reevaluated its position after the mutinies, it abandoned the idea of a multiracial officer corps until after rapid Africanization occurred. Under pressure from the UNIP government, Lea had to double the officer production goal to seventy by 1966. While there were vacancies for African cadets at both Mons and Sandhurst, Lea was doubtful that the government would be able to attract enough qualified applicants. Educated Africans were more likely to take jobs in the private sector, and the British government was not forthcoming with places at either academy for Africans.[58]

In light of the events in East Africa, all these recommendations came with a warning. The governors and Major General Lea made it clear that Pan-Africanism was becoming a potent force in influencing the ideas and behaviors of African leaders in emerging nations. Concurrently, both Ghana and the Soviet bloc were putting pressure on Britain and the West to end white rule in southern Africa. The British government could only count on Kaunda to resist this pressure for so long before he would need to take an active role in challenging white rule in Africa. The most pressing concern of the British government was maintaining military influence. However, military and political considerations were not aligned concerning the pace of training potentially risking British influence: "Failure to move fast enough even at the risk of substantial loss of military efficiency, may therefore cause extremist pressures to grow so fast that all control over ordered progress and the retention of the British alignment in the military sphere will be lost."[59] The experience in Kenya and in East Africa demonstrated to British policy makers that African soldiers and politicians were not willing to follow the British down a slow road toward decolonization.

Major General Lea and the British military staff in Northern Rhodesia were in a less than ideal situation prior to independence. The effort to retain as many federation personnel as possible did not fare as well as the British government had hoped. The Northern Rhodesia Army had billets for forty-five European officers and twenty-three European other ranks in the two battalions of the Northern Rhodesia Regiment. However, it filled only seventeen officers' billets and eight other ranks.[60] Similarly, the Northern Rhodesia Air Force had a full complement of sixteen European officers but only nineteen of the eighty required enlisted personnel.

The MOD felt it was in British interests to remain engaged in the country for three reasons: to help maintain a British presence, to reduce the likelihood of assistance being sought from nations unfriendly to Britain, and to facilitate the reentry of British forces if necessary.[61] British defense officials wanted the training mission to create a multiracial officer corps rather than a solely African one.[62] The British intention to retain some European officers in the army indefinitely would eventually put them at odds with the Kaunda government and the UNIP.

The independence ceremonies occurred on 24 October 1964. When the Union Jack was lowered in Lusaka, the Republic of Zambia was born. While many in the new nation had come together under the banner of the UNIP to fight against settler power, they were far from a united group. After independence the UNIP had to work out what its new political objectives and interests were. Kaunda and the UNIP were influenced by Kenyan politician and author Tom Mboya's ideas on East African unity and federation.[63] The problem was that the UNIP did not grasp the finer points of Mboya's proposals. He made it clear that simply being black was not enough to get Africans to cooperate politically and economically. The traditional relationships inside Zambia came to the surface, and the simple unity in opposition to colonialism began to fade away. British policy makers had to consider the declining level of goodwill for direct involvement in the affairs of these newly independent states in future assistance programs.

The first batch of officers in the Zambia Army began training prior to independence. In February 1964, twenty-three officer cadets were in training at Mons, RMA, or the School of Military Training, Ndola. The eight warrant officers selected for training went to Ndola to go through a special commissioning course.[64] Due to the lack of qualified personnel in the army, the Zambian government shifted its focus to recruiting African school leavers to train as officers. The Zambians mirrored the process of accessions in Britain; an Officer Selection Board (OSB) put applicants through a series of written and physical exams to determine their leadership potential. After passing through the OSB, the potential officers went to a preparatory course at Kalewa Barracks in Ndola. During the 1965 OSB process, fourteen applicants were selected to attend the prep course at Kalewa. The three-month course consisted of basic military instruction, drill and ceremonies, and a period of training at the Outward Bound School in Mbala. This school included courses in rock climbing, sailing, backpacking, and free-fall parachuting, in order to challenge the officer cadets both mentally and physically in rough terrain.[65]

After officer cadets returned to Kalewa from the Outward Bound School, they received their overseas training assignments. By 1965 other Commonwealth countries, including Canada, India, and Pakistan, offered military training assistance to the Zambian government. These institutions were acceptable to the British government because they followed the British military tradition. All these commissioning courses, which were based on the curriculum from British commissioning courses, focused on the gentlemanly characteristics of officership, many of which were learned in the officers' mess or through athletic competition. These were reinforced in the classroom, where a code of honor set the conditions for behavior at both the individual and the collective level.[66]

The course of instruction at RMA involved significant university-level academic study. The subject areas included math, current affairs, military history, and the sciences. Initially, it took two years to complete the course. It was not until the reorganization of the officer training programs in 1972 that the course was reduced to one year and focused more on practical military training. In addition to academic subjects, the officer cadets learned basic infantry platoon tactics, skill at arms training, and field craft in the training areas around the academy. Overseas field training exercises augmented the on-campus instruction. Francis Sibamba was one of three officer cadets from the 1965 OSB selected to attend RMA. During his time at RMA, he went on training missions to Cyprus, Germany, and France. Participation in exercises with NATO forces while attached to the British Army exposed Zambian officer cadets to the professionalism of Western armies. Those Zambian cadets who attended RMA returned to Zambia with certain expectations about levels of training and professionalism.[67]

From 1964 until the establishment of the Zambian Military Academy in 1971, three Zambian cadets went on to every Sandhurst intake. Even though Zambian cadets were in every RMA intake, the amount of time required for the course was just too much of a burden for the new army to shoulder. After selection at the OSB, it took almost two and a half years to produce a lieutenant ready for service in a line infantry battalion. Due to the long period of training required by RMA, most Zambian officers received their training and commissions through Mons Officer Cadet School. The six-month course at Mons reduced the time required to nine months.[68]

Although the military was attempting to become a completely Africanized force, it was far from a respected institution in Zambia. Sibamba commented that the army had a poor reputation among Zambians because of the "colonial hang-over."[69] The Zambian people still saw the military as a reflection of colonialism and thought that soldiers were uneducated and poorly disciplined. The new Zambian government hoped to change this impression through the Africanization of the officer corps and promotion of Africans to high-level command.[70]

Unilateral Declaration of Independence

The events of 1965 complicated Zambia's security situation. Prior to November of that year, the greatest security concerns that the country faced were conflicts in Angola or Mozambique spilling across their borders. In November 1965 the disagreement between Rhodesia and the British government over the prospect of independence was at an impasse. In October talks between Harold Wilson's government and the Rhodesian Front cabinet broke down over the principle of equal voting rights for African citizens.[71] On 11 November 1965, the Rhodesian government led by Ian Smith unilaterally declared independence, announcing:

We Rhodesians have rejected the doctrinaire philosophy of appease-
ment and surrender. The decision which we have taken today is a
refusal by Rhodesians to sell their birthright. And, even if we were
to surrender, does anyone believe that Rhodesia would be the last
target of the Communists in the Afro-Asian block? We have struck
a blow for the preservation of justice, civilization, and Christianity;
and in the spirit of this belief we have this day assumed our sovereign
independence. God bless you all.[72]

While Smith assured Rhodesia's African neighbors that they had nothing
to fear, he also warned them not to meddle in Rhodesian affairs. Both
Zambia and Britain were in an awkward position. The British government
ruled out the possibility of using force to bring the Rhodesian government
back in line, and the Zambia government depended on rail lines from Victoria Falls to Beria to export copper and import petrol.[73]

Initially the Zambian government encouraged Britain to use force to
end the rebellion in Rhodesia, as Britain had done in British Guyana in
1953.[74] Kaunda insisted that if the British government did not dispatch
troops to Zambia to deal with the Rhodesian problem, he would appeal
to other nations to do so.[75] The Organisation of African Unity (OAU) put
enormous pressure on Kaunda to host an all-African force to invade Rhodesia. Even though Kaunda was sympathetic to the goals of the OAU, he
was a pragmatic leader and knew that an invasion of Rhodesia by African
forces could end in disaster for him and Zambia's small army.

Harold Wilson was concerned about what the reaction of the British
public might be to using military force in Rhodesia, fighting "kith and
kin." Even so, plans were underway to deploy a battalion to Zambia. The
British army issued a warning order for Operation Amberley, as it was
titled, with Royal Marines earmarked to spearhead the effort.[76] The operational plans for the introduction of a single battalion group into Zambia
required deploying an infantry battalion from Aden and sustaining it via
an air bridge. Defense planners in Whitehall concluded that dispatching
a battalion and the huge number of aircraft needed to maintain the force
for any length of time would inhibit the ability of the British government
to respond to any other contingency worldwide.[77] However, the Wilson
government concluded that dispatching a battalion would be too much
provocation and scrapped the plan. To pacify the Zambian insistence on

British military forces, Wilson agreed to send a squadron of RAF Javelin fighter aircraft to protect Zambian airspace. Stationing RAF jets in Zambia was only a show of force; they were of no tactical value. By 1964 the Javelin was an outdated aircraft, the first variant having entered service in 1947; the Hawker Hunter fighters of the Royal Rhodesian Air Force (RRAF) were certainly capable of defeating the Javelins in air combat. By the end of 1966, the Javelins were retired from RAF service.[78]

With the British unwilling to reinforce Zambia with ground forces, Kaunda decided that the military needed to be built up at a swifter pace than had previously been planned. When he announced the expansion on 9 December 1965, it came as a complete surprise to British officers in the Zambian defense establishment.[79] When the Unilateral Declaration of Independence was announced, the Zambia Army included only twenty-two hundred regular soldiers. The main concern of Zambian policy makers was that the Rhodesian government would interfere with common services on the Zambezi River, specifically electricity from the Kariba Dam.[80] The establishment of the third battalion of the Zambia Regiment accelerated, and the battalion was activated in 1966. Lieutenant Francis Sibamba was posted to the newly established Third Battalion, Zambia Regiment (3ZR) after he graduated from RMA. In his memoir, he made it clear that the possibility of facing the Rhodesian Army posed moral problems for African officers in the Zambia Army. He befriended a Rhodesian cadet, Andrew Blaine, during his Sandhurst days. When 3ZR was deployed to the Zambezi to guard the border, he was faced with a vexing moral problem: "Facing Rhodesian soldiers, you can imagine my conscience playing havoc at the thought of shooting Andrew, taking him captive, or vice versa!"[81]

European officers serving in the Zambia Army also faced the prospect of fighting their Rhodesian counterparts. In some cases, these were men with whom they had served in the Federal Army. While this certainly caused sleepless nights for some of these officers, the British government was concerned about the prospect of seconded officers caught in an engagement with Rhodesian troops. In 1966 this only seemed like an unfortunate possibility, but the seriousness of such an incident mounted as the Rhodesian situation worsened. Harold Wilson and Ian Smith met for negotiations on board HMS *Tiger* in December 1966. The negotiations revolved around the British position of no independence before majority

rule. Smith refused the British proposal of independence based on the
1961 constitution, with amendments made to give Africans more seats in
the assembly immediately.[82]

The failure of the *Tiger* talks and the ineffective economic sanctions
made the situation worse. In 1967 the British government reached the
point of planning for military intervention against the Rhodesian Front
government. Such a scheme was simply too politically risky and resource-
intensive, however, and the Wilson government dropped the idea.[83] In
1967 and 1968 the Zambian government became increasingly concerned
by the activities of liberation movements in Mozambique, Angola, and
Rhodesia. Some of the liberation fighters infiltrated their respective target
countries through Zambian territory. In August 1967 a group of ninety
guerrilla fighters from the Zimbabwe African Peoples Union (ZAPU)
and the African National Congress (ANC) slipped into Rhodesia in the
vicinity of Victoria Falls from Zambia. The ZAPU fighters hoped to start
a Maoist insurgent movement in the Tjolotjo Tribal Trust Land, while
the ANC fighters planned on infiltrating South Africa through Botswana.
Rhodesian intelligence soon had information on the size and whereabouts
of the group and destroyed it.[84] This incident upped the ante for Zambia: not only had these men come from its territory, but the participation
of the ANC in the operation brought South Africa into the simmering
conflict. Concerned by the possible infiltration of guerrilla fighters from
Zambia into South Africa, the Pretoria government deployed a force of
three thousand militarized South African Police officers to patrol the
Zambezi in cooperation with Rhodesian forces. These officers completed
a counterinsurgency course prior to deployment and were more soldiers
than policemen. The South African government also sent aviation support, with its forces adding to the formidable helicopter fleet the Rhodesian Air Force already possessed.

The Zambian government faced off against two unfriendly forces
across the Zambezi whose combined military power dwarfed the small
Zambia Army. In response to these emerging threats on their border,
Kaunda's government pleaded with the Britain for more modern heavy
equipment. Kaunda also sent representatives to the United States to try
to secure American arms. These efforts failed, and the Zambian government had to make do with the arms and training the British were willing
to provide; fortunately, this did include the sale of British surface-to-air
missile systems. The Zambian defense staff resolved that it was necessary

to form a fourth battalion of the Zambia Regiment to meet all the nation's security demands. In addition to the new infantry battalion, the Zambian government intended to expand the ground-based air defense system by creating an antiaircraft missile battery and an antiaircraft battery armed with 20mm antiaircraft guns.[85]

In light of the rapid expansion of the Zambian defense forces and the deteriorating situation on almost all of Zambia's borders, the British government wanted to renegotiate the defense assistance scheme. On 21 February 1968, the Zambian minister of foreign affairs signed a new status of forces agreement (SOFA) for the British training mission.[86] The most notable aspects of the agreement were the limitations put on British officers serving in the Zambia Army. The British government worked throughout 1967 to prevent the possibility of its officers ending up in a combat situation. When Zambia became independent, Major General Lea noted that a training team arrangement was not useful in Zambia. However, allowing troops to remain part of the indigenous command structure reduced the control that senior British officers had over their actions and movements. This same issue had become a problem in Kenya in 1967. The British government hoped to avoid a similar situation in Zambia.[87]

In order to prevent the possibility of a British officer ending up commanding troops against Rhodesian, Portuguese, or South African forces, the SOFA prohibited British officers from commanding Zambian units that were on operational service on the Rhodesian border.[88] By the end of 1967, all British officers who occupied combat positions in the Zambia Army were transferred into advising and training positions. Also, starting in 1967, those British officers were not replaced when their terms of service in Zambia expired.

Even though the British training mission became smaller each year, the Zambian government admitted in 1967 that immediate "Zambianization" was impossible and that it needed to continue recruiting expatriate contracted officers from both the United Kingdom and Ireland. In a letter to Harold Wilson, Kenneth Kaunda wrote, "In spite of various communications which have passed between our two governments regarding the Defence Force, I am alive to the necessity of maintaining a loyal and efficient Defence Force, and to this end I intend to continue to recruit a certain category of expatriate officers from the United Kingdom and the Republic of Ireland."[89]

While this scheme did contain certain advantages for the British government, it was disapproved by the Foreign and Commonwealth Office (FCO). The British recognized that if they did approve the scheme to subsidize this recruitment, they would commit the Zambia Army to continuing to seek services from British and Commonwealth sources. However, the focus of the British government at the time was simply to get the Zambian government to agree to signing the SOFA to remove British troops from combat roles and provide legal protections for them and their families.[90] Even before the agreement was signed, a memorandum of discussion was signed in the summer of 1967 that agreed to most of the provisions of the draft until the final agreement was signed.

In November 1967 trouble on the Congo border tested these guidelines. The government decided to deploy two companies of First Battalion Zambia Regiment (1ZR) to the area, both commanded by British officers. Even though this was the type of situation the British were trying to avoid, they approved the deployment of these two officers. Since the operation did not involve a situation where the enemy might be Rhodesian or South African, this use of British personnel was seen as acceptable.[91] This distinction demonstrated that the British were willing to use force against Africans but not against settler communities.

In actuality, the British were growing impatient with their own training mission. Not only were the constant costs of the mission a source of irritation, but the personnel requirements were becoming a burden to the British Army. In London the MOD hoped to run down the army component of training mission as soon as possible.[92] In the same memo the defense staff made it clear that they were also concerned that British forces would be engaged in operations against the South Africans, Rhodesians, or Portuguese inside Zambia's borders.

The Zambia Army was extremely reliant on British and contracted expatriate officers. Colonel Bade, the defense adviser, noted that the Zambia Army was also having a difficult time retaining and recruiting contracted expatriate officers due to poor rates of pay and terms of service. In 1966 the Zambian government went to great effort to reduce the cost of expatriate personnel by normalizing their pay scales with local Zambian officers.[93] Colonel Bade also emphasized to the MOD: "Whatever happens in the end will be a mess, and no doubt the blame will be laid at our doorstep."[94] From the British perspective the training mission in Zambia was winding down. By December 1968 there were expected to be only twenty

British officers in country, whose tours were scheduled to end by July 1969, completing the army component of the mission.

The Zambia Army, like the Kenya Army, was quickly filling its officer ranks with qualified African infantry officers. However, the greatest need for officers was in the supporting arms and specialized combat arms units. One British captain detailed from the Royal Artillery to command the Zambian Light Battery was filling multiple positions in 1967. He was serving not only as the commander of the battery but also as director of signals for the entire army simply because the Zambians could not find anyone to replace him.[95] The problem was twofold: the Zambian government refused to offer terms that were attractive to European expatriate officers, and Zambia was facing enormous administrative issues that were bogging down its government. Even though the SOFA was agreed upon and was ready for signature in early December 1967, it was not actually signed until several months later. The British High Commission in Lusaka learned that the Zambian Ministry of Foreign Affairs was in a state of administrative disarray, often losing paperwork and correspondence.[96] Nonetheless, the Zambian government finally signed the agreement, and the British Army hoped that the end of its training mission was in sight.

As the British training team officers left Zambia, there was still a need for expatriates to fill the gaps in capabilities. In 1967 Kaunda had visited India and explored the possibility of establishing a military-to-military relationship. The Indian government insisted that if the Zambians were to accept military assistance, they would have to agree to India being the sole provider or receive no assistance at all. The British government first learned of the possibility of South Asian military assistance when the Zambians planned a recruiting mission for both India and Pakistan in 1968. The Zambian government wanted to send two British training team officers to recruit Indian and Pakistani officers to serve on a contract basis in the Zambia Army.[97] Initially the proposed recruiting mission caught the British government off guard, particularly since the entire trip had been planned with the intent of sending British personnel without informing the High Commission. However, once both the Commonwealth Office and the MOD had a chance to weigh in on the matter, they agreed that any measures that the Zambian government took to improve the state of their forces within certain boundaries should be encouraged.[98]

In February 1968 the Zambia Army was still struggling to build up its officer corps. Of the 228 officers in the army, 32 were on loan from the British Army, 94 were expatriates serving on contracts, and the remaining 102 were Zambian. Of the Zambian officers two were majors, with six more expected to be by April 1968. Additionally, from February 1968 on, no more Europeans were to be appointed to command infantry companies. The NCO corps was actually further behind in the Zambianization process than the officer corps. Of the 474 senior NCOs in the army, only 168 were Zambian—the rest were British, European expatriates, or Malawian.[99] There were problems emerging in the army by this point. On orders from President Kaunda the army commander started an investigation into political activity within the service. The investigation did uncover an active United Party cell in Arakan Barracks. While this was a point of concern for the government, particularly because this was an opposition party, it signaled the need to ensure that the army remained apolitical. Factionalism within the military was also beginning to be a concern for both British officers and Zambian policy makers. As the number of Zambian officers and NCOs increased, so did concerns about their ethnic background. Initially the Zambia Army had instituted a quota policy for officer selection. This was followed in 1968 by an order that required that the allocation of overseas training courses be representative of the country's ethnic diversity.[100]

The training of officers in counterinsurgency operations took center stage during the early part of 1968. Expatriate and African officers were required to attend three officer study periods on the subject between January and March. Colonel Bade attended one of the sessions and noted: "I was surprised to see how very bad were the expatriate officers at tactical appreciations and orders. The African officers made little contribution and did not take criticism easily."[101] This made it very clear to the MOD that even though the training mission was rapidly coming to a close, the Zambia Army was far from capable of operating on its own, even with the help of expatriates. The problem was not only the capabilities of the officers in the Zambia Army but also related to the lack of specialty officers. As of May 1968, the brigade workshop and army workshops were critically short of qualified technicians. The Zambian government counted on the upcoming recruiting mission to India and Pakistan to help alleviate these shortfalls.[102] The shortfalls were compounded by the fact that in December 1968 fifty expatriate officers and NCOs left the army.

The British and the Zambians were growing impatient with the progress of the training mission. In March 1968 a graduation parade was held for a batch of Zambian Air Force (ZAF) officers who qualified as pilots. Colonel Bade attended and commented: "In his address the President, who was the reviewing officer, characteristically omitted the passage which the drafter had included praising the RAF for its part in building the ZAF. Gratitude it seems is not a Zambian trait."[103] Even though patience was wearing thin on both sides, building up the army into a self-sustaining organization was a long process. To alleviate the lack of technical personnel, several Zambians went to specialty courses in Britain: two to an automobile engineering course, one for training in nursing, and one to train in ordnance. It would be the early 1970s before very many Zambian officers had undergone specialist training to take up these positions within their own army.

As the activities of guerrillas increased on Zambian borders, so did the tensions with their neighbors. In April 1968 Portuguese aircraft bombed three Zambian villages where guerrillas had allegedly been based prior to infiltrating into Angola. The ZAF had only a few transport aircraft at the time and was essentially useless.[104] The Zambian government did actively try to prevent guerrillas from using their country as a base. Zambia Army units that found armed guerrillas inside the country would arrest them, but if the guerrillas did not carry weapons, Zambian law prevented authorities from taking any action. At the same time, the army developed a friendly relationship with a battalion of the Movimento Popular de Libertação de Angola–Partido do Trabalho (MPLA) that occupied a camp directly across the Zambian border. The MPLA battalion commander even invited an expatriate officer to come and tour his facilities and observe his battalion training. Apparently, the British officer was very impressed by the state of the MPLA camp, saying it was well laid out and had a very efficient operations room.[105]

The political chatter and ethnic divisions in the army also continued to be a problem. One of the major political divisions among troops was based on ethnic identity. As the December 1968 elections grew closer, discussion of politics in the officers' mess became more common. The political division between UNIP and United Party supporters occurred largely along ethnic lines; the Bemba officers tended to support the UNIP, and the Lozi officers supported the United Party. This type of vocal support of an opposition party did not last long in Zambia. The UNIP was attempting to create a one-party state and was making policies to facilitate the process. In April 1968 Kaunda announced economic reforms that made it advantageous to be a member of the UNIP.[106] That same month some Zambian officers went so far as to discuss the possibility of a military coup in the mess. While they all agreed that a coup was not in the interests of Zambia, one Zambian company commander boasted that he was in a position to organize one. Unbeknownst to these officers the Zambian Intelligence Service kept a close watch for this type of activity and cataloged all such discussion, no matter how inconsequential.[107] It seems that even though these officers discussed politics and joked about coup attempts, for the most part they limited their political activity to the officers' mess.

The Zambianization process was moving along at a quick pace. In February 1968, five Zambian officers passed the examination for promotion from captain to major, and an additional thirty-eight would be eligible to take the exam in December 1968. The most senior Zambian officer in the army, Major Patrick Kafumukache, took up the post of military secretary to the president of Zambia in May 1968. This was the first of a number of high-level advisory positions awarded to Zambian officers.[108] Part of the difficulty in placing Zambians in these positions was that the men in these posts needed staff college training. Since Zambia did not have the capacity at the time to support a staff college, as in almost all other cases men had to be sent overseas. There were plans in place to send five men to staff colleges in 1969, in Britain, Canada, and Pakistan.[109] The difficulty in sending men on these courses lay in making sure that by the time they went they had accrued enough field and operational experience to be able to learn and understand staff-level functions.

The June 1968 recruiting mission to India turned out to be a resounding success. The mission was able to recruit ten officers and sixty NCOs for service in the army and another fifty-two for the air force. While the mission was successful in recruiting trained personnel, the British advisers were unsure how African troops would react to the influx of Asian officers and NCOs. As it turns out, these fears proved unfounded, particularly as the Zambian government built up its defense relationship with both India and Pakistan. This partnership was increasingly important to the Zambia Army. Even though the SOFA was signed in February 1968, by December the Zambian government had given its required twelve-month notice to terminate the agreement early.[110] This initially came as a shock to both military and diplomatic planners in the British government. The Zambianization of the army was incomplete, as was the training of the technical arms, and the Zambia Air Force was in no way ready to operate on its own; it did not even have a full complement of Zambian pilots.[111]

The British discovered that the lack of Zambian pilots and the delayed delivery of jet aircraft to the Zambia Air Force was a major reason the agreement was terminated. The continued violations of Zambian airspace by both Portuguese and Rhodesian aircraft had become the most pressing defense concern for Kaunda and his cabinet. British instructors in the RAF component of the training team insisted on thorough and lengthy training courses for Zambian pilots. By 1968 they produced only twelve fully qualified pilots.[112] The training team also participated in running the ZAF. The government of Zambia had secretly entered into negotiations with the Italian government to provide jet aircraft and a training team to the ZAF. The Zambian vice president, Simon Kapwepwe, boasted in an article in the *Zambia Mail* that where the British were able to train only twelve personnel a year, the Italian training team would train four hundred a year. Interestingly, the ZAF numbered only five hundred personnel at the time.[113]

The Zambian government was under pressure from all sides to reduce Britain's role in Zambia's defense forces. The planning had already begun for the Non-Aligned Conference to take place in Lusaka in 1970, and that same year Kenneth Kaunda was elected chair of the OAU. All these organizations were staunchly opposed to the British relationship with the Republic of South Africa and the lack of action on the Rhodesian issue. The Italian defense industry did well in this deal. In addition to training the ZAF, it was also secretly supplying aircraft to the Rhodesian Air Force.[114]

Until 1969, British influence in shaping the Zambian Defense Forces was almost total. However, the Zambian decision to terminate the SOFA led to the departure of the remaining army training team components in 1969. There was no agreement in place regarding the end of the RAF portion of the training team until September 1969.[115] When RAF personnel finally departed Zambia in December 1969, the impact on the army was blunted by the fact that expatriate officers serving on contracts remained in Zambian service and far outnumbered the seconded British officers. Command of the Zambia Army remained in the hands of a contracted expatriate Briton, Major General Tom Reid, yet his contract was due to expire in 1970, and a renewal was uncertain. However, the departure of British officers was not without its consequences. During the course of the year in 1969, the number of expatriate officers continued to fall, and Zambians filled many of the vacated posts. Based on the number of Zambian officers trained, the army was prepared for the departure of the British and expatriates, but in actuality it could not afford to lose the assistance that the training team provided. By the beginning of 1970, the number of expatriate officers and NCOs dwindled to sixty. Of the expatriates who remained in Zambian service, many were of mediocre quality, disillusioned, and/or simply waiting for their contracts to end.[116]

Once British officers departed, many in the Zambia Army realized that they were not prepared to stand on their own. The most senior Zambian officers in the army had only five years of service. The British high commissioner to Zambia, Sir John Laurence Pumphrey, thought that the outlook for the army was grim: "There is little doubt that Zambianization is moving too fast. The Zambian officers and NCOs are young and largely inexperienced in military matters. Above all, with a very few exceptions, they lack the power of leadership."[117] This lack of leadership, combined with a playboy culture popular in the officer corps, made the focus for many Zambian officers social obligations rather than the more serious task of soldiering. A lack of discipline among officers of course led to a discipline problem among the other ranks. Even though British officers had not been serving as operational commanders for at least six months prior to their departure, their presence as training officers and staff officers within units allowed them to exercise a measure of oversight over such issues among the officers.

The discipline and training problems in the army did not improve in 1970 and 1971. When Major General Reid's contract expired in December 1970, a Zambian officer was appointed to command the army. Colonel Kingsley Chinkuli was promoted to the rank of major general and became the first Zambian general officer.[118] Lieutenant Colonel Patrick Kafumukache, who had served as the aide-de-camp to President Kaunda, was seen as a front-runner for the position until he got drunk at a state dinner during a visit to the Caribbean.[119] Chinkuli was one of the first three Zambian graduates of Sandhurst in 1965 and had rotated through company, battalion, and brigade commander billets prior to becoming army commander.

Once a Zambian officer was in command, Kaunda summarily dismissed most of the European expatriate officers still serving in the army. His decision to immediately Zambianize the entire army was a response to the return of a Conservative government to Britain and the possibility of British arms sales to South Africa. It seems, however, that the army was not completely Zambian—Indian officers were allowed to remain, as were technical specialists and medical officers.[120]

The Zambians also moved away from British equipment and weapons. The Yugoslavian government was interested in Zambia as a market for both construction materials and military hardware. Kaunda also was an admirer of Marshal Josip Tito. President Kaunda had expressly stated that Zambia could no longer buy arms from nations that supported racist regimes. This, combined with the pressures of having being elected chairman of both the OAU and the Non-Aligned Movement, led the Zambians to look east for arms suppliers.[121] While the Zambian government was successful in changing arms suppliers to nonaligned nations, training assistance was a much more difficult task.

When the Italian Air Force training team replaced the RAF, the language barrier immediately became an issue. Only three of the Italian trainers spoke English. This problem was compounded when Yugoslav Air Force officers came to Zambia to assist in the training effort.[122] The quality of these trainers was questionable; in the first month that the Italian team was there, an Italian instructor crashed one of the Beaver trainer aircraft. When the Zambian government figured out that the language issue was a significant barrier to progress, it turned again to English-speaking nations for assistance.

The Zambian government did not intend to turn to communism; in fact, it had a frosty relationship with both the Soviet Union and East Germany. Since the Zambians were not moving wholesale into the Eastern Bloc, Christopher Diggines, the deputy high commissioner in Zambia, still thought HMG had an opportunity to preserve some level of influence in the military through training assistance in the United Kingdom. Zambian authorities, while eager for the British to leave Zambia, were not eager to give up the courses the British allowed them to attend in Britain. Diggines proposed that allowing Zambians to continue attending courses in Britain with few obligations attached to their attendance would help expose the strings that were attached to military aid from the Eastern Bloc. In doing so, Diggines thought that the British might even be able to recover some orders for military hardware that they had lost to Yugoslavia.[123]

Colonel Alexander R. Kettles, now defense adviser to the high commissioner, noted that continued aid to Zambia would not be wasted "What is important to us," he said, was that Zambia remain closely tied to the United Kingdom in terms of equipment and training, and that Zambia be "predisposed" to look to the United Kingdom for "support in all fields."[124] The Zambia Army received three spots at RMA and nine spots at Mons in 1971. In addition, it had forty-two spots for officers in both staff and line officers' courses. Other ranks were also allocated fifty-one spots. The Zambian government on one hand wanted to pull away from Britain but from a practical standpoint could not seem to find any other provider of such quality and diverse training taught in English.

Zambia confirmed this dependence in its bids for course allocations for 1972, asking for sixty-six slots at various British schools. The British were keenly aware that the Zambia Army was well under establishment. The Zambians need to form a new antiaircraft battery, and a fourth infantry battalion made the situation even worse. In 1971 the army was tasked with administering the Zambian Youth Service and a new National Service scheme.[125] The push to produce officers was not simply to equip the expanding army but also to commission a large batch of officers before the Zambians were forced to train officers on their own. In 1971 the Zambians established an officer cadet school and began training the first intake. British analysis of the school, and the Zambia Army generally, led the British to conclude these officers would probably be poorly prepared to perform their duties.[126]

With these factors to consider, the MOD was still able to offer the Zambian government only a fraction of the 1972 training allocations that it had requested. Zambia was offered eight for 1972, one fewer than had been allocated in 1971. Since the Zambians requested twenty-four slots, this seemed like a diplomatic slap in the face from the British government.[127] Only three nations received more spaces at Mons that year (Uganda, Nigeria, and Saudi Arabia). There were only fifteen Sandhurst slots available for cadets from sub-Saharan Africa, and of those Zambia received three in 1972.[128]

William Wilson of the Central and Southern Africa Department of the FCO made the case that should the British be completely supplanted in Africa, training Zambian officers in British institutions could counter communist influence. Britain had important economic interests in both black- and white-governed countries in southern Africa and wanted to encourage détente between them. If the level of communist influence in the military of a frontline state became too great, the British felt that the region would become more polarized and violent. The suspicion was that the involvement of Cuban and Soviet forces in the area could escalate from financial and logistical support to the introduction of forces into the region.[129]

The turn to the East for military assistance was beginning to cause a great deal of damage to the efficiency of the Zambia Army. Until 1969 the army had exclusively British military hardware; what soldiers trained on in Britain was what they were to use when they returned to Zambia. With the introduction of Eastern Bloc equipment, however, very few soldiers were trained to employ and maintain all the various types of hardware that a Zambian unit possessed. The Zambia government was attempting to turn away from the British so quickly that it was not exercising any future logistical planning. It collected various pieces of equipment from a multitude of suppliers with little thought given to the ease of ordering replacement parts or integrating the hardware into its current order of battle.[130]

By 1971, the Zambia Army was dealing with security threats on every part of the border. The majority of the infantry companies in the army were deployed to border areas to prevent incursions from either the Rhodesians or the Portuguese. These rotations did not end on the border with Mozambique until 1975, Rhodesia in 1980, and Angola in 1990. Having such a high percentage of the army actively engaged in operations made it nearly impossible to train or undertake a large brigade exercise.

In addition to the lack of opportunities to train as large units, the Zambia Army was not impressed by the training teams brought in after the British. For example, in 1971 a Chinese military training team arrived secretly in country and also sold the Zambians weapons such as the Chinese-made version of the AKM assault rifle and other light infantry weapons. According to the Francis Sibamba, second-in-command of Second Battalion, Zambia Regiment, the training was not very beneficial because the Chinese approached the issue as if the soldiers were untrained and could be molded from scratch. Their training syllabus was not prepared to deal with soldiers who had already been trained along Western lines. According to Sibamba, "I am convinced that these foreign instructors also learnt a thing or two from their students on the conventional tactics of modern warfare in which the Zambia Army was well vested."[131]

Conclusion

In spite of British military assistance, the Zambian turn to the nonaligned powers was complete by 1972. Soviet-style military hardware quickly replaced British-supplied equipment, as the AKM became the standard-issue rifle of the army. The Zambia Army purchased BRDM Armored Reconnaissance Vehicles and T-34 tanks from Yugoslavia and China. The USSR sold Zambia the BM 122mm Rocket System.[132] While military suppliers from 1972 on were almost exclusively Eastern Bloc nations, the Zambia government did not allow the military to become politicized. It continued to count on the Pakistani and Indian governments for training assistance. Indian officers who had been recruited in 1968 remained in the Zambia Army even after European officers were dismissed in 1970. A large number of Zambian officers attended higher-level courses in one of the two countries, and this type of English-language instruction continued to be preferred over training at other institutions.

After 1972 the Zambia Military Academy was the primary commissioning source for Zambian officers. The initial academy cadre had visited military schools around the world, including India, in preparation for the assignment. Zambia finally established a staff college in 1996. Eastern Bloc training teams occasionally sent to Zambia trained special units of the army, such as a North Korean team that trained the Zambian Commandos.[133]

The British training mission in Zambia left the country in poor circumstances. The dissatisfaction with the military assistance program was the result not of a poor relationship with the Zambian government but of British policies on South Africa and Rhodesia. The army component of the British Joint Services Training Team acquitted itself well, according to the British and Zambian governments. Training in Zambia began after the independence of the East African nations, and at the very moment that weaknesses in those missions were identified. The British government initially anticipated a long-term training mission in Zambia that would require a British presence in the country well into the 1970s. The East African mutinies of 1964 changed the way the British looked at their training plan. Prior to 1964 they had emphasized quality training that was extremely time-intensive. This type of arrangement kept white British officers serving in colonial armies for years after independence. The mutinies in East Africa made them reconsider this approach. They decided that quality military training must be traded for timeliness. The military mission in Zambia had a shorter time frame than others in East Africa, with the hope that the Zambia Army would be more loyal to the government if it felt it benefited from independence.

The British mission in Zambia was not completely successful. But was it a complete failure? While the new army was not nearly as professional as the British had hoped it would be, it was able to defend Zambia. There were numerous cases throughout the 1970s where Rhodesian and South African forces inserted special operations units into Zambia, but at no point were they bold enough to send conventional troops against the Zambian forces. The Zambian military also remained relatively aloof from domestic politics, in comparison to some of its neighbors. Military officials in Zambia often are involved in politics after their retirement. While in service, however, such behavior was frowned upon by the majority of the officer corps. In 1973 the UNIP declared Zambia a one-party state, and even after this point military officers discouraged political participation among their fellow officers. In Zambia, military coup attempts occurred in 1980, 1989, 1990, and 1997. However, all these attempts originated in small factions in the military and were put down by the army at large before these factions were able to come close to taking power.[134] In contrast to the role of the military in places like Uganda, this is an excellent record of civilian control of the army in a young nation.

The British were not able to retain Zambia within their sphere of influence. The politics of the era in southern Africa and the economic interests that were at stake made South Africa a divisive issue between the United Kingdom and Zambia. Yet it is important to note that the British left such a professional impression on the military that the Zambian officer corps saw itself as a part of the Western military tradition.[135] This went further than simply a style of marching or uniform design but manifested itself in their approach to training and professionalism and how the army saw itself in society. Technical knowledge from communist and nonaligned powers was happily accepted, but Anglophone military norms and culture were embraced and ingrained in the Zambia Army.[136]

The Rhodesian Army and the Liberation Forces

Throughout the late 1970s, *Soldier of Fortune* magazine published sensational articles about the Rhodesian Army's special units, highlighting their elite nature and their victories against "communism." The magazine implied that the Rhodesian Army was composed of a small number of highly professional white soldiers who were able to hold back the threat of communism and protect Western values in Africa. This portrayal in such sensationalistic American publications seems to have mirrored how the Rhodesian settlers saw themselves. However, the reality of their army differed greatly from this popular perception.

Since its establishment as a permanent force, the Rhodesian Army relied on a combination of European National Servicemen and professional African soldiers to fill its ranks. In spite of mandates that some young Europeans serve in the army, the Rhodesian government had to rely on volunteers from the African population to meet its recruiting goals. In 1973, a time when the Zimbabwe War for Independence was escalating in intensity, the Rhodesian Army had already established itself as a British-trained force with experience in both conventional and counterinsurgency operations. At the same time, the forces of the liberation movements were attempting to create their own cohesive military units. Portions of the liberation movement were training to fight a conventional war with the Rhodesians, whereas others were attempting to instigate a Maoist revolutionary spirit among the peasants. To understand the dynamic in 1980 when all these forces were combined, the experiences of each of the contributing armies must be taken into account. While there were other minor contributors to the military conflict in Rhodesia, this chapter focuses only on the experiences of those organizations that eventually became parts of the Zimbabwe National Army.

Rhodesian Security Forces

The Rhodesian military was a direct consequence of the spirit of conquest in southern Africa that created the colony of Rhodesia. The British South Africa Company formed its own police force in 1893. This paramilitary organization took part in the ill-fated Jameson raid in 1895 and was the primary force used to put down the 1896–1897 Ndebele Rebellion. This rebellion, now known as the First Chimurenga (or liberation struggle) shaped the perception of the security policy in that colony. The European population was extremely concerned about the possibility and related expense of another uprising among the African population. The settler state had a monopoly on military training and organized violence in an attempt to avoid any similar incidents.

At this time, only a small number of Africans were in colonial service, and these men were employed in a segregated division of the British South Africa Police (BSAP). When the First World War came to Africa, the Rhodesians were eager to serve. The Rhodesian government formed the all-European Rhodesia Regiment as its contribution to the war effort; however, the small European population in the colony was not able to provide replacements for the losses sustained by the regiment. To stanch the losses among the European population, the Rhodesian authorities established the first large unit of armed Africans in Rhodesian history: the Rhodesian Native Regiment.[1] From 1916 until 1918, this regiment served with distinction in the East African campaign. Upon the war's end, however, the regiment quickly demobilized. From 1918 until 1940, the only armed African force in Rhodesia was the BSAP's Askari Platoon. This small unit guarded Government House in Salisbury and provided instructors to the African Constable Training Depot of the BSAP.

World War II brought with it a revival of the regular African infantry regiment in Rhodesia. This all-African regiment, the Rhodesian African Rifles (RAR), was formed in 1940 and saw active service in North Africa and Madagascar, and later in Burma. At the end of the war the regiment demobilized, but it was reestablished in 1947.[2] It went on to serve as the

Rhodesian contribution to the Malayan Emergency, as well as in other imperial defense missions. When Southern Rhodesia entered the Federation of Rhodesia and Nyasaland, the RAR was the only regular infantry regiment in the small Southern Rhodesia Army. In the 1950s the European community performed peacetime National Service in the Royal Rhodesia Regiment. This created a balancing act within the defense apparatus in Rhodesia; a small number of African military professionals received armed power, but steps were taken to ensure that every male member of the European community in Rhodesia was trained and ready for military service, should the need arise. The RAR was a one-battalion regiment and would continue to be so until after the Unilateral Declaration of Independence (UDI) and the beginning of the liberation war.

The federation period ushered in a great deal of military expansion in Southern Rhodesia. As discussed in chapter 2, the Royal Rhodesian Air Force (RRAF) both expanded and modernized its equipment during this period. The Rhodesia and Nyasaland Army (R&N Army) followed suit, establishing the Armored Car Squadron and adopting the modern FN FAL rifle as the standard-issue battle rifle. In 1950, many of the Southern Rhodesian specialized territorial units (such as engineers, artillery, and signals) suffered from a lack of supplies and qualified staff. The Rhodesian Artillery was shut down at the time; there was no one serving who was qualified to operate the guns.[3] The creation of the R&N Army allowed the expansion of these units into joint regular/territorial units in which regular officers staffed a portion and the unit was supplemented by the territorial component. This increased the level of technical skill of the army and gave it the opportunity to use weapons that had not previously been available.

The 1960s brought changes for both Africa and the army. The mutiny in the Congo of the Force Publique led to the establishment of the first all-European regular infantry regiment in the R&N Army, the Rhodesian Light Infantry (RLI). In addition to the RLI, the R&N Army also reestablished the "C" Squadron, Rhodesian Special Air Service (RhSAS), a unit that recruited from Rhodesia for service in Malaya. The RhSAS replaced the RAR as the federation's contribution to imperial defense. In 1962, the "C" Squadron participated in military exercises in Aden with the Twenty-Second SAS (the Artist Rifles). While the Rhodesians were enthusiastic about the exercise, their British counterparts were not impressed with their performance and declined to include them in the Middle East Command order of battle. The British Army required that the RhSAS undergo an additional year of training before it would be considered an operational unit by British standards.[4]

The operational experience of the Rhodesian Army during the Federal period consisted of internal security operations. Due to the demands of internal security operations, it was extremely difficult for these forces to conduct anything larger than battalion training exercises. The focus of both the training exercises and official operations at the time was internal security and the provision of support to the civil authorities; however, the chief of the Imperial General Staff made it clear that the army's lack of preparedness for conventional war had to change.[5] In 1962 the R&N Army reorganized itself from a regional command structure to a two-brigade structure, with the brigades located in Southern Rhodesia and Northern Rhodesia, respectively. The intention was to make it easier for units in the brigade areas to conduct integrated training, yet this arrangement simply made it much easier for the R&N Army to be divided up since operational control of the units in each territory was already granted to their respective brigade headquarters.

The Federal era gave the army access to a level of funding that had not previously been available. The prosperous copper industry in Northern Rhodesia provided tax revenue that allowed for the expansion and modernization of the army. It also allowed for a renewed emphasis on the Territorial Force (TF). While the concept of a territorial force is similar to that of the British Territorial Army or the US Army National Guard, British defense advisers made sure to note that the TF in Rhodesia was very different. While the TF was similar to these other institutions there were significant differences: "It is misleading to make too close a comparison between the TF and the British TA. Although the system of drill halls and training are very similar the RN Army is kept to a much higher state of readiness for internal security operations. It is possible to call up units of the TF at very short notice by proclamation of the Governor General."[6] Participation in the Rhodesian Federation TF was not limited to Europeans. The Asian and mixed-race populations also had to perform mandatory military service. The Rhodesian government continued this practice of mandatory service even after the federation was dissolved.

When European boys left secondary school, they generally went directly into their National Service training. In 1962, roughly 1,800 Europeans were presented for service. Of these, 540 received deferments, 237 were rejected on medical grounds, and 1,083 became soldiers.[7] From the time these boys were twelve years old, they were prepared by the Rhodesian government to enter the army through mandatory cadet programs. All medically fit Rhodesian men were required to undergo some sort of military training; their obligation was satisfied when they finished their four years' service with the RRR. After UDI and as the liberation war escalated, this service obligation was repeatedly extended.

When the federation dissolved, the armed forces divided up between the member territories. Southern Rhodesia (now simply referred to as Rhodesia) received the largest share. The RLI and RAR formed the core of the Rhodesian Army and were backed up by support units of the old R&N Army. Since the TF was composed primarily of Europeans, it also transferred to Rhodesia. Despite the division of the armored car squadron equally between Rhodesia and Zambia, most of the soldiers from the unit transferred into the Rhodesian Army. From this group of transferees, the Rhodesian Army formed a new Rhodesian Armored Car Regiment. In the early part of 1963, the Chiefs of Staff Committee suggested that the RAR be abandoned in favor of the establishment of two long-service (twelve-month National Service periods) TF Regiments. The concern was that the "Askari must therefore be regarded as an unacceptable security risk in the [combat arms] units, which can only be replaced by Europeans. We recognize however, that Africans will continue to be employed in administrative units."[8] The difficulties with finding European manpower made the disbandment of the RAR impossible.

The British were concerned that, upon the dissolution of the federation, European members of the Federal Army would flock south, leaving the northern territories undefended. Even though the Rhodesian Army attracted more former Federal officers than the northern territories, it still had trouble recruiting enough European personnel to meet operational requirements. According to the first post-Federation defense report, the chief of the General Staff, Major General R. R. J. Putterill, noted, "Filling the establishment of the new Army has presented many problems. Due to the attractive terminal benefits offered, many members elected to be released from the R&N Army, and the Southern Rhodesia Army started well below its authorized establishment in both European and African personnel."[9] Due to this apparent lack of enthusiasm for service in Rhodesia, the Defense Staff believed that they would not be able to man the RLI properly until 1966. This recruiting challenge was compounded by the RLI's transition from a regular infantry battalion to a commando unit with airborne capabilities. This expansion required higher physical standards and soldiers willing to volunteer for airborne duty.[10]

The RhSAS also suffered from personnel shortages between 1963 and 1965. The squadron only become operational in 1963, and by 1964 the number of soldiers serving in the unit had dropped to twenty.[11] Rhodesian authorities had no problem recruiting African soldiers; the manpower pool seemed limitless and was significantly cheaper. The Rhodesian Ministry of Defence went so far as to suggest that the army form another battalion of the RAR. Even though the suggestion was made in 1963, the Second Battalion of the RAR was not formed until 1975, specifically due to a lack of funds.[12]

The Rhodesian Army did not rely as heavily on commissioning sources in Britain as some other British colonies did. The larger settler community in Rhodesia, as compared with Kenya, allowed for the establishment of an officer cadet school at the School of Infantry in Gwelo. This school produced the majority of the officers needed by Rhodesian Army. Once Rhodesia separated from the Federation, the government made no effort whatsoever to recruit Africans into the officer corps. As was the case in other Commonwealth countries, European men eighteen years of age and with a General Certificate of Education were eligible to apply for officer training.

The regular officer course at Gwelo was one year in length and mirrored the curriculum at Mons Officer Cadet School. It consisted of three phases, each putting an increasing amount of leadership responsibility on the individual officer cadet. The first phase was roughly two months long and consisted of the normal basic training given to all soldiers in the army. In addition to the field craft and weapons training in this phase, officer cadets took classes in current events, leadership, and military history. These included visits to RRAF bases, the BSAP headquarters in Salisbury, and factories in Gwelo. This phase ended with a series of written exams, followed by a weeklong escape and evasion exercise.[13]

The second phase of the officer course was four months long and addressed duties more specific to the role of officer. This military training included platoon-level battle drills, the use of crew-served weapons, and riot control procedures. At this point in the course, cadets rotated in and out of platoon and company commander positions and had their performances evaluated. The focus of the classroom and field training during this phase was conventional warfare. Leadership training included courses on administration, military law, and additional instruction on military history. At the end of the phase, there were written examinations on all these subjects as well as an oral exam on conventional war tactics. The final exam for this phase was a major conventional war exercise in which each student was graded on his performance as a platoon leader, company commander, or company second-in-command.[14]

The first two phases were very similar to the officer training offered in most Western armies, with a focus on conventional military operations. The third phase centered on training officers to perform in counterinsurgency operations. This phase lasted four months and covered subjects such as joint operations, civil-action programs, combat tracking, and the use of close support aircraft. The field training during this phase required cadets to plan company-level counterinsurgency operations leading regular troops. The students also continued to receive courses on military law, staff duties, and military history. The cadets had a weeklong bush survival course in which they would live off the land without shooting any game. The cumulative field exercise was a ten-day counterinsurgency exercise in which African soldiers posed as enemy guerrilla fighters. All the branches of the Rhodesian Security Forces participated in this exercise to impress upon the cadets the joint nature of this type of warfare. After the final field training exercise, the cadets went on a ten-day visit to South Africa to become familiar with the South African Defence Force (SADF). The trip was meant to emphasize to cadets that the Rhodesian Army did not have the capacity to fight a large-scale conventional conflict on its own, and that it would need the support of South Africa to do so. During the visit the cadets toured the army, navy, and air force facilities and became familiar with the organizational structure and deployment system of the SADF.

Once the cadets graduated from the School of Infantry, they were commissioned as second lieutenants and posted to their respective units. Those graduates who went to infantry units were fully trained (except for those officers who were posted to the RLI and thus required parachute training). The new officers posted to engineering, artillery, or other support units needed further training at other army installations; if the training was extremely specialized, they were sent on to courses in the United Kingdom prior to 1965, and to South Africa thereafter.[15] Officer training in Rhodesia was comparable to most military courses of instruction in the Western armies and held officer cadets to a high standard of professionalism. As a point of comparison, in the 1960s, Officer Candidate School in the US Army was only five and a half months long.

The UDI severed all military and political ties with the United Kingdom. Officers and cadets who were training in Britain were forced to declare their allegiance, either to the Crown or to the Rhodesian cause. Commanders of British training institutions were instructed to withdraw all personnel in training who were members of the Rhodesian forces or who held Rhodesian citizenship. They were allowed to choose between repatriation to Rhodesia or to file an application to transition into the British Army. There were five Rhodesian individuals training in UK military institutions at the time of UDI. Of these five, only two asked to transfer to the British Army. There also were two men from the RRAF in the United Kingdom at the time; only one opted to remain in the UK and transfer to the RAF.[16]

British personnel who were filling training or technical positions in Rhodesia were withdrawn from the now renegade colony. With the end of the defense relationship between Rhodesia and the United Kingdom, the Rhodesian government was forced to search for new suppliers of weapons and training. The economic sanctions placed on Rhodesia by the United Kingdom and the UN made this somewhat difficult.[17] During the course of the rebellion against the United Kingdom, no nation officially recognized Rhodesia. However, both the Portuguese and South African governments were sympathetic to Rhodesia's position and were willing to provide assistance. The Portuguese hoped to prop up the Rhodesian government so that it would not become another potential safe haven for guerrillas. The South Africans hoped to maintain the buffer zone to the north against the infiltration of nationalist forces.

The South African government became Rhodesia's main supplier of defense materials, as well as other products banned by the sanctions. The British government sent warships to the coast of Mozambique to enforce the sanctions and prevent petroleum products from offloading in Beria. These patrols were successful in preventing some tankers from docking.

Yet they were not effective in blocking the supply of petroleum products to landlocked Rhodesia. Rather than receiving their supply from Beria, the Rhodesians began importing oil (and almost everything else) from South Africa. Pretoria was not alone in ignoring the sanctions. The United States continued to buy chromium from Rhodesia until the late 1970s, and governments throughout Europe were willing to set up "backdoor" deals with the Rhodesians.[18]

In the first several years after UDI, the insurgency was limited and the Rhodesian authorities considered it a police problem. The BSAP viewed the issue as one of small-scale terrorism; it took the lead, and the military provided assistance on a case-by-case basis. At this point in the war, operations were small enough that the regular army was able to handle them with limited help from specialist units in the TF. The first incident of the war occurred prior to UDI. In July 1964, a group of five members of the Zimbabwe African National Union (ZANU) crossed into Rhodesia from Zambia and killed a Rhodesian civilian. The group that claimed responsibility called itself the Crocodile Gang. The killing was part of a series of acts of sabotage and arson directed against the Rhodesian government. While the event did not achieve iconic status in the story of Zimbabwean independence, it was shocking to the European community.[19] Peter Godwin, author and former member of the BSAP, witnessed the aftermath of the event as a child and remarked that seeing the body lying with the knife still in it brought an end to his childhood sense of security.[20] Even so, the event was treated as an isolated incident and as a matter for the police.

A significant portion of the Rhodesian military were dedicated Rhodesian Front supporters. In 1967, Lieutenant Colonel R. Wilson, head of the School of Infantry, resigned from the Rhodesian Army and fled to London. He claimed he no longer sympathized with the Rhodesian cause and decided to take advantage of the generous terms offered by HMG to Rhodesian Army officers and civil servants who were fired or felt compelled to resign on political grounds.[21] He was debriefed by both the Foreign and Commonwealth Office and the Ministry of Defence when he arrived in London and gave the British government a detailed description of the politics at work inside the Rhodesian Army.

He identified three groups of officers within the Rhodesian Army: those who were fiercely loyal to the regime, a middle group who generally tried only to ensure continued employment and eventual retirement for themselves, and an antiregime group. Most of the officers who commanded major units were also thought to be loyal to the Rhodesian Front regime. The short list of officers who were against the regime included the general officer commanding at the time, Major General Sam Putterill, as well as the commander of the First Brigade, Brigadier Robert Prentice. These were the only two notable opponents to the regime on the list; the rest of the men were minor staff officers. Even Major General Putterill was quiet about his opposition to the regime because he knew that the army, as a whole, would not support him against the government.[22] Putterill rebuffed the attempts of the British representative stationed in Rhodesia to contact him. He made it clear that unless the British government had something specific to say to him, he did not wish to meet, regardless of how well concealed the meeting might be. During his time in service, Putterill confined his acts of resistance to the regime to butting heads with Clifford DuPont, the officer administrating the government.[23]

The British considered the junior officers and other ranks in the army avid supporters of the Rhodesian Front government. This was particularly true of those individuals who joined the regular forces after UDI; few doubted that their loyalties were to Rhodesia first and the British Crown second, if at all. In 1967 the operational demands on the military increased to a point that required large-scale involvement of the TF. The Federal Defense Act of 1955 established the peacetime National Service system as it stood at that time. However, over the intervening years the way in which training and territorial service were carried out had changed dramatically.

The depot of the Royal Rhodesia Regiment handled all initial entry training for National Servicemen entering the army. By 1967, the depot averaged eight courses of 150 trainees per year. The training period was four and a half months long; however, at the beginning of each course, twelve men were selected for special training. Of this group three were selected to attend officer training and three NCO training. The other six were placed in engineer, artillery, medical, or signals training. Those trainees selected to become officers and NCOs went through their respective training courses concurrently with their course work. At the end of the four-and-a-half-month cycle, the newly minted second lieutenants and sergeants returned to the groups with which they started in order to serve as those groups' leadership cadres. The other change from the previous system was that the graduates went directly to operational areas. At the end of their training period, the course group, now re-formed as a company, went to either Wankie or Kariba, where they served in the field for fourteen weeks before being released to their respective TF battalions.[24]

Admittedly, during this period of the war of liberation there were few confrontations between Rhodesian forces and the guerrilla fighters. Most of the time that these young men spent out in the field consisted simply of hours of uneventful patrolling through the bush. One former National Serviceman commented that his first period of operational service was defined by long days and nights of endless walking, followed by several days of rugby matches and drinking at the local pub.[25] Even though many soldiers grew bored with their duties, there was enough guerrilla infiltration on the border to cause the government some concern. Another unexpected turn occurred in 1967. Instead of holding their annual training camps, active TF units were ordered to perform operational service in Tribal Trust Lands and on the Rhodesian border.

The increasing dependence on the TF for operational duties meant that there was a continuous shortage of regular instructors for the training courses. The South Africans agreed to send the Rhodesians two warrant officers to serve as instructors at the School of Infantry: one at the School of Engineering and one at the School of Signals. They also allowed an increasing number of Rhodesian officers to attend the South African Defense College, since Camberly (the British Army staff college) was no longer an option.[26] In exchange for their services, South African special operations soldiers utilized Rhodesian parachute training facilities and drop zones.[27] In 1967, the dependence on the SADF was not all-encompassing, but it was rapidly growing. This was the same year that African National Congress (ANC) guerrillas were caught infiltrating Rhodesia in an attempt to reach South Africa. The response from Pretoria was to send two thousand paramilitary South Africa Police to patrol the northern border of Rhodesia. While the Rhodesian government readily accepted this assistance for the security and political benefits, Rhodesian soldiers were less than enthusiastic about their presence.

At the time some groups like the Anti-Apartheid Movement claimed that the South African Police committed to Rhodesia were simply soldiers given police uniforms. In some cases, this was true. For instance, the South African pilots who flew the "police" helicopters sent to Rhodesia were almost always South African Air Force pilots.[28] However, these police units were of questionable quality. Lieutenant Colonel Ronald Marillier noted:

The SAP men who initially arrived were very enthusiastic, but had no idea of the difficulties of fighting a COIN [counterinsurgency] war, having had no military training. They were not initially effective at COIN operations, but were useful "boots on the ground" in the Border Control role, in that they covered areas left exposed since Rhodesian units were heavily engaged elsewhere. The effectiveness of SAP [South African Police] companies depended very much on the ability and enthusiasm of their officers, especially their Company Commanders. There were some ineffectual commanders, and as a result bad mistakes were made, sometimes ending in tragedy. Where there were good and effective Company Commanders, the results were sometimes very good.[29]

Early on, these units were sent to quiet areas to patrol. As the intensity of the war picked up, however, they were required to patrol active combat zones. While some of these South African Police companies did do their jobs well, many were poor-quality units and were given little responsibility.

Throughout 1967 and 1968, the liberation movements successfully sent some large infiltration units into Rhodesia. Even though some units were able to make it into the country undetected, they did not perform well against the Rhodesian Army. By the end of 1968, 160 liberation fighters and 12 members of the security forces had been killed. Sending large military units into Rhodesia was not producing the kind of results that the liberation movements desired. Furthermore, they could not continue to sacrifice so many trained men. The military arm of ZANU, the Zimbabwe African National Liberation Army (ZANLA), turned to the Chinese for both aid and inspiration. ZANLA decided that rather than using a Che Guevara–style "Foco" approach focusing on small armed commando groups, a Maoist insurgency might be better suited to liberate their country.[30] Subsequently, ZANLA would transition into a period in which it repeatedly tried to insert small armed groups into the country to mobilize the peasantry. In 1969 and 1970, when the liberation armies began changing their approach to the war, guerrilla activity slackened, giving the Rhodesian government the sense that it was winning the war.

The Rhodesian Army continued to train despite the operational constraints under which it operated. Overseas recruiting continued to be an important source of manpower for the regular army. Young men with no prior military experience were recruited from countries as close as Botswana, where two eighteen-year-old Europeans volunteered for officer training.[31] Recruits came from all over the world, but with varying amounts of military training. Peter McAleese was a British subject who had previously served with the Parachute Regiment in Cyprus, the SAS in Aden and Indonesia, and later as a mercenary in Angola. He applied to join the Rhodesian Army in 1976. Even though he had an extensive military record and was extremely qualified, he was almost turned away because he had been a mercenary. He did join the army but was required to undergo the Rhodesian SAS selection process as a private in spite of his having been an NCO in the British SAS.

The group with which he went through selection was quite multinational: it included South Africans and Australians, and one of the instructors was an American. After he passed selection and became part of an operational team in the regiment, he noticed that many of the Rhodesian NCOs were immature and, at times, arbitrary with the use of their authority. He did not resent having to serve as a private but recalled that on one occasion a Rhodesian sergeant had asked him to shoot a civilian. Deliberately, he missed.

According to McAleese, the pay in the Rhodesian Army was quite poor. Even though he reached the rank of staff sergeant, his lifestyle remained very modest. By 1978, the Rhodesian SAS had a large number of expatriates serving in the regiment. McAleese noted that of the forty men in A Squadron, thirty-three were expatriates.[32]

McAleese's comments on the Rhodesian NCOs were not without merit. Those soldiers selected at the beginning of their National Service period for service as NCOs did not receive much additional training. They were taught how to give battle orders for patrols, general leadership principles, and the duties of platoon and section leaders. Their initial training course ended with an evaluation of the NCO candidates that determined what rank they would receive, between lance corporal and sergeant. The regular army system of promotion was much different. The RAR, RLI, and RhSAS selected men with extensive experience who were judged to have leadership potential, and sent these men to attend regimental junior NCO courses. These courses were two months long, after which the graduating soldier was promoted to lance corporal. The regular courses were more in-depth than the National Service course and held the men to a higher standard (since they were already experienced soldiers). After soldiers reached the rank of corporal, the army required those interested in promotion to senior NCO ranks to take a promotion exam and attend further courses, including the Junior and Senior NCO Drill and the Junior and Senior NCO Weapons/Tactics course. If a soldier was able to pass the promotion exam and attend the requisite courses, he was promoted (based on the needs of the army).[33] Since soldiers were able to volunteer for service in the regular army from the TF, the standard of training among NCOs varied from highly experienced to "wet behind the ears."

In 1970, Rhodesians completely severed their relationship with the Crown when the unrecognized state declared itself a republic. The move was a reaction to the failure of another round of talks with the British government. Ken Flower, the head of the Rhodesian Central Intelligence Organization, said that the "government propaganda sought to convince the electorate that if Rhodesia could afford to reject the best terms Britain could offer, then why not sever all links?"[34] The chiefs of both the Rhodesian Army and the RRAF opposed the move. Major General Putterill sent a letter to Prime Minister Ian Smith detailing his opposition: "There is a worthy tradition of keeping our Forces non-political. A Republic declared in existing circumstances would be a political act, and our acceptance of it would commit our forces politically."[35] The declaration was the breaking point for Putterill, who retired from the army to become a vocal opponent of the government until the end of the Smith regime.

Although this was a significant political development, it did not have a dramatic impact on the course of the military conflict. Only a handful of officers resigned or retired after the declaration of the republic, demonstrating that the Rhodesian Front had a much higher level of support in the armed forces in 1970 than it did in 1967.[36] There were still a number of attempts by the British government to bring a peaceful end to the Rhodesian standoff. In 1970, when Edward Heath's government came to power, the Rhodesians reached out to the British to see if some deal could be made. Since 1964, Smith had been trying to get the British to agree to grant Rhodesia independence on the basis of the 1961 Rhodesian constitution. This document gave enormous power to the European population and set an extremely slow pace for the implementation of majority rule. The Smith government insisted that this was a fair and equitable way to solve the situation; Smith also claimed that the African population of Rhodesia would accept the 1961 constitution. Heath's government agreed that if the African population truly wanted independence on these terms, then it would acquiesce.

A royal commission headed by Lord Pearce traveled to Rhodesia in 1972 to take the pulse of the African and European population on this issue. The commission was able to poll about 6 percent of the population and determined that an overwhelming majority of Africans would not accept independence under the 1961 constitution.[37] While the Pearce Commission was touring Rhodesia, there was an increase in urban violence and unrest. Ken Flower assured the Rhodesian and British governments that the BSAP had things well in hand.[38] However, neither he nor Ian Smith anticipated that the war was about to escalate.

During 1970 and 1971, ZANLA began infiltrating Rhodesia from Mozambique and establishing a guerrilla network in the eastern region of the country. In November 1972, the army intercepted a large ZANLA column in Mzarabani Tribal Trust Land; only then did the government in Salisbury realized how much progress the guerrillas had made.[39] After this point in the war, the military knew that it needed additional manpower. The period of National Service increased from nine to twelve months in 1972.[40] Call-ups of the TF units also increased after 1972. The military could not sustain itself through an expansion of National Service alone. In 1973, the RAR formed a second battalion to meet the dramatic increase in operational tempo. The added advantage for the government was that African troops were paid far less than European soldiers. In May 1973, the government established the first "no-go" area in the country along the Mozambique border. This area was off-limits to civilians in an attempt to create a free-fire zone for the security forces. Anyone who was not part of the Rhodesian Security Forces found inside the "no-go" area was considered a guerrilla.[41]

During the British counterinsurgency campaign in Malaya, the primary goal of government forces was to separate the populace from the guerrillas. In 1973, the Rhodesian government embarked on a similar effort to prevent a Maoist insurgency from receiving assistance from the peasant population. Wickus de Kock, the minister for security, announced the beginning of a pilot protected villages scheme at the end of the year. Africans in newly established "no-go" zones were forced from their homes and resettled in the new protected villages, which were fenced in had a strict curfew in place. Administration and defense of the protected villages were the responsibility of the Ministry of Internal Affairs. Prior to the escalation of the war in 1972, Internal Affairs personnel did not receive military training because their primary duty was administration of the African Tribal Trust Lands. As the war spread throughout the country, however, the Internal Affairs service became a paramilitary force.[42]

The responsibility for military operations spread across the government, from the air force to Internal Affairs. This meant that once the conflict was over, the British government overlooked men who had significant amounts of both military training and experience but who were not in the army and potential training assets. Men with this kind of experience could have trained the new Zimbabwean Army; however, paramilitary forces were demobilized before they could be made a part of the training mission.

By the end of 1973, 8,000 people were forced from the "no-go" areas. The transit camps and protected villages were known for their poor conditions and inadequate security. Public health crises were common, and the guerrilla element often infiltrated the lightly defended villages. Over the course of the conflict, the government resettled almost 250,000 Africans in either consolidated or protected villages.[43] The scheme cleared citizens from many parts of the country so that the security forces could operate freely, but this redistribution of the population did not prove to be the solution the government hoped it would be. This tactic gave security forces an advantage on a local level. However, it proved to be the start of larger strategic problems that began to confront the Rhodesians in the late 1970s.

Tactical Success, Strategic Failure

The Rhodesian Army invested a great deal of effort into what it called Fire Force tactics, developed in 1974 and the army's primary tactical innovation of the war. When ground units located a guerrilla element, they would radio back to the regional headquarters for reinforcement. The Fire Force element, which was always on standby, flew into the area using helicopters and deployed as a blocking force that allowed the ground-based units to push the guerrillas out of the designated areas. While these elements maneuvered into place, a helicopter gunship would circle above and harass the guerrillas, and a command helicopter would direct the movements of the ground forces. As the war progressed, the Rhodesians transitioned from using helicopter insertions of the blocking forces to parachute insertions. This tactic allowed them to make the most of their resources because they did not have enough manpower to completely cover the terrain.[44]

Rhodesian Special Branch experimented with using "turned" guerrilla fighters as pseudo gangs, with some success. In 1973 the Central Intelligence Organization (CIO), in partnership with the security forces, formed the Selous Scouts, a multiracial army unit specifically tasked with pseudo operations.[45] This unit was partly funded by the South African Security Branch and occasionally had South African Police personnel attached to its operations.[46] Interestingly, this was the first unit in which African and European men served in the ranks together. It was also the first unit in which African NCOs were given power over European soldiers.[47] Even though this unit seemed very progressive by Rhodesian standards, the officers were still all white until 1979.

The political situation grew worse as the war escalated. One of Rhodesia's few allies, Portugal, gave up the fight to retain its own colonies in 1975. The Carnation Revolution, a military coup by junior army officers, brought down the Estado Novo and returned Portugal to democracy.[48] The Portuguese people were tired of war; 11,000 metropolitan Portuguese soldiers were dead and another 30,000 wounded. By June 1975, the Portuguese withdrew from Mozambique, and Frente de Libertação de Moçambique (FRELIMO) took control of the government. With the Portuguese gone, FRELIMO was able to actively assist the Zimbabwean liberation movements by providing a safe haven of operation and a port to receive equipment.

Around this same time, the commitment of South Africa to Rhodesia was starting to wane. B. J. Vorster's attempt at détente with the African frontline states had significant consequences for Rhodesia. In 1975, as an act of good faith on South Africa's part, the South African Police units deployed along the Zambezi were withdrawn. The South Africans left most of their equipment for the Rhodesians to use, and their helicopter pilots remained. This was a significant blow to the Rhodesian defense system. Even though many of the South African units were of marginal quality, their presence still provided a measure of deterrence.

With the majority of the South African forces gone, the Rhodesians had to find some way to meet their manpower shortfalls. One of the immediately apparent ways of doing that was to change the required National

Service period. A new National Service Act passed in 1976, extending the initial service period from twelve to eighteen months. The opportunities for service expanded as well, from only the army and the air force to include the BSAP and Internal Affairs. The three-year period of service in the TF, following the initial service period, remained unchanged. However, it was not simply Rhodesian citizens who were liable for service now; it was all European, Asian, and mixed-race residents between the ages of eighteen and twenty-five. The act defined "resident" as any male inhabitant who had lived in the country continuously for six months or more.[49] There also were significant safeguards put in place to keep young men and families from fleeing Rhodesia. There were limits on the amount of money that could be taken out of the country, and European men between the ages of sixteen and twenty-five who had not completed the first phase of service were not allowed to leave the country without government permission.

Volunteers from Abroad

The extended period of National Service and the increasing use of the TF in an operational role began to take a significant toll on the country's economy. The effects of sanctions also were becoming more noticeable by the late 1970s, and continuous TF call-ups taxed the civilian workforce. After 1973, the Rhodesian government was able to tap into new sources of recruits for its regular forces. The attention brought to Rhodesia by the international press, as well as the United States' withdrawal from the Vietnam War, left a pool of trained soldiers with combat experience seeking victory against communism that they missed in Vietnam. Not only were some Americans attracted to the ongoing fight in Rhodesia, but former servicemen from Britain, Australia, and South Africa immigrated to Rhodesia to join the regular army. Opponents of the Rhodesian effort often accused the government of recruiting and employing mercenaries who were unstable and did not care about the safety of civilians. A ZANU publication published an interview with an anonymous Frenchman who claimed to have been in a mercenary unit in the Rhodesian Army. The unnamed Frenchman claimed, "The officer corps was made up of former mercenaries. The majority of the staff, at least a dozen, had seen action in Angola."[50]

While there were indeed foreigners in the Rhodesian Army, these foreigners certainly did not dominate the organization. Their reasons for joining the settlers' cause were as wide-ranging as the countries from which they came. Peter McAleese was one who could be accused of being a mercenary, having worked as one in the Congo prior to coming to Rhodesia.[51] His motivation for serving in Rhodesia, however, was not based on monetary gain; he claims he was just a fighting man looking for another war in which he could serve.[52] McAleese was one adventurer among many who migrated from conflict to conflict in an attempt to satisfy his addiction to combat.

The security situation only got worse as the 1970s continued. While the Rhodesian Army retained the tactical advantage in firefights with guerrilla forces, the liberation armies had overall numbers on their side. The Rhodesian Army needed more soldiers; National Service and TF call-ups were so frequent that the economy suffered from a severe labor shortage. In 1977, the Third Battalion of the RAR (3RAR) was established, and the initial training period for regular army African soldiers was cut from six months to three.[53] The Third Battalion never operated as cohesive a force as did the other two battalions. It was used as a training unit to supply various other units with African troops.

Mixed-race and Asian soldiers held curious positions in the Rhodesian Army. Since the onset of National Service during the Federal period, they were liable for conscription on the same terms as European men. However, they did not train alongside European men, and they served in segregated units under white officers and often worked in noncombat service positions. Unlike Africans and Europeans, mixed-race and Asian soldiers could not serve in the regular army. If they wanted to serve full-time in the army after their National Service term expired, they signed yearlong contracts as "continuously embodied volunteers" and were paid significantly less than European soldiers.[54] The Rhodesian Army placed most of these men into protection companies and reinforcement holding units. These formations guarded static locations or protecting road-building crews. In 1978, these units combined into one unit: the Rhodesian Defense Regiment. These units often were considered subpar by the rest of the Rhodesian Army, in part because they received only five weeks of infantry training.

H. A. Berriff was a young European National Serviceman in 1973 posted as the mess NCO to a mostly mixed-race unit. Even though he just finished basic training, he was promoted to corporal and as such was set apart from the mixed-race soldiers. He recalled that these conscripts did not care about fighting and often left their weapons lying around the camp. They also were very jumpy soldiers and would start firing at the slightest provocation, a habit that was attributed to the poor quality of their short training. Overall, the mixed-race soldiers earned their reputation as poor soldiers because they did not want to be in the army. One Indian soldier commented to Berriff, "What are we fighting for? We can't even buy houses in the European areas of town even though we are born here in Rhodesia."[55]

Even though mixed-race soldiers did not want to take part in the conflict they were forced into, they still wanted equal treatment. In 1974, mixed-race and Asian soldiers went on strike in an attempt to force desegregation in the army. They insisted, "A bullet knows no colour!"[56] They also were not afraid to protest their position within Rhodesian society. In 1977, five hundred mixed-race soldiers signed a petition objecting to the racialized conscription system and being forced to participate in the war. They wanted an end to the conscription of mixed-race and Asian men. However, since both of these groups could vote on the same terms as European Rhodesians, the Rhodesian Front government insisted that they had all the same obligations as Europeans.[57] In protest, the highest-ranking mixed-race soldier in the army, a warrant officer 1, resigned.[58]

The End Is Near

By 1978, the security situation in Rhodesia was spiraling downward. The cost of the war had increased to £500,000 a day, and tax increases on the white population were required to accommodate the growth in the defense budget.[59] Even though the South African troops were gone, monetary assistance from South Africa continued. By this time, the South African government was funding up to 50 percent of the Rhodesian defense budget.[60] However, this still was not enough money to replace the losses in manpower, both in the field and due to emigration. In 1978, TF soldiers were serving approximately 190 days a year on operations: six weeks on operations, followed by six weeks at home. The strain on the white community was becoming unbearable. As a result, Ian Smith decided to negotiate with those whom he considered to be the moderate African nationalist leaders.

Smith portrayed the negotiations as a "Rhodesian solution" to the issue of majority rule. He approached the three African leaders who still remained in Rhodesia, and who were not in prison. Abel Muzorewa was a bishop of the United Methodist Church, as well as the leader of the United African National Council. Senior Chief Jeremiah Chirau was the chief of Mashonaland and the head of the Zimbabwe United People's Organization, which was secretly financed by the Rhodesian government, thus making Chirau a paid servant of the government. Reverend Ndabaningi Sithole had previously been the leader of ZANU but was forced out of power by Robert Mugabe in 1975. These three men together represented the political parties in Rhodesia that lacked an armed wing, and thus had sat out the liberation conflict. Smith believed that if he entered into a power-sharing agreement with the parties led by these men, he might be able to win international recognition for Rhodesia.[61]

Ken Flower, the head of the CIO, made it clear to Ian Smith and the rest of the cabinet that guerrilla forces were spreading throughout the country; it was imperative to secure African allies against the militant liberation movements.[62] Smith's government was encouraged by the cautious enthusiasm of Western nations over the possibility of a settlement. The three African leaders agreed to enter into a government with the Rhodesian Front in March 1978. Even though the country's name changed to Zimbabwe-Rhodesia and Abel Muzorewa became the first African prime minister, power remained firmly in the hands of the settler community. Whites retained a minimum of twenty-eight seats in the parliament; the remaining seventy-two were open to Africans. Whites also retained control of the security forces, Internal Affairs, the judiciary, and their privileged property rights.[63]

The Internal Settlement did not live up to the hopes of the Western powers, and Zimbabwe-Rhodesia remained unrecognized. The military conflict escalated as the guerrilla forces began to make use of more sophisticated weapons. In September 1978, Zimbabwe Peoples' Revolutionary Army (ZIPRA) guerrillas used a shoulder-fired surface-to-air missile to shoot down a civilian Air Rhodesia flight from Kariba. Eighteen of the fifty-six people on board survived the crash. However, fourteen of those eighteen were killed by guerrillas who found the crash site.[64] In retaliation, the Rhodesian government launched further raids on the frontline states. In October 1978, the Rhodesian Air Force attacked ZIPRA's "Freedom

Camp" at Westland Farms in Zambia. The large Rhodesian formation took over Zambian airspace and warned the airbase at Lusaka that if any Zambian aircraft attempted to intervene, they would be shot down. The strike was extremely successful in military terms; it also provided excellent propaganda for the settler community. A recording was made of a Rhodesian Air Force officer, the so-called Green Leader, talking to Lusaka tower. The recording was repeatedly replayed on the Rhodesian Broadcasting Network during the next several weeks.[65]

Even though the Rhodesians occasionally scored major tactical victories, the security situation was still grim. The culture of the Rhodesian Army was changing; in May 1978, the first Asian officer was commissioned into the Rhodesian Army. Reverend Val Rajah was an Anglican priest who commissioned into the Rhodesian Corps of Chaplains as a captain. His duties were confined to ministering to the spiritual needs of mixed-race trainees at Llewellin Barracks in Bulawayo, but this was a dramatic jump forward for non-whites in the Rhodesian forces. After the Internal Settlement, conscription extended to include young African men. Conscription of African men caught the British government completely off guard. It concluded in October 1978 that the Rhodesian Forces would not introduce the conscription of Africans because of the potential drawbacks.[66] The official decision occurred on 8 January 1979 and was followed shortly thereafter by the first multiracial National Service intake in February 1979.[67] Intake 183 was also the first time that a multiracial instructor cadre was used in the conventional army.[68] The Selous Scouts often used both African and European NCOs as instructors in their selection and training courses prior to this time. However, this was due to the special nature of their operations; the practice was unheard of outside of this special unit. After this point the size of the army continued to expand through the use of African troops. Although they were subject to National Service, they still were not paid the same rate as whites and still were required to serve in separate units. Conscripted Africans went to the RAR, whereas whites went to the RR.

The first African officers were commissioned only a short time prior to the integration of National Service training. In 1977, the first group of African officer cadets passed out of officer training and into service in the Rhodesian Army. In July 1977, three African officers commissioned into the RAR: Lieutenants Tumbare, Mutero, and Choruma. All three were long-serving NCOs in the RAR. Tumbare had accrued twenty-nine years in the army at the time he was commissioned.[69] General Peter Walls, the commander of the Rhodesian Army, said on the occasion: "The Army has always been prepared to accept black men on commissioning courses if they measured up, potentially, to the standards required of leaders."[70] Interestingly, this was the same line used by white members of the Federal Assembly when questioned about the lack of African officers in the Federal Army. Rhodesian authorities embarked on a publicity campaign to highlight the "shoulder to shoulder" nature of the war, often showing African and white troops fighting together in the field.[71]

Assegai, the official magazine of the Rhodesian Army, was widely circulated inside the army and sent abroad to public libraries and universities. While it focused primarily on professional military topics and army news, there was also a significant amount of ideological content on the government positions and the anticommunist nature of the conflict. The cover of the September 1977 issue of *Assegai* showed Lieutenant Tumbare, a member of one of the first groups of Africans commissioned, accepting an officer's sword from the widow of Lieutenant Colonel Kim Rule. In his will, Lieutenant Colonel Rule asked that his sword be presented to the first African officer commissioned into the Rhodesian Army.[72] The article and cover were used to further the impression that the Rhodesian Army truly was integrated. The December 1977 issue of that same publication had a white and an African soldier on the cover, loading up ammunition together. One of the features in that issue was a story on joint training between the RR and the RAR. Again, the magazine attempted to highlight the single week of joint training between the two units and marginalize the unequal pay, unequal accommodations, and unequal treatment of African soldiers.[73]

After the first class of African officers commissioned in late 1977, the second group started training. The following year, seven more African officers were commissioned. None of the seven were commissioned into line units in the army; four were commissioned into the "administrative stream" of the army, one was commissioned into the Army Educational Corps, and the final two were commissioned into the Administrative Branch of the Rhodesian Air Force.[74] Even after African officers had officially been commissioned, some members of the Rhodesian government viewed the program with suspicion. During a parliamentary session in

July 1977, Mr. R. W. McGee, the member representing Matobo, questioned the legitimacy of the commissioning process when he asked the government how many African officers had been granted their commissions after failing their written exams. He also inquired as to why some officers were separated during training, and whether such training was actually equal in standard. In response, the government said that the commissioning standards remained high and that no officers failed their written exams; the only reason for the separation was to accommodate those for whom English was a second language.[75] The white community was still extremely uncomfortable with the idea of African officers. By the end of 1978, there were ten African officers in the Rhodesian Army. While Africans soon were brought into the National Service scheme, they were not permitted to undergo National Service officer training.

The Expansion and Decline of the Security Forces

The expansion of the conflict in the late 1970s necessitated a further expansion of Rhodesian forces beyond the inclusion of Africans in the officer corps and the conscription of Africans. An altogether new organization was established by Bishop Muzorewa's party, called Pfumo Revanhu, or "spear of the people," also known as the Security Force Auxiliaries (SFA). This organization was composed of Muzorewa's followers but also from the Sithole political party and from the surrendered personnel of ZANLA and ZIPRA.[76] The extremely high unemployment rate among Africans in Rhodesia made recruiting very easy. These men received a short (six- or eight-week) training course before being sent out on operations in a zone from which the rest of the security forces were barred. Often a single white officer, NCO, or Special Branch agent commanded these patrols. While the Rhodesian regime advertised the SFA as an illustration of the unified nature of the fight in Rhodesia, some international observers insisted that it was nothing more than a criminal organization.[77]

The SFA did not generally operate in the field with the regular security forces. The only connections between the defense establishment and the SFA were the Selous Scouts and the Special Branch liaison officers who served with the auxiliaries. The SFA units did not even operate in the same parts of the country as the regular forces but were relegated to the "frozen zones" that by January 1979 covered about 15 percent of the country. These forces operated with little or no supervision and at times were guilty of stealing from and terrorizing the African population.[78]

The auxiliaries' loyalty was never assured; there was a widespread problem with desertion after they received their training and weapons. The closer the country came to a settlement, the more discipline in the SFA weakened. As early as January 1978, the British government received intelligence indicating that Africans in rural communities lived in genuine fear of the auxiliaries; over time, the problem simply got worse.[79] By the time the December 1979 Lancaster House Agreement was reached, many SFA units had to be disbanded because they were no longer effective in the field.[80]

In the late 1970s, the Rhodesian government also attempted to use the maximum possible number of white personnel. After the changes to conscription in 1977, there were very few deferments available for National Service; deferments for university students were abolished in September 1977. Even clergymen, judges, MPs, and civil servants were required at least to register themselves with the Ministry of Security Manpower.[81] Even with this expansion, the entire security establishment could only field roughly sixty thousand men if all the reserve forces were called out for active service.[82]

With the addition of African conscription and the extension of call-up periods, the Zimbabwe-Rhodesia government was still stretched too thin and could not sustain itself indefinitely. The security forces were losing control of large swaths of land to the liberation armies because they did not have the personnel necessary to provide adequate ground coverage. In rural areas, European farmers resorted to hiring heavily armed private security guards to protect their land and livestock from theft and damage.[83] In 1979, Rhodesia was swarmed by armed groups, both African and European. With the army regularly engaging in operations against the liberation armies, the SFA moving about the country with little supervision, and private armies of farm security guards operating with impunity, mass chaos in the country was only a short step away.

In August 1979, the Commonwealth Heads of Government met in Lusaka. The conference concluded with an invitation by the British government to host a constitutional conference. The idea was that both the liberation organizations and the Rhodesian government might come together to negotiate an end to the conflict and set up the basis for an independent Zimbabwe. The conference, held at Lancaster House in London, was chaired by Lord Carrington, the foreign secretary. Both ZANU and ZAPU attended the conference under the banner of a united Patriotic Front, which initially was hesitant to attend due to its increasingly successful campaign within the country. However, the governments of Mozambique and Zambia were just as war-weary as the Rhodesians and insisted that the Patriotic Front attend.[84]

The conference ended on 21 December 1979, with the signing of the Lancaster House Agreement. All sides declared an official cease-fire and also agreed to hold free elections in 1980 to create a new Zimbabwean government. The armed groups in the country were supposed to disarm and the political parties engage in peaceful campaigning during the run-up to the election. Until the election results were finalized and the new government in place, the country was to return to British control. Only a few days after the agreement was signed, the Commonwealth Monitoring Force, a peacekeeping force made up of soldiers from throughout the Commonwealth, began to arrive in Rhodesia. The largest contributing nation was the United Kingdom. These soldiers and a force of British policemen flown in specifically to monitor the election in March were supposed to ensure the free and fair nature of the proceedings. However, all three sides in the conflict engaged in some form of intimidation; in the end, Robert Mugabe and ZANU achieved electoral victory.

The Liberation Armies

At the end of the conflict in Zimbabwe, thirty-seven thousand liberation fighters reported to assembly points in accordance with the provisions of the cease-fire agreement. Of this number, seventeen thousand were members of ZANU's military wing, the Zimbabwe African National Liberation Army, and twenty thousand were members of ZAPU's military wing, the Zimbabwe Peoples' Revolutionary Army.[85] While these forces served different political parties, they had the same strategic goal of bringing majority rule to Zimbabwe. The soldiers in these armies ranged from highly trained infiltration specialists to young boys pressed into service with little or no training.[86]

It is difficult to present an overview of the training pipeline of the liberation armies because of their ad hoc supply system and training structure.

While training sometimes occurred inside Rhodesian borders, the threat from security forces was often too great to train any more than a handful of fighters in any one place. Both ZANLA and ZIPRA had to look outside Rhodesia for training bases. By 1979, both groups had bases in Tanzania, Botswana, Mozambique, and Zambia (to name only the major training areas). In 1965, ZANLA established a training base in Itumbi, Tanzania. Initially, only Tanzanian Army instructors staffed the base; ZANLA cadres took part only in the political indoctrination of recruits because they lacked the military skills to contribute in any other way.[87] In the 1960s, this training concentrated on commando tactics: infiltration, sabotage, demolition, small-unit tactics, and some marksmanship training.

In actuality, however, the training in Tanzania left much to be desired. The recruits were left to their own devices much of the time. They were expected to cook their own meals and lead their own physical training sessions without any supervision; the training cadres often did not show up to the camp until 9:00 a.m. Marksmanship training was almost non-existent; the recruits were given extensive lectures on the use of firearms, but they had little hands-on experience with any weapon.[88] There were chronic shortages both of weapons and ammunition in these training camps. Even when supplies were available, training followed the Russian model, which concentrated on promoting area fire rather than actual marksmanship. Area fire is the use of a unit's firepower directed at an area where an enemy is or is thought to be. The primary purpose of area fire is suppression; it is not expected to actually hit the enemy. After receiving instruction on how a weapon should operate, the trainees were allowed to fire five rounds. Often, this would mark the last time a trainee handled a weapon until arriving in Rhodesia to fight.[89] Some guerrilla fighters never had the opportunity to train with a gun before they arrived to fight with the Rhodesian Army. ZIPRA alluded to this problem in 1977 in its official publication, the *Zimbabwe Review*. The magazine was an external propaganda magazine printed in English that ZIPRA sent to libraries, and universities all over the world. Prior to the meeting of the Organization of African Unity's Liberation Committee, ZIPRA pointed out that most of its fighters had to train with wooden replicas rather than actual weapons.[90]

By the late 1960s, however, ZANLA replaced its commando-style training with an increased emphasis on revolutionary warfare. Robert Mugabe commented on this change in strategy in a 1978 interview: "When we began the armed struggle in 1966 all we had were some small commando groups. . . . There was no preparation work carried out among the people so when our groups arrived in the villages, the people were suspicious of them." He went on to say that "there was a complete revision of our manner of carrying out the armed struggle. We began to realize that the armed struggle must be based on the support of the people."[91] The two liberation armies received support from different parts of the communist world. Their supporters influenced the development of the liberation armies' military strategy through the types of training and equipment they provided. ZANLA's main supplier was China. Prior to 1969, cadres went to China to undergo military training. These "train the trainer" courses were designed to produce instructors who would be able to train the everyday ZANLA fighters. However, in 1969 the Chinese changed their model of support, and rather than bringing ZANLA members to China, the Chinese sent instructors to ZANLA camps in Tanzania.[92] Chairman Mao's three phases of revolutionary warfare appealed to the ZANLA cadres: (1) phase one: organization, consolidation, and preservation of base areas; (2) phase two: progressive expansion by terror and attacks on isolated enemy units to obtain arms, supplies, and political support; and (3) phase three: destruction of the enemy in battle.[93] ZANLA never matured beyond the second phase of warfare before the end of the conflict.

From the early 1960s to 1979, the recruiting patterns of both liberation armies went through three phases: voluntary recruitment, press-ganging, and finally back to voluntary recruitment. Initially, both forces targeted expatriate communities in Zambia. When it became clear that they were not achieving their recruiting goals, they resorted to press-gang tactics. They struggled with high desertion rates both during training and in the field. A large number of impressed fighters turned themselves over to the Rhodesians, and some ended up as members of the Selous Scouts. From time to time, one of the liberation armies attempted to steal recruits from the other. In 1967, ZANLA recruiting officers launched an armed assault on a ZIPRA training camp with the intention of scattering the ZIPRA recruits and then impressing them into ZANLA service. The Rhodesian authorities often publicized guerrilla abductions of students from mission schools for service in their armies.[94] By 1973, the large number of refugees that were flowing into both Zambia and Mozambique made impressments unnecessary.

After ZIPRA refused to participate in training under Chinese instructors, it became more involved in training abroad in both Russia and East Germany. The training in these countries focused on how to conduct a conventional war against Rhodesian forces as opposed to the guerrilla tactics used in the past. Unlike ZANLA, ZIPRA possessed heavy weapons, tanks, and armored personnel carriers. ZIPRA had two separate organizations, the guerrilla unit and the conventional brigade. The conventional brigade was task organized like a Soviet combat unit with armor, infantry, artillery, and even engineering and signal support. The guerrilla unit continued to send fighters into Rhodesia in small groups throughout the conflict. However, after ZANLA relocated most of its forces to Mozambique in 1975, ZIPRA could not keep pace with the number of fighters sent into Rhodesia. In 1977, ZANLA had three thousand guerrilla fighters in Rhodesia, whereas ZIPRA had only two hundred.[95] At this point, ZIPRA was planning for Operation Zero Hour, the moment when its conventional forces would move across the Rhodesian border and engage in a full-scale assault on the Rhodesian Army. In 1979, ZIPRA had fighter pilots in training in Russia in preparation for Operation Zero Hour. When the conflict ended, ZIPRA had twenty thousand fighters in various stages of training around the world.[96]

The conventional brigade was the only part of the liberation movement that had any training in conventional warfare or experience in leading units larger than a handful of men. Yet once the war ended, a large number of liberation fighters marketed themselves as guerrilla commanders. Since the rank structure of the liberation movement was less rigid than that of the Rhodesian Army, it is sometimes difficult to grasp where, exactly, specific men fell in the organization. The term "commander" was applied much more broadly in ZIPRA and ZANLA than it was in Rhodesia. A man who led a group of four or five men was labeled a commander in the same way that Robert Mugabe was commander in chief of ZANLA. Some commanders attended command courses abroad, but this was the exception to the rule. Preparation of new commanders was limited to on-the-job training. Some men were extremely successful and were both tactically and technically proficient. Others failed both themselves and their men and terrorized their own people, using their status as freedom fighters to protect them from retaliation.

From 1975 until 1978, ZANLA and ZIPRA attempted to combine their efforts under the umbrella of the Zimbabwe Peoples' Army (ZIPA). The experiment demonstrated the weaknesses in the command structures of each organization. The spokesman for ZANU, Eddison Zvobgo, commented that one of the problems that both of the organizations suffered from was that they "had little experience coordinating military programs."[97] The leaders of the liberation movements also made it clear that their weakest point was their logistical structure. Even though the ZIPA experiment lasted almost four years, the combined military council never managed to coordinate logistics or operations between the two forces. Some of the lack of cooperation was due to a genuine mistrust between the parties. However, two organizations that already possessed severe limitations in their command and logistical capabilities could hardly have been expected to coordinate the efforts of a combined army at a more proficient level.

The ZIPA experiment never really worked in practice, no matter how much the liberation parties pushed the idea in the public eye. Both armies continued to suffer from endemic command problems. One of the most serious for both groups was a lack of discipline among the guerrilla forces once they crossed into Rhodesia. One ZIPRA detachment in Rhodesia simply refused to work with its own high command from 1976 until the cease-fire at the end of the war.[98] ZIPRA leadership attributed this breakdown in the command structure to heavy casualties, as well as anger that the leaders in Zambia were enjoying a comfortable lifestyle while the guerrillas suffered from a severe lack of supplies. However, the Rhodesian Selous Scouts believed that the actions of this rebel detachment (and others like it) were the result of tension between the guerrillas and the ZIPRA conventional brigade, which remained outside of the country.[99] The relationship between the guerrilla fighters and their leadership was fragile. When on operations, the guerrillas had little supervision and at times operated in direct contravention of what their commanders envisioned.

ZANLA also experienced dramatic showdowns between its guerrilla fighters and the chain of command. In 1974, a group of ZANLA fighters led by Thomas Nhari, a senior ZANLA commander, mutinied against the ZANU Supreme Military Council. Nhari and his followers claimed that ZANU had grown too close to the Chinese and that because of this relationship ZANLA was cut off from Russian weapons suppliers. The mutineers called for the replacement of the entire council and access to Russian weapons and training. ZANLA's commander, Josiah Tongogara, was able to marshal enough freshly trained troops to put down the mutiny.[100] Internal conflicts persisted in ZANU/ZANLA. In March 1976, Robert Mugabe was able to centralize authority in his position on a new central committee. He abolished the political commissar training academy and focused all political training on ZANU history; with this move, he began building his cult of personality.[101] In January 1978, another group of ZANLA cadres was accused of conspiring to engage in a coup from within the party. Mugabe personally oversaw a contrived courtroom drama that convicted the men of conspiring to engage in mutiny, after which they were thrown in pit cells for several months.[102]

Even though the guerrilla forces were constantly plagued by internal political problems, they were able to insert enough fighters into Rhodesia to stretch the security forces to their limit. Direct confrontation with Rhodesian Security Forces often ended poorly for the guerrillas. Even low-quality Police Reserve units were able to repel guerrilla attacks. The Rhodesians felt that their Fire Force tactics were the answer to winning the war. After 1976, however, there were just too many fighters coming into the country for Fire Force units to be able to respond to all reports of insurgent activity.

Tactically, the Rhodesians were more skilled. When they met liberation forces in combat, they often outperformed them; the RAR was actually the most effective unit in the army. However, the Rhodesians failed strategically. They could not match the liberation armies' mobilization of the masses. While Rhodesian Army units might only occasionally encounter guerrilla fighters on patrol, there was an overwhelming land mine and ambush threat throughout the country. This limited the mobility of Rhodesian forces and hampered the Rhodesian economy. The consequences of economic sanctions, a limited white workforce, and security threats throughout the country crippled Rhodesia. They were unable to overcome the strategic obstacles that the liberation armies put in their path. Even though the conflict never matured into Mao's third phase of warfare, the Rhodesian regime was weak enough by the late 1970s to be forced to admit defeat and accept an agreement implementing majority rule.

Conclusion

On 21 December 1979, representatives from all the warring parties met at Lancaster House in London and signed an agreement for the cessation of hostilities. They agreed to the tenets of a new constitution and to British supervision of free and fair elections. The Lancaster House Agreement provided the basis for the creation of the Zimbabwe National Army out of the collected forces of the combatants (ZANLA, ZIPRA, and the Rhodesian Army). These three organizations brought to the bargaining table completely different levels of military training. The Rhodesian Army had well-established, but race-based, systems for training its officers, NCOs, and enlisted men. Additionally, it maintained a competent administrative and logistical structure that both liberation armies lacked. One of the major questions that remained unanswered at the time of the Lancaster House Agreement was whether European soldiers would remain in the army and be available to help integrate the forces. Even though there were African officers in the Rhodesian Army with years of military experience, many had been serving in officer roles only since 1977 or later. As in the previous two examples of Kenya and Zambia, there were no African officers above the rank of captain at the time of independence in 1980.

Although the British Army had dealt with this type of situation before, it had not previously integrated a guerrilla force into a conventional army. The guerrilla fighters had years of experience operating in the bush and mobilizing the population. This type of combat experience, while useful, was not applicable to serving in a peacetime conventional force. Even those members of the guerrilla movements who had received formal training in China or the Soviet Union were taught how to fight as guerrillas, but not how to command a platoon of thirty men assaulting a fortified objective. Even the ZIPRA conventional brigade was a problematic factor. All those soldiers had been indoctrinated by Soviet Army doctrine focusing on the use of large mechanized formations. Even if the new Zimbabwe National Army could obtain a sufficient number of tanks and armored personnel carriers, that part of Africa was not ideally suited for large-scale armored combat.

The Rhodesian Army could not simply become the new Zimbabwe National Army, but in 1979 it appeared that it was the only part of the equation that did not require complete retraining. As they had done in Kenya, British training teams set up a program to prepare former guerrillas to attend Sandhurst and then work their way up through the officer ranks. However, it was difficult to see how these teams could convince guerrilla commanders who had been fighting for well over a decade that they needed to start their military careers all over again. In agreeing to be the honest broker in Zimbabwean independence, the British government took on a military training task unlike any other it had encountered, at least since 1945. It would have to call on thirty-five years of experience in transitioning colonies to independent nations to figure out how to begin to turn Rhodesia into Zimbabwe.

How Do You Create an Army?
British Postconflict Planning

Planning for the postconflict environment in Zimbabwe began long before the war was actually over. While the Unilateral Declaration of Independence resulted in de facto independence for Rhodesia, the British government assumed that Her Majesty's Government would be responsible for the transition to majority rule at some point. The British learned important lessons while training armies in Africa for the three decades preceding Zimbabwean independence. Kenya was the first time British military planners had to deal with the issue of Africanizing a white-led force in an area where a white settler population remained. In Zambia, British planners wrestled with the prospect of creating a multiracial force that reflected Zambian society. In both cases there were setbacks that had a dramatic impact on the way the British approached military training. The East Africa mutinies of 1964 made HMG question the value of training African soldiers to a high standard if it took so long that it created animosity among those being trained.

The British were fearful that the same type of sentiment created in East Africa would be replicated in Zambia, and HMG decided that it was preferable to accelerate Africanization rather than focus on rigorous and professional training programs. As noted in chapter 2, this was accompanied by significant pressure from the Zambian government to quickly Africanize high-level command positions. Defense and Foreign Office planners had to come up with training and transition schemes in mere months prior to the colonies becoming independent. In the late 1970s, as the Rhodesian situation dragged on, the war became increasingly unwinnable for Ian Smith's regime, and the British began to make plans for an independent Zimbabwe.

Rather than be caught unprepared for the eventual transition from colonial rule to independence, the Ministry of Defence (MOD) began planning for a new Zimbabwe Army in 1976. These policy discussions took
place at a difficult economic and operational time for the British defense
establishment. In 1975 inflation had reached a decade-high level of 24
percent. The economic crisis of 1976 forced HMG to accept spending
restraints imposed by the International Monetary Fund in exchange for
an economic rescue package.[1] The Defense White Paper of 1975 reevaluated what kind of military commitments the British government could afford. The Priority 1 commitments were the maintenance of NATO forces
in Germany, the Atlantic submarine forces, and UK nuclear deterrent.
Everything else was a Priority 2 task.[2] The white paper also called for a
reduction in the overall manpower of the regular army by fifteen thousand soldiers and a greater reliance on the Territorial Army.[3] All the while,
the army was pulling soldiers from the garrisons in Germany, Cyprus,
and England to meet the demands of operations in Northern Ireland. The
army also suffered from a shortage of officers and senior NCOs, the most
critical groups of personnel for overseas training missions.

The two primary factors to shape British planning for the end of the
conflict in Zimbabwe were money and manpower. British interests in the
region were a secondary factor throughout the process. However, world
events also influenced the way the British approached their postconflict
planning. By 1975 the South African government had entered a period of
détente with the international community. South African prime minister
B. J. Vorster attempted to appease Western powers by scaling back support
for Ian Smith's Rhodesian government. Vorster withdrew South African
forces from Rhodesia and reduced the amount of South Africa's financial
support to the Smith government. These actions by the South Africans, as
well as the continued infiltration of liberation forces into Rhodesia, made
it clear to the British that the time was right to start thinking about the
postconflict era.

Planning for a New Army

The first question that British officials raised in their postconflict planning
process was about the role of British forces during the pre-independence
stage. Both the Foreign and Commonwealth Office (FCO) and the MOD

assumed that the conflict would eventually come to a negotiated end. The liberation armies did not have the military power to overrun the Rhodesian Security Forces (RSF); conversely, the Rhodesians did not have the manpower to suppress the growing insurgency in the Tribal Trust Lands. Since the British continued to insist that the Rhodesia problem was an internal matter (Rhodesia had been a Crown colony in rebellion since 1965), HMG assumed it would be responsible for some sort of interim governing arrangement between any negotiated agreement and formal independence. Along with this assumption came the problem of preserving law and order during the interim. There would be a large number of armed men in the country beyond the constitutionally legitimate RSF.

The FCO envisioned that the liberation organizations and the frontline states (Zambia, Mozambique, and Botswana) might call for the introduction of British forces into Rhodesia. The major concern the FCO had about deploying British forces during the interim period was how these soldiers would be perceived. Since the Rhodesian Front government would still be in control until elections were held, HMG feared that the presence of British troops would be seen by Africans as a move to support the white regime.[4] There was also the problem of command and control. In Northern Rhodesia the colony simply remained under the control of the Colonial Office until elections were held and an independent government was prepared to rule. The situation was markedly different in Rhodesia; it was never under the supervision of the Colonial Office, and when the British reestablished control, it simply meant that a British governor would return to the country. Even so, the governor would have little power in the day-to-day operations of the country and would not be in control of the security forces. The only statutory force in the country was the Rhodesian Security Forces. Since Rhodesia achieved responsible government in 1923, the governor was only a ceremonial position like the governor-general in most dominions. The British government refused to accept responsibility for the situation without accompanying authority.[5]

The defense planners looking at the military integration problem initially decided that the model they used in Kenya and Zambia might also work in Zimbabwe. The Rhodesian Army was already a British-trained force that had African NCOs, an NCO academy, and established schools based on British models. The office in the MOD responsible for overseas military assistance, DS11, felt that it would be best to have the Rhodesian

Army infrastructure train the guerrillas selected for integration as enlisted men into the new Zimbabwe Army. The British government would focus on sending black officer cadets to Sandhurst. Because a similar method had worked in Kenya and Zambia, the MOD was confident it would work in Zimbabwe.[6]

In December 1976 the MOD formed a working group to examine how to preserve law and order between the end of the conflict and independence. London had already determined that it was advantageous for Britain to maintain a long-term defense relationship with Zimbabwe after independence. The relationship would be beneficial to the economically depressed British defense industry in the late 1970s, and it would allow the British government to moderate the types of technology Zimbabwe acquired. The British were worried about upsetting the balance of power in southern Africa by giving sophisticated military hardware to Zimbabwe; such acts would doubtlessly upset South Africa.[7] Therefore, the British had to be extremely careful of what types of resources they made available to Zimbabwe. This hearkens back to a similar situation they faced during the late 1960s, when attempting to equip the Zambia Defense Force.

When the working group began discussions on the future of the Zimbabwean military, the MOD had already established some procedural guidelines. The Defense White Paper of 1975 stated that the United Kingdom could not support anything more than a brigade diverted from Priority 1 to Priority 2 tasks. In 1975 the British had already violated that provision by the number of soldiers deployed on operations in Northern Ireland. Any sort of British military mission sent to Zimbabwe would be capped at two hundred personnel. The British were in no position to pay the complete cost of a training mission and had to assume that there would be a significant Commonwealth contribution. The MOD also hoped that it would be able to convince the new Zimbabwean government to shoulder the costs of the military mission. The working group had to examine five issues: (1) the future structure and control of the Zimbabwe armed forces; (2) the control, integration, and deployment of guerrilla forces; (3) portfolios of defense and law and order in the interim administration; (4) the form and nature of the Commonwealth mission; and (5) the future of individual senior members of the armed forces after the establishment of the interim administration.[8]

The findings of the working group were based on the assumption that the RSF would remain relatively intact and that the guerrillas would be absorbed into it. This was a dramatic misreading of the political and military situation in southern Africa. The fall of the Portuguese empire and the rise of the Frente de Libertação de Moçambique (FRELIMO) government in Mozambique also led to an increase in capabilities and success rate of infiltration attempts of the Zimbabwe African National Liberation Army (ZANLA) forces. While the Rhodesians continued to achieve tactical victories against the guerrilla fighters, there were quickly becoming too many infiltrators for the RSF to stop. The momentum of the conflict had shifted in favor of the guerrilla armies. British planners, however, continued to assume that the Rhodesian government would retain enough political capital to preserve the structure of the government and military in the country's postcolonial phase.

This does not mean that the British did not recognize the goals of the guerrilla armies. The first draft of the working group's report pointed out that there were four major problems facing any integration of the security forces in Zimbabwe: (1) ideological differences over the system of government; (2) bitterness resulting from the fighting; (3) inequality of training; and (4) notions of discipline.[9] These four points also succinctly sum up how the situation in Zimbabwe was different from any previous training mission the British had faced. The working group understood that the aim of the guerrilla armies was to dispense with the British system and create a military force similar to that created by FRELIMO in Mozambique.[10] Until 1994 the armed forces of Mozambique were a political extension of FRELIMO. They were truly a revolutionary army and were often pointed to as being at the forefront of the revolution. They also pointed out that the Rhodesian personnel who remained in the army would have to be vetted for loyalty to a majority-ruled government. Additionally, all the foreign nationals who joined the Rhodesian Army could not remain in service if the liberation parties were going to agree to be a part of the new army.[11] These were just a few of the hurdles that the working group knew it had to overcome to create a functioning force.

The MOD ruled out the deployment of British troops to maintain law and order; the British government not only was unwilling to take on the mission but also was unable. However, an unidentified Canadian Army colonel on loan to the MOD authored a report suggesting the possibility of sending an observer force to Rhodesia to supervise the transition of power when the time came. He asserted that neither the Rhodesians nor the guerrilla armies were prepared to maintain law and order and needed to be retrained. The key reason he cited for needing such an observer force was to safeguard the human rights of individuals on both sides. To maintain any semblance of impartiality, neither of the combatant forces could be trusted to ensure law and order unsupervised. He suggested that a British officer take command of all the forces in the country and that a Commonwealth observer force ensure that the transition process was peaceful.[12] At the time this report was published, it was ignored. The British government was more interested in exploring low-cost options such as a UN observer mission rather than funding such missions on its own. However, as the end of the conflict approached, HMG had to reevaluate this option.

The final draft of the working group report was released on 20 December 1976. As the working group studied the problem, it became aware of two issues that would seriously endanger any possibility of success in Zimbabwe. If the guerrilla armies were not satisfied with the agreement at the end of the conflict, they could simply leave some of their forces outside of the country rather than bring them in for integration. If this occurred, it would seriously threaten any security arrangement in Zimbabwe. There was also a real possibility that interethnic fighting could break out during the interim government period. There would have to be a balanced approach to preserving law and order so no particular ethnic group would be favored, including the settlers.[13]

Even though the working group acknowledged that there had to be balanced representation in the new army, it was hesitant to get rid of the Rhodesian Army altogether. The group felt that "the quality of training of the current Rhodesian forces [wa]s far superior to any African force . . . it [wa]s far better than any African force that might replace it."[14] The working group felt that the RSF was the best choice to maintain law and order during the interim. In reference to the training of the new army, the group recommended three possible solutions: (1) training soldiers in the United Kingdom at British Army schools, (2) sending British officers and NCOs to serve on secondment to the Zimbabwean Army, or (3) sending specialists and technicians to Rhodesia to help train technical branches.[15] The notion of seconding officers was immediately ruled out. The challenges in trying to manage British officers seconded to the Zambia Army during

the UDI period were difficult enough to manage; the MOD did not want
to repeat the experience with Zimbabwe and South Africa.

The most heavily favored option was a combination of sending specialists to Zimbabwe and bringing some trainees to the United Kingdom.
The working group thought that if British Army specialists went to help
train the new army, it would also open up the possibility of a renewal of
defense sales to Zimbabwe. The British also thought that the new Zimbabwean government could pay for the cost of any specialists sent to train
its soldiers. This, combined with the prospect of sales to the new country,
made it theoretically possible for any training mission to Zimbabwe to be
at best profitable, and at worst cost-neutral. The Zimbabwean Army that
the working group envisioned was a slightly more Africanized version of
the RSF. The group specifically noted that "the current forces [we]re too
well trained to sacrifice them, they and the current structure should be
maintained."[16] The examples of Zambia and Kenya were particularly useful to the members of the working group. The members of the working
group looked at the process of Africanization in Zimbabwe as a gradual
process based on the training and fair treatment of soldiers of all races.

Negotiating an Army

When the working group wrote the initial report, it had little to no idea
of how the Rhodesians or the guerrillas would react to a negotiated settlement. By 1977, negotiations at Geneva between the warring factions had
broken down. However, the Geneva talks gave the British government a
better idea of what type of postconflict settlement each side might accept.
Additionally, the DS11 staff section proposed demobilizing all the armed
groups, including the RSF. Group Captain H. Davidson, a member of the
working group, felt that once a cease-fire was in place, there should be a
progressive disbanding of the forces on both sides. While this occurred, a
Commonwealth force could deploy to Zimbabwe to start rebuilding the
military. Davidson felt that once the Commonwealth forces arrived, the
only remaining units of any military force should be engineering, logistics, and transportation units that could be used to form the foundation
of the new Zimbabwean Army.[17] This method would facilitate a screening
process that would allow for the commissioning of long-serving African
senior noncommissioned officers and warrant officers, the screening of

former RSF members who wanted to reengage in the Zimbabwe Army, and selective recruitment of guerrillas. Like the previous plans that originated in the working group, this one assumed that the RSF, rather than the guerrillas, would form the majority of a new Zimbabwe Army.

The British would have had a difficult time convincing any of the warring parties to disband their forces. Ian Smith and the Rhodesian Front refused to disband the RSF or replace any officers with guerrillas. Robert Mugabe was guarded in his views on the postconflict military. However, he indicated that he did not expect the RSF to completely disband. Even so, Mugabe did expect the new Zimbabwe Army to be based on his own Patriotic Front forces. Abel Muzorewa also wanted guerrillas to make up the majority of the new army but wanted to retain some RSF units to counterbalance any possibility of a coup by PF elements. There was another important interest group in these negotiations: the presidents of the African states bordering Rhodesia. These frontline presidents wanted the entire RSF disbanded and an all-African force in its place.[18] The frontline states suffered at the hands of the RSF. During the war the RSF sent forces into Zambia, Mozambique, and Botswana to destroy guerrilla bases and the local infrastructure.

The British faced an unpleasant reality in 1977. They realized they would not be able to control the military transition in Zimbabwe as they had in Kenya and Zambia. In Zimbabwe, the RSF did not hold a monopoly on the use of force (as the colonial military forces had in both of the previous examples). A number of planners in the FCO repeatedly asked the MOD how the establishment of the army in Mozambique worked out, thinking that the British might use Mozambique as a model for Zimbabwe. Much to their disappointment, the MOD pointed out that no Portuguese troops remained in Mozambique after independence, so there was no need for any sort of integration process.[19]

After some initial posturing by both the Rhodesians and the guerrillas, the British informed them that it was unreasonable for either side to expect the disbandment of the other's forces (particularly since neither side was defeated in the field). After the parties agreed on this point, the British diplomatic focus turned to convincing guerrilla leaders that during the interim administration the only force capable of maintaining law and order would be the RSF. If the FCO could manage this, it would ensure that the RSF would be the basis for the new Zimbabwe National Army

(ZNA), and the RSF would be in a position to be the primary training organization during the transition to independence.[20] The latter point, in particular, was important to the British government because it absolved the British of financial responsibility for training the ZNA.

The guerrilla leaders were more willing to compromise on this issue than Ian Smith was. The FCO suggested that a British general take command of the ZNA during the transition and training period, as in Zambia. While Joshua Nkomo and Robert Mugabe were open to discussing the idea, Smith firmly rejected it. Nkomo was a pragmatist; he had been a railway workers' union organizer before the war, and he was openly willing to accept an integrated ZNA. Mugabe kept his thoughts from the British. The only indication that the FCO had of his opinions was intelligence gathered from those around him.[21] By November 1977, the Rhodesian government seemed to be ready to compromise on certain security issues. The commanders of the RSF, Lieutenant General John Hickman (commander of the Rhodesian Army) and Lieutenant General Peter Walls (commander of Combined Operations), were both open to the prospect of integrating the guerrillas into the new ZNA. Naturally, they wanted to maintain the overall integrity of the RSF, but the simple fact that they admitted the need for some integration was a major step.[22]

The MOD and the FCO were not accustomed to negotiating the terms of a military integration. In Kenya the MOD and the Colonial Office simply directed it. In Zambia the negotiations took place among the governments of the Central African Federation so that they could divide up the forces. The Colonial Office and the MOD controlled the actual training and integration of the Zambia Army. Up to this point, the British had not experienced a situation in which they were responsible while lacking real control. The British recognized to a certain degree how the experience in Zimbabwe was different from their past training missions, and as a result consulted other world powers. Field Marshal Lord Carver, appointed British special commissioner on Rhodesia in 1977, consulted the US State Department on the creation of the ZNA. The Americans also felt that the guerrilla armies were not up to the task of maintaining law and order, nor did they think the guerrillas should be considered real armies.[23]

The FCO did not just turn to Western powers for advice. The British defense adviser in Zambia consulted with the Zambian defense chief, General Kingsley Chinkuli. The Zambians were intimately familiar with the guerrilla armies, having hosted them for a decade. Chinkuli thought it was impossible for the new ZNA to be based on the structure used by the guerrilla armies, agreeing that they had to adopt the British style of the RSF.[24] This view was clearly reflective of the Zambian experience. Chinkuli was a product of the British military system, having graduated from Sandhurst. Zambian military culture drew its traditions from the British Army. Regardless, this was exactly the type of advice that the British wanted to hear.

Based on the collective wisdom of the MOD and FCO and consultations with other countries, Lord Carver put together a proposal for the formation of the ZNA. He asserted from the opening of the proposal that the British goal was "to produce an army that [wa]s truly national, impartial and efficient."[25] Carver saw the Rhodesian African Rifles (RAR) battalions as the core of the new ZNA. He proposed that the force should be made up of no more than ten thousand men. In addition to the technical units and supporting arms, there should be seven infantry battalions: four drawn from former guerrillas and three others from the RAR battalions and from new recruitment. Africans would train to fill open positions in the technical and supporting armies, but these forces would remain largely unchanged. The Selous Scouts, Grey's Scouts, Rhodesian SAS, and Rhodesian Light Infantry (RLI) would all disband. Additionally, all foreign members of the RSF would be discharged. Finally, National Service would end and the existing Territorial Army be replaced by a reserve element of the ZNA. The new reserve would consist of two parts: the Regular Army Reserve and the Zimbabwe National Guard. The Regular Army Reserve of four thousand men could bring the regular element up to operational strength. The Zimbabwe National Guard was to be approximately ten thousand men distributed throughout the country, similar to the situation with the existing Territorial Army.[26]

Lord Carver saw the plan for the actual transition as unfolding in two distinct phases: first, members of the guerrilla armies would be assigned to units to be incorporated into the ZNA as either regular or reserve soldiers, then eligible men in the RSF would terminate their engagements and reattest into the ZNA.[27] This plan kept the RSF mostly intact and absorbed some guerrillas into its ranks. Lord Carver's proposal remained the basis for the British approach to the integration problem well into 1980. Even during the Lancaster House talks, the British plan changed very little from this 1978 proposal. However, Lord Carver was not there to see it through. He took up the position of special commissioner in January 1977, but in March 1978 he resigned. He was increasingly frustrated by the lack of progress toward an independence agreement and could no longer stand the stagnation.[28]

The FCO knew that the RSF could not retain all of their special operations units. The Selous Scouts and the Rhodesian SAS were particularly hated by the guerrilla forces for their ability to strike deep into Zambia or Mozambique, as well as for their ruthless efficiency. The guerrilla forces also felt that certain Rhodesian generals should not have a place in an independent Zimbabwe. Lieutenant General Peter Walls was chief among those considered unacceptable. Walls was a former SAS officer who had risen through the ranks of the Rhodesian Army and commanded some of its crack units, and he was known as a hard-core Rhodesian Front supporter. The British hoped to make the transition process smoother by replacing Walls with a British commander. They first considered this possibility in July 1977; yet again, they looked to their experience in Zambia. General Tommy Reid was the commander of the Zambia Army until his dismissal in 1970. With his experience in establishing a newly independent army, the FCO felt he was a prime candidate to command the ZNA.[29] Yet by the time the Lancaster House Agreement was signed in December 1979, Walls was considered an acceptable interim leader of Zimbabwean forces, at least until they found a more permanent solution. This demonstrated the paucity of choices available.

The British government's formal appraisal of the military integration process ended with Lord Carver's report to the FCO, not because of any lack of interest but because Carver's plan seemed to be sound. Until they could reach a settlement in Rhodesia, there seemed to be no use in coming up with a more detailed plan. Between the release of Lord Carver's report and the Lancaster House talks, significant changes occurred in the Rhodesian situation. The Rhodesian Army began commissioning African officers on an extremely limited basis in 1978 and 1979. Additionally, the internal settlement in 1979 with Bishop Abel Muzorewa stalled the international resolution of the problem for almost a year. As the parties finally came to the negotiation table at Lancaster House in 1979, the British prepared themselves to act as a small-scale peacekeeping force during the transition period between settlement and independent elections.

The Lancaster House Conference took place from 10 September to 15 December 1979 and was signed on 21 December 1979. The three warring parties, ZANU, ZAPU, and the Rhodesian government, met to discuss the terms of a cease-fire and a pathway to independence. The FCO hosted the conference in London, with Lord Carrington presiding. Land reform and the future of the settler community in independent Zimbabwe were key issues in the negotiations. The attendees wrote a framework for the Zimbabwean constitution. Even though the guerrilla movements were not in favor of the agreement as it was written, the presidents of the frontline states (Mozambique, Zambia, and Botswana) were tired of hosting the guerrilla armies and pressured them to put an end to the conflict.

Introducing the Commonwealth Monitoring Force

The warring parties came out of the Lancaster House Conference with an agreement to return governing power to the British until free and fair elections were held in Zimbabwe. The MOD named the mission Operation AGILA. The British Army received a warning order in November 1979 telling it to be prepared to deploy a three-hundred-man force to monitor the transition to majority rule in Zimbabwe. However, this number was based on the assumption that the Rhodesians would provide all logistical and communications support for the British unit. A twelve-man reconnaissance team led by Major General John Acland, which left for Rhodesia in late December 1979, discovered that the Rhodesians were both unwilling and unable to support the British mission.[30] Any support services that the British needed, they would have to bring themselves. The lack of local support required the British to more than triple their force to one thousand men.

Because the British did not have the capacity to fly all the necessary vehicles and helicopters to Rhodesia, they relied on US Air Force C-5 Galaxy cargo planes that the US government pledged to the operation. The monitoring effort would not have been possible without the contributions of troops from four Commonwealth nations, including 159 Australians, 75 New Zealanders, 51 Kenyans, and 24 Fijians. The force was named the Commonwealth Monitoring Force (CMF), due to the large Commonwealth contribution to the mission, with Major General John Acland of the British Army in command. The CMF personnel began to arrive on

22 December 1979, and soon thereafter were deployed to their respective assembly points (APs). These APs were to allow guerrilla forces to gather during the interim period so the CMF could ensure they were not violating the cease-fire agreement or engaging in election-related violence. During this period, personnel from the CMF also monitored the RSF.[31]

The guerrillas poured into the APs by the thousands after the cease-fire began on 28 December. The CMF personnel at the APs had orders to welcome the guerrillas and attempt to disarm them. In fact, unarmed men were turned away. By 9 January 1980, there were 20,634 guerrillas at the APs around the country; by the time the CMF left the country, there were roughly 22,000 men at the APs. When the CMF initially deployed, it assumed that each entity (RSF, ZANLA, ZIPRA) would be responsible for its own logistical support. The British brought enough logistics personnel to provide for the 1,300 men of the CMF, yet they soon discovered that the guerrillas at the APs had no logistical capability whatsoever. Additionally, the Rhodesians did not have the available personnel to support the APs. Therefore, the CMF and the British government were responsible for supplying, feeding, and administering the APs.[32]

The logistical needs at the APs became the overriding concern for the CMF for the remainder of its deployment. Providing food became one of the primary challenges of Operation AGILA. The guerrillas who reported to the APs did so under the impression that they had won the war and were staying there as the first step on their journey to becoming soldiers in the new Zimbabwe Army. This was in part because Robert Mugabe told the ZANLA fighters that anyone who wanted to be a soldier in the ZNA would have a place there. Until there was constitutional change, however, the RSF was the only de jure military force in the country. Therefore, Lord Soames, the new British governor, looked to the RSF for the maintenance of law and order during the interim period. The guerrillas challenged their status and asserted de facto equality with the RSF. They also insisted on better food and a role in maintaining law and order until the elections.[33]

This created a number of problems for the CMF and the future of the military integration process in Zimbabwe. According to the cease-fire accords, the guerrillas were supposed to turn in their weapons to centralized armories at the APs. Each of the guerrilla armies, ZANLA and ZIPRA, sent liaison officers to work with the CMF to bring the guerrillas in and order them to disarm. Yet these liaison officers were often unsuccessful in convincing the guerrillas to give up their arms. The guerrillas were afraid that as soon as the CMF left the country, the RSF or one of the other guerrilla armies would attack. Their fears were not unwarranted; violations of the cease-fire were common on both sides. The Rhodesian Air Force frequently flew aircraft low over the APs, which reinforced the concerns among the liberation fighters.[34] However, the incidents were kept out of the press to maintain the fragile peace that had been achieved.[35]

The RSF attempted on numerous occasions to end the cease-fire. Lieutenant General Walls sent a cable to his commanders on 19 January 1980, with a plan to attack the guerrillas at the APs and assassinate Mugabe, but some Rhodesian officers told the CMF about the plan.[36] Were it not for the intervention of the CMF officers at the various headquarters, the RSF commanders might have been tempted to implement Walls's secret orders.[37] Even with the RSF provocations, the situation was slightly less tense as the logistical conditions improved. However, the roughly twenty-two thousand guerrillas who reported to the APs during the cease-fire were only a fraction of the men that ZANLA and ZIPRA had under arms. Both parties kept portions of their forces outside the country in case hostilities resumed. There also were bands of guerrillas who simply did not report to the APs. The RSF informed *The Times* about one such group that burned a man to death in a village after the guerrillas' demands for food were not heeded.[38] Such incidents were highlighted by the RSF but disavowed by the guerrilla forces. The guerrilla units were accustomed to operating in the bush with a great deal of autonomy; they seldom came into contact with a command element. However, the guerrilla commanders were reluctant to admit that they had only limited control over their men.

Some elements of ZANLA and ZIPRA operated outside of the APs during the lead-up to the elections in February. There were accusations from all sides that electoral intimidation was occurring in the countryside. As a result, the CMF had to be very careful in the way it approached the situation. The fact that it was led by the British was evidence enough to some that the mission was biased and supportive of the white government. At various points when CMF observers made public statements about election tampering and intimidation by guerrilla forces, both ZAPU and ZANU cried foul. Lord Soames made it clear that he had no delusions about the way the elections would go, saying, "It would be impossible to hold an election in Southern Rhodesia, as in any other African country, which was completely free from intimidation."[39]

Even so, the election went forward, and when all the votes were counted, ZANU clearly won the parliamentary majority. Out of the one hundred seats in the House of Assembly, ZANU won fifty-seven, ZAPU twenty, the Rhodesian Front twenty, and Muzorewa's party, called the United African National Congress, three. While the British government hoped for a more moderate government, it was eager to divest itself of the entire situation. The CMF observers declared the election fair, and Robert Mugabe formed a new government. The official date of independence was set for 18 April 1980. The CMF was scheduled to leave the country before the end of March. At that time, there were still three armies present in Zimbabwe that had hardly begun to merge into one.

Training a New Force

The British intended for the RSF to both train and form the new ZNA. The FCO and MOD agreed that the United Kingdom was only capable of offering token financial support to the effort. Yet much of this planning was done in a vacuum, and prior to the British acquiring any real knowledge regarding the conditions on the ground in Zimbabwe. During the Lancaster House Conference, both ZANLA and ZIPRA portrayed themselves as experienced and efficient fighting forces. While ZIPRA did have a well-trained and well-equipped conventional brigade, most of the guerrilla fighters were poorly trained and equipped. The CMF provided these men the most basic supplies, such as shoes and clothing. Some of the guerrilla fighters did not even know how to disassemble their weapons, let alone clean them.

After the elections in February, it was clear that integration plans needed to be put in place if Zimbabwe was to have one official armed force by the date of independence. The results of the elections frustrated the plans of the FCO and the MOD. Since ZANU won a resounding parliamentary victory, it was fair to assume that it would insist on playing a large role in the country's new defense arrangements. As Mugabe began forming his new government, it was clear that he did not trust anyone else with the defense minister's portfolio. In addition to his role as prime minister of Zimbabwe, he also acted as the minister of defense. Reporting directly to

Mugabe was the Joint High Command (JHC). This temporary body was made up of the commander of ZIPRA, Lookout Masuku; the commander of ZANLA, Solomon Mujuru; the commander of the Rhodesian Army, Lieutenant General Andrew Mclean; and the chair of the JHC and commander of the Combined Operations Headquarters, Lieutenant General Peter Walls.[40]

The JHC was supposed to establish a framework for an integration program and a unified command structure. However, the JHC quickly turned into a forum for deception and stalling tactics. Even though Masuku and Mujuru did not have formal ranks, they were granted lieutenant general status. This made getting anything accomplished in the meetings extremely difficult; even the chair of the JHC held the same rank as all the members. If one person did make a decision, Lieutenant General Walls had no authority to force any of the other members to comply.[41] At first this was simply an irritating problem, but as time went on it developed into a debilitating issue.

In February the CMF and the RSF began training roughly twelve hundred guerrillas from both forces. The training was rudimentary; the RSF was in the lead, with the CMF monitors supervising and assisting with planning. The goal of this initial training push was to have some trained Africans available other than those in the RAR. It was not coordinated with any larger training plan or with the FCO and MOD's preliminary plan. There was relatively little oversight or reporting on this initial effort because it was viewed as an RSF rather than a CMF operation.[42] While this ill-led training program got underway, the British finally began sending officers to assess what kind of training the new Zimbabwean forces needed.

Major General Kenneth Perkins, the assistant chief of the Defense Staff for Operations, visited Zimbabwe in March 1980 to assess the needs of the UK military assistance program. He met with Robert Mugabe on 14 March 1980 to set the stage for his visit to the various defense establishments in the country. While Mugabe was a shrewd politician, he was not well versed in military matters; in many meetings he did more listening than speaking. One request he did make in his first meeting with Major General Perkins was that the ZNA train according to British standards. However, in this same discussion Mugabe pointed out that the two guerrilla commanders would be inclined to seek assistance elsewhere.[43] Indeed, both Mujuru and Masuku had received their military training from courses in the Soviet Union and were aware that both the USSR and China were offering no-cost training and low-cost equipment. Mugabe had the power as both prime minister and defense minister to decide where Zimbabwe would turn for military assistance, and he used his position to play on British fears that Zimbabwe would turn into another African satellite of the communist bloc. Lord Soames himself pointed out that to counter both the communist threat and the specter of South African power, the British would "continue to need as many friends as we can muster in black Africa—and the Third World."[44] While the British were not keen on paying for the retraining and restructuring of the ZNA, they were more concerned about losing even more influence in southern Africa.[45]

Major General Perkins proposed a relatively limited aid package to Zimbabwe. The main element of this aid package was a training team of between fifty and seventy men. The team would be responsible solely for training Zimbabwean instructors, who could then train the rank and file of the ZNA. This training team would also be prepared to give advice on the amalgamation process, as well as open up some courses in the United Kingdom to selected Zimbabwean students.[46] The white military leadership also offered numerous suggestions. The Zimbabwe Air Force commander Air Marshall Frank Mussell wanted to reestablish a relationship with the Royal Air Force so that he might begin sending personnel to the United Kingdom for training. However, Lieutenant General Walls, ever the pessimist, felt that after the election whites would resign from the army in great numbers, and insisted that the British needed to do something to forestall this. He proposed the development of a personnel exchange program with the British Army to provide some incentive for white officers to stay in the ZNA.[47]

From past experience in Kenya and Zambia, the British knew that staff work was a weakness of the newly independent African armies. In order to prevent this problem from also occurring in Zimbabwe, Perkins proposed that the British run a three-week accelerated staff college course for officers of the new ZNA. This course was intended to help integrate guerrilla officers into the conventional military planning process, as well as to be a cost-saving measure for the British. If the Africans were staff college–trained, a significant number of British officers would not need to be loaned to Zimbabwe to run the ZNA (which had been the case in

Zambia).[48] When Perkins corresponded directly with the former guerrilla commanders Masuku and Mujuru, he suggested that basic officer and staff training should occur in Zimbabwe and that only selected individuals should be allowed to attend Sandhurst. Additionally, the United Kingdom would provide the ZNA with significant guidance in establishing a military academy and staff college. This point in itself is a remarkable departure from the way the British had trained African armies over the previous two decades.

In all the previous examples mentioned in this book, the British insisted that new officers should either be long-serving NCOs or commissioned through Sandhurst. Historically, this was the best way to maintain British influence over the independent armies. If officers were indoctrinated into British military culture as second lieutenants, they would be predisposed to accept British military assistance throughout their careers. Sandhurst civics training was another method used to ensure that an army remained apolitical after independence. While there were practical reasons for the decision to abandon this model, it was still contrary to the desired British goal in Zimbabwe. As was the case in the early 1960s when Zambia was sending officers to Sandhurst, there simply were not enough spots available to meet the country's need. Previously, both Zambia and Kenya had made up for the lack of Sandhurst spots by sending men to the Mons Officer Cadet School, a six-month-long commissioning course. However, the Cadet School closed in 1972 when Sandhurst transitioned to a forty-four-week curriculum from a two-year training model. Yet unlike Zambia and Kenya, the MOD made no effort to make additional spots available for the ZNA at Sandhurst.

Major General Perkins was not hopeful at the conclusion of his visit to Zimbabwe. He was not impressed with the training that he observed during the trip. He pointed out that the ZIPRA recruits were doing far better than those from ZANLA, a common view among the British and Rhodesian officers. He also noticed that morale in the RSF was extremely low; many of the men were concerned about their careers and pensions. This problem presented two immediate challenges: the possibility of an abrupt loss of technical knowledge, and entire units of the ZNA defecting to South Africa.[49] This was a legitimate fear on the part of the British and a situation that did occur on a number of occasions. The Pathfinder Company of the South African 44 Parachute Brigade was composed of former members of the Rhodesian SAS.[50] The South African Army established the 3 Reconnaissance Commandos when most of the Selous Scouts defected.[51]

Perkins was also aware of the other critical challenge facing the UK mission to Zimbabwe: funding. Even the small mission that the MOD envisioned was projected to cost £2.5 million. However, the total budget allocated to UK military assistance around the world was only £5.189 million. Of that, only £200,000 was allocated to Zimbabwe.[52] When the MOD and FCO planned the overseas military assistance budget, they presumed that the Zimbabwean government would pay for the assistance package. As a result, the British government only allocated enough money to pay for the Zimbabweans to attend certain courses in the United Kingdom. This budgeting issue was a consistent problem for the MOD and the FCO. British policy interests necessitated a significant training package, yet the necessary funding was just not available in the age of austerity that the British found themselves in.

Even so, the MOD continued making plans for a British-funded training mission. The FCO and Lord Soames had to petition the Exchequer and the prime minister's office for additional funds. Major General Acland, the CMF commander, projected that the training mission in Zimbabwe would be at least two years. On 2 March the CMF pulled back all of its personnel to the air force base in Salisbury in preparation for their return home. The only remaining British soldiers in the field were forty men who volunteered to stay behind as an ad hoc training team. The CMF mission ended on 16 March when the main body of the force left the country. By the end of the month it was clear that the monitoring force left too soon. The training team reported that the situation at the training camps was tense at best. The guerrilla trainees felt they were being mistreated by white Rhodesian trainers and on a number of occasions engaged in small-scale mutinies.[53] The British trainers often were required to serve as peacekeepers in addition to their duties as training officers.

While the FCO was concerned about the problems with military integration, they were more concerned with the wider security issues in the country. Even though whites in Zimbabwe had lost political control, they retained almost all commercial power. The FCO was concerned that if the whites began fleeing the country in large numbers, the economy would collapse and Zimbabwe would be an easy target for communist influence. As a result, the FCO wanted to ensure that whites in Zimbabwe felt they had a future in the country. The primary conduits for ensuring this attitude were the security forces. The British believed that if white morale in the security forces was high, that confidence would translate to the white civilian community. Consequently, the FCO made it clear to the MOD and Major General Perkins that supporting the confidence of the white community and the emergence of a viable amalgamated army were directly related.[54]

With this in mind, Lord Soames knew that the first six months of independence were critical. He estimated that between 30 April and 30 June, 25 percent of the white officers in the army would resign, as would 50 percent of the white SNCOs. Most of those officers were in key technical fields that could not be replaced internally; their absence would put the very fabric of the army at risk. The MOD proposed that a team of fifty-eight British trainers replace the ad hoc CMF team. Soames asserted that this number was too small to make any real difference considering the number of men that needed to be trained. His great fear, like that of many other British policy makers, was that the Zimbabweans would look to Eastern Europe to make up the difference.[55]

By Independence Day, 18 April 1980, there was still no singular army and even less agreement on how the amalgamation process should proceed. Major General Edward Fursdon, the military adviser to Lord Soames, painted a grim picture upon his departure from Zimbabwe. He pointed out that the ad hoc training team had a particularly difficult task and that the former Rhodesian Army personnel were at best not very helpful, but at worst were actively causing problems. However, the guerrillas were also a source of constant worry for the trainers. Not only did they occasionally mutiny, but they also were terribly undisciplined. The JHC had achieved very little by this point in time. The only issue it had managed to agree on was that the army should be organized using a British framework. This was largely because the RSF was already structured in this way, and the guerrilla commanders had no alternative structure to propose.[56]

Crisis of Command

The euphoria of the independence celebrations was short-lived. Even though the country officially was independent, it was no closer to genuine stability. On 9 May 1980 Margaret Thatcher met with Robert Mugabe in London to discuss the future of British involvement in Zimbabwe. During the meeting Mugabe praised the efforts of the RSF and their senior commanders, pointing out that they had accepted the new government and were willing to stay on as long as the government needed them. He claimed that the real problem in the integration process was the former ZIPRA guerrillas. He cited acts of sabotage within the country and insinuated that these ZAPU men were preparing to overthrow the government. Mugabe also complained that the integration effort was not going well. He asserted that the Rhodesian commanders had been too harsh in the beginning and had lost their credibility. He begged Thatcher for more trainers to help build up the ZNA as quickly as possible. While Thatcher said she was open to the possibility of sending a larger team, she made no promises; she did ask the MOD to look into it.[57]

Supporting the new government in Zimbabwe was a priority for the Thatcher government. Mrs. Thatcher knew that Mugabe could very easily look to the Chinese or the Soviet Union for military support. Naturally, HMG wanted to limit the amount of communist influence in the region. More important, though, the British wanted to prevent communist forces from staging on the border of South Africa. The involvement of Cuban, Russian, and East German forces in Angola compounded the paranoia of the South African defense establishment. If Zimbabwe became host to more communist forces, there was a possibility of an even larger regional conflict developing. This prospect was even more dire in light of the South African development of a working nuclear weapon in 1979.[58]

With this in mind, the MOD went to work to find officers and senior NCOs to support an enlarged training mission. The goal was to increase the size of the training mission from 58 to 127 personnel as soon as possible. While this seemed like a relatively small number of soldiers, and certainly was far fewer than the number required by Operation AGILA, the type of men the MOD needed were in short supply. Battalion adviser positions were the most critical to fill. The ideal candidates for these positions were majors who had finished a period of company command, served on a battalion staff, and, if possible, had passed staff college. Unfortunately, officers of this description were in short supply in the army, and any reassignment would result in an operational shortfall elsewhere. Even though the army had expressed its manning concerns to the MOD,

Lieutenant General John Stanier, vice chief of the General Staff, made it clear that regardless of any manning concerns, the Zimbabwe British Military Advisory and Training Team (BMATT) was a national commitment of high priority. The British Army's goal became having all additional men in place by 8 October 1980.[59]

Major General Fursdon returned to Britain in early June. His time as Lord Soames's military adviser was his last military assignment prior to retirement. However, before he left the army he met with the vice chief of the General Staff to advise him on a way to move forward in Zimbabwe. Fursdon reiterated the difficulties that the BMATT would continue to face in Zimbabwe, focusing particularly on the deadlock within the JHC. Without any decisions coming out of the JHC, it would be impossible for the men on the ground to set any sort of policy or blueprint in place to provide for the future needs of the mission. The only issue the JHC had agreed on was that the ZNA would be composed of four infantry brigades with support services, and four special units, including a parachute regiment, commando regiment, horse mounted unit, and SAS unit. The JHC had not come up with an integration plan and had left it to the BMATT to propose a training scheme.

The urgency of Mugabe's requests for training assistance and the lack of funds available narrowed down the training options. Fursdon recommended that the BMATT run three four-week courses concurrently: one for senior leaders (majors and lieutenant colonels), one for junior officers (lieutenants and captains), and one for NCOs. At the end of their respective courses, the graduates could meet up to form the leadership element of a battalion. They would join the rank and file of the battalion and lead them through a four-week basic training period that would involve minimal British participation. This method of training became known as the "sausage machine." Ideally, it would take eight weeks to train a new battalion. While units were waiting to enter the "sausage machine," they would participate in the Soldiers Engaged in Economic Development scheme and thus spend their time working on farms and in industry.[60] This eight-week training scheme applied only to infantry soldiers. Specialists such as cooks, clerks, signalers, and drivers would train concurrently but in separate courses. This concept met with little resistance in the JHC, and with no other options available, Zimbabwean officials put the plan into action.

As these plans were finalized, the BMATT and ZNA were faced with a fresh challenge. Lieutenant General Peter Walls promised Mugabe that he would continue in his position through independence to provide some continuity and encourage former RSF members to stay on in the ZNA. However, by July 1980 Walls was hinting that his retirement was quickly approaching. The question arose of who would command the Zimbabwean forces after Walls left. The British felt that the situation was so fragile between ZIPRA and ZANLA that the appointment of someone from either of those two groups would be disastrous. By the same token, the British were not sure how the Zimbabweans would respond to the appointment of another Rhodesian officer to the position. That summer, Mugabe mentioned to Robin Byatt, the British high commissioner, that he might initially be interested in having a British general fill the position after Walls left.[61]

The placement of a British general at the head of a newly independent force was not a unique idea. The army had provided British commanders to African forces since the decolonization process began. This was the case in Zambia, Kenya, Nigeria, Ghana, and many other former colonial possessions. Lord Carrington and Prime Minister Thatcher were both open to the prospect of placing a British general in command of the force. One of their main concerns with the plan was the prospect of British responsibility for the actions of the Zimbabwean military. If a British general commanded the force and the Zimbabwean government decided to become involved in a war with the South Africans, the British government would be thrust into the middle of the conflict. It also would be saddled with unwanted responsibility if there were any breakdowns in order in Zimbabwe. While Lord Carrington did consider the possibility of the appointment of a general from a Commonwealth nation, he concluded that the resulting drop in white morale would be even more damaging. Therefore, Carrington asked the MOD to look into the possibility of appointing a British general to take Walls's place. He hoped that the MOD would be able to find a retired officer who would be able to fill the position on a contract basis; this would officially distance HMG from the events in Zimbabwe.[62]

The MOD moved quickly to find acceptable candidates for the job in Zimbabwe. It immediately agreed with Carrington's assessment of the situation and had identified at least three candidates for the position by 1 August.[63] General Edmund Bramall, the chief of the General Staff of the

British Army, visited Zimbabwe in August; after touring the country he met with Mugabe, who expressed his frustration with the lack of progress in the amalgamation process, a problem he attributed to the former RSF officers. When General Bramall mentioned that they had come up with some possible candidates to replace Lieutenant General Walls, Mugabe toned down his enthusiasm for British assistance. He said he needed more time to consider the matter and also indicated that he was now thinking of asking other Commonwealth nations to provide commander candidates. He claimed he needed another two weeks to think about what to do.

Some in the British High Commission felt that Mugabe was having trouble pushing the idea of a British commander through the ZANU Central Committee. However, it is more likely that he was buying time with the British to figure out what alternatives he could find to a British officer while still drawing on British training resources. Mugabe alluded to the fact that he was delaying in a conversation with General Bramall, when he said that he might not even nominate a successor to Walls until all of the force commanders had a better attitude toward the amalgamation process.[64] In late July and early August, the FCO hoped to convince Walls to stay on as long as possible, offering even to pay for his leave expenses. While Byatt made overtures to Walls, the MOD continued to look for retired British officers to take the position, should Mugabe make up his mind to accept one. The MOD was able to narrow down the list to three potential candidates of the proper rank and experience. By the first week of August, however, all three had declined the assignment.[65]

On 14 August, Lieutenant General Walls gave an interview on South African TV in which he stated he did not believe that majority rule in Zimbabwe would succeed, and that there was still a very high probability of civil war breaking out again in the country. This was the last straw for Mugabe; he had tolerated Walls's demands and obstructionist attitude because Zimbabwe lacked experienced generals. However, Mugabe would not tolerate public disloyalty from a military commander. Walls was immediately placed on the retired list, and the ZANU government used the Emergency Powers Act to bar Walls from returning to Zimbabwe. Walls's abrupt departure from the JHC left a significant power void. With this turn of events in mind, the MOD made it clear that it was willing to offer up a serving officer, but Mugabe seemed deaf to this suggestion. Rather than immediately fill the position with a ZANLA officer, Mugabe insisted on leaving it vacant.[66] The JHC meetings were now led by Alan Page, the permanent secretary for defense, until the new ZNA commander was appointed.

Playing the Game

The back-and-forth between Mugabe and the FCO regarding Walls's replacement became the standard Zimbabwean strategy: delaying the British while appearing to remain interested, in large part because of the British sphere of influence. All the while, Robert Mugabe shopped around for military assistance and neglected to mention it to the British, unless he could use it as leverage to obtain concessions. During the meeting on 9 May, Mugabe had held with Thatcher, he assured her that Zimbabwe was looking only to the British for military assistance. By that point he had already been approached by the Nigerians, who had offered a training team. In June 1980, a Nigerian military delegation covertly visited Zimbabwe to assess the situation and write up a military assistance proposal. Through various intelligence channels, by the end of July the British managed to acquire a copy of the report. The delegation met not only with Mugabe but also with General Solomon Mujuru, the ZANLA commander. Both the Nigerian visit and the meeting between the Nigerians, Mugabe, and Mujuru were kept secret from the rest of the JHC.

The Nigerians had come to evaluate the possibility of training ZNA and ZAF officers. However, when they arrived, Mugabe asked if they could send a group of instructors to train around twelve thousand soldiers by December 1980. Since the Nigerians had not expected this request, they told Mugabe they would have to take the request back to the Nigerian government for consideration. It was not only with the British that Mugabe was being duplicitous. He told the Nigerian delegation that he had told the British he was asking for Nigerian assistance, even though he had done nothing of the sort.[67] In the short term, the Nigerian delegation could not promise much. Training pilots for the ZAF would take between two and three years. However, the Nigerians were able to accommodate the training requirements of some one hundred ZANLA officer candidates at the Nigerian Defense Academy. The course was scheduled to begin the first week in July and run until the first week of December.[68]

The Nigerian defense delegation recommended that the government support Mugabe's request for a military training team. However, since the British had agreed to increase the size of the BMATT, Mugabe backed away from his efforts to find a Nigerian training team. Of course, this did not keep him from sending additional ZANLA troops to Nigeria for military training without informing the British or the JHC. The training program did not progress well, not simply because of a lack of instructors but also due to a lack of agreement on how the army should be run. In June, more than five hundred former guerrillas were imprisoned for mutinying against their trainers at Llewellin Barracks. A battalion of the former RAR put down the mutiny.[69] The former guerrillas found the official forms of training extremely taxing. Often, they simply refused to wake up for morning physical training or to perform any sort of labor detail. Even the potential officers did not want to do any additional work beyond what was required of the rank-and-file soldiers.[70] During the war these men had operated with a considerable degree of independence; now they were being asked to adhere to a strict system of discipline. Many also lacked the education necessary to perform as part of a modern military force. Roughly 25 percent of the former guerrillas were completely illiterate; only 40 percent spoke English (at a very basic level).[71] Of the five hundred former guerrillas who had mutinied, four hundred were discharged; these men had been part of the total twelve hundred soldiers who had been trained up to that point. Clearly this was the type of setback that Mugabe was referring to in his complaints about a slow integration process.

The escapade with the Nigerians was the first of many for the Mugabe regime. The Zimbabwean officer candidates left for Nigeria on 6 July; all were former ZANLA fighters. British intelligence and the FCO monitored the progress of the training course and discovered that in addition to the one hundred officer candidates, twenty ZANLA officers would be attending the next two Nigerian Staff College courses.[72] The Nigerian government was extremely secretive about the training of Zimbabweans at its Defense Academy; however, the British were not particularly concerned. The British defense adviser in Lagos said of the Nigerian Army, "[They] have an inflated idea of their own capabilities. Therefore apart from CSC [Command and Staff College] the level of instructive expertise will not be high."[73] The Zimbabweans later learned that they also should not expect too much from the Nigerian Army. By October, the Zimbabwean officer candidates had finished the basic course at the Nigerian

Defense Academy and were commissioned in the ZNA. However, even the ex-ZANLA fighters were appalled by the conditions and training they received in Nigeria. These men stayed on in Nigeria for another three months for the Platoon Commanders Course at the Nigerian School of Infantry, but the damage was done. After their experience, the Zimbabweans had little interest in an increased partnership with the Nigerians.[74]

Faced with competition for influence, the British upped the ante slightly by increasing the number of liaison visits by Zimbabwean officers to British Army schools in the United Kingdom. The British also agreed to attach nine Zimbabwean officers and NCOs to British regiments for one month each. The commandant of the ZNA School of Infantry flew to Britain to visit Sandhurst to help him formulate a blueprint for the Zimbabwe Military Academy. Zimbabwean personnel were allotted spaces in a variety of courses in the United Kingdom. These courses included the Signal Officer Course, Officer Engineering Mechanical Course, Junior Regimental Officer Course, and Parachute Jumping Instructor Course, to name a few.[75] The British government had to find ways to remain competitive, particularly because the security situation in Zimbabwe had not improved since independence.

A Plan Takes Shape

Security incidents in Zimbabwe increased after the April independence ceremonies. The withdrawal of the CMF, as well as the disbandment of the RSF Territorial Force and the BSAP Field Reserve, left many areas of the country with a limited security presence. In some parts of the country guerrillas who had not reported to the assembly points took responsibility for maintaining law and order. Their definition of law and order often ended up looking suspiciously like political terror, intimidation of opponents, and retribution for whites and ZAPU supporters.

In July 1980 the BSAP changed its name to the Zimbabwe Republic Police. There was no amalgamation of forces as there had been with the military. Africans were the majority in the BSAP prior to the conflict, so it was far easier to Africanize the force. White officers remained for the time being but were asked to retire at their earliest opportunity. When the Zimbabwe Republic Police attempted to reassert control in many of these areas, they were attacked by ZANU forces. By the end of August policemen in the northeastern region of Zimbabwe were regularly being ambushed and sustaining casualties.[76]

By 1 September, 3,000 former guerrillas had completed ZNA basic training. These men made up the first three battalions. An additional 1,900 remained in training but would eventually form the Fourth and Fifth Battalions. By 30 October, the BMATT expected to have an additional 3,250 men trained and formed into the four remaining battalions. The additional 650 men who would form the Parachute Regiment and 400 who would compose the Air Force Regiment would finish their training at the same time. While on the surface it seemed like the BMATT was making excellent progress, there were still 14,500 men taking part in Operation SEED (Soldiers Engaged in Economic Development), 7,047 ZIPRA men at APs, and 14,078 ZANLA men at APs.[77] What compounded the problem was that Robert Mugabe had promised a place in the army to any guerrilla fighter who wanted one. To exacerbate the difficulties even more, there simply were no more tents or buildings available in the country to house the large number of men coming into the ZNA.

The logistical problems in Zimbabwe continued to mount as both personnel and equipment were shipped into the country from old guerrilla bases in both Zambia and Mozambique. In September 1980 the ZNA received a large shipment of heavy equipment given to ZIPRA by the USSR. This shipment included T34 tanks, armored personnel carriers, and artillery pieces.[78] This presented a new set of challenges to the ZNA such as how to train on and maintain such a wide variety of equipment, especially since the technical manuals provided were written in several different languages. This was also a challenge for the BMATT. Major R. A. Boys, who was a member of the team that trained the First Field Regiment, Zimbabwe Artillery, pointed out:

> This has proved a very interesting and demanding job. The regiment has 32 British 25-Pounders and 40 Soviet M76 guns. This combination, together with the different command and control philosophies, certainly has forced the instructors to return to basic principles. As an example one only has to consider the optics. The British dial sights (dated 1919) are in degrees, the compasses in 6,400 mils and the Soviet dial sights in 6,000 mils. The author can also testify personally to the problem of translating Rumanian and Czechoslovakian firing

tables into a common format based on 25-pounder computation drills.[79]

This was not just an artillery problem; most of the British personnel had to learn about the Eastern Bloc equipment as they taught the ZNA soldiers how to use it.

In an effort to increase the capability of the ZNA to provide for itself and manage its own logistics, BMATT began a quartermaster course in September 1980. The course was four weeks long and intended to provide a basic understanding of supply management. However, the course did not succeed in turning the men into the logistics professionals the ZNA so desperately needed. At the same time, to accommodate the incredible excess of soldiers that the ZNA was taking in, the government announced that it would house at least seventeen thousand ex-guerrillas in private homes in Salisbury. This decision came from outside the military chain of command. Most of these men were former ZANLA fighters who were allowed to keep their weapons with them.[80] This plan was of tremendous concern to both the white population and the ZAPU party members. Mugabe's order to position seventeen thousand armed men loyal to ZANU in the capital did not suggest an environment of reconciliation and unity. The move was meant only to secure the ZANU government in its place of power. During the formation of the ZNA battalions, battalion commanders were selected based on merit and performance in the leader course. Former ZIPRA members consistently outperformed the former ZANLA fighters and therefore were far more often selected to command the ZNA battalions.[81] Mugabe wanted a ZANLA security force prepared to defend the government against any possible ZANU- or RSF-concocted coup.

The logistical problems that the ZNA faced were only one component of their consistent growing pains. The JHC continued to stagnate, even without Walls's presence. Lieutenant General Andrew "Sandy" Mclean, the commander of what had been the Rhodesian Army, was tasked with temporarily chairing the committee. However, his negative and sometimes despondent attitude did not improve the situation. This attitude was contagious among the white officers; Brigadier Palmer predicted that there would be a substantial exodus of white officers between October and December 1980. This would create such a significant skill deficit in the army that the BMATT would not be able to resolve the situation for several years. There was a group of young Turks, lieutenant colonels who were dedicated to making it work, but the old guard regularly brushed their good ideas and recommendations aside.[82]

The drain of white personnel combined with the stagnation of the JHC gave ZANLA the opening they needed to assert their influence in the defense forces. Mujuru increasingly asserted his authority and freely stated that he believed that before long ZANLA would be in control of the armed forces. He continued to make side deals with the Nigerians and other parties outside of the knowledge of the JHC. He also regularly encouraged whites to leave the army over the course of the next six months. He did not understand that the skills of the white servicemen and officers in technical arms were one of a handful of things keeping the ZNA from collapsing in on itself.[83] Mujuru relied on the contributions of other nations to give the ZNA the skills it needed to remain a functioning force. He was often very candid with Brigadier Palmer about his plans and goals; he put great faith in the idea that Nigeria would eventually come in and take over the training of the entire army. It was a commonly held belief among the ZANLA commanders that the British had clear neocolonial ambitions and were attempting to reassert control over Zimbabwe. These commanders did not understand that the British reluctance to commit resources to Zimbabwe was a sign of shrinking British power in the region.

As Mujuru expanded his control, Lookout Masuko, the former ZIPRA commander, grew tired of Mujuru's backroom dealings. He even considered walking out of the JHC altogether. Palmer felt that during September 1980, ZIRPA/ZANLA relations were at an all-time low. However, he was unable to anticipate the events that would take place over the coming months. By September, seven of the nine battalions were either trained or in the training pipeline. Palmer commented that they were "making good progress, by African standards, and morale is good."[84] While he did not explain exactly what he meant by this comment, a report by one of the battalion liaison officers offers some insight:

I recently spoke to a major who is our liaison officer with 21 Battalion: the first amalgamated ZIP-ZAN battalion. He told me that much of the work which he does in fixing things for the battalion, could be done by an NCO in the British Army but that an officer was necessary since everything required a good deal of negotiation and diplomacy. I asked him how he thought the battalion would get along if he and his sergeant were withdrawn. Without a moment[']s hesitation he said that the whole thing would grind to a halt in a matter of days. I have no doubt that he is right and that our wheel-oiling will continue to be essential for some time to come.[85]

The not-so-subtle implication here is that even after a period of training the former guerrillas were only capable of performing functions at a junior NCO level. Granted there were exceptions to this rule, but it was clear that the ZNA was nowhere near capable of operating like a serious military force. It was clear to Palmer that the BMATT would need to remain in Zimbabwe beyond the scheduled end date of April 1981 if the country were to have even a small chance of success. Palmer also encouraged the MOD to consider sending select African personnel to Sandhurst and Camberley, free of charge. He insisted that men sent to these courses could become "the seed corn of pro-British influence in the long term."[86]

The goal of the mission, to combine all factions into a loyal and responsive military, was continuously in peril. Palmer ended his report on the future of BMATT by saying, "BMATT struggles to produce order out of chaos and sometimes even succeeds! In my view our continued presence here in strength next year provides the one hope for the future, both militarily and politically."[87] Brigadier Palmer also included in an annex to his formal report a tentative plan for the future of BMATT. Since the JHC was deadlocked, he unilaterally decided on issues related to the ZNA and prioritized training needs. He said that the need for staff-qualified officers should be the first priority of the training mission; at least three hundred staff officers were required in 1981. This was closely followed by officer cadet training, which included a focus on the training of infantry officers because that was the vast majority of the officer corps. Finally, he saw the training of quartermaster officers, administration officers, and regimental quartermaster sergeants as key to the stability of the force.[88]

The security situation in Zimbabwe was continuously eroding. In late September there were regular pay problems in the army. They were even more severe at the APs, where gun battles flared up between men who had been paid and men who had not. Mugabe created even more difficulties for the ZNA in a speech to the House of Assembly on 18 September 1980.

While he pleaded for the violence to stop and asked all parties to come together, he also froze all promotions of ex-RSF personnel. This made it clear to many white officers that they would be marginalized in the ZNA if they remained in the force. Additionally, Mugabe announced that all the members of the JHC would remain of an equal status and that a single commander would not be appointed until the forces were amalgamated.[89] The consequences of these policies can be seen in the disbandment of the RLI. The three-hundred-man battalion had forty-two officers; of those only seven decided to remain in the ZNA. The rest either left military service completely or joined the South African Defense Force.[90]

Some of these men understood that the opportunity for whites to play a role in the new army had already passed. The stubbornness of the RSF officers and men at the initial stages of integration made them enemies of ZANLA and the new order that now occupied the government. As of October 1980, none of the ex-RSF units had been integrated into the newly formed battalions. The white officers thought it was best to maintain the integrity of units like the RAR in an attempt to preserve professional standards. However, it was clear to many RAR officers that they were being left behind. If they were to have any chance at playing a role in the new army, they needed to be integrated. In late September, African officers of the RAR petitioned Mugabe directly for the integration of their battalions into the new ZNA units.[91] However, their request went unanswered and they remained a separate force. Interestingly, they were considered the only disciplined force left in the ZNA. Mugabe seems to have understood the stabilizing influence that both the experienced officers and the RAR had on the force, but he did not seem to think they warranted a place in the future ZNA. In October 1980, there were 700 white officers left in the army. At least 300 resigned in April 1980. The MOD estimated that by April 1981 there would only be 350 white officers left.[92]

By October 1980 a plan embraced by the JHC began to take shape. It focused on keeping Mugabe's promise of allowing any man to serve who wanted to, while at the same time creating an army that better fit Zimbabwe's needs. The Ten-Year Austerity Plan, as it was known, was intended to form a 58,000-strong army supported by a 2,600-man air force. The ZNA would be divided into two parts. The primary component would be composed of five equally balanced infantry brigades that would be the first line of defense for the country. The secondary component would consist of five or six infantry brigades and would serve as a secondary line of defense; this second component would focus primarily on agro-industrial work and secondarily on military training.[93] This closely reflected the lines on which the Zambian military operated. This component of the ZNA was modeled on the Zambian National Service, which went through initial military training but then spent most of its time focusing on public works projects with short periods of military training interspersed. The plan also recommended that Zimbabwe hold off on any large military hardware acquisitions for at least ten years. The designers of the plan hoped that after two or three years the army could begin reducing in size. Mugabe had given the JHC little feedback on the plan by the end of October, and Brigadier Palmer was barred from seeing him since General Bramall's visit. One British staff officer concluded after visiting Zimbabwe:

> My visit left me with the impression that Zimbabwe has a chance but for the next year it will be touch and go. Zimbabwe's chance is not a particularly good one but without BMATT it would be even less good. BMATT have achieved much, will continue to have an important role for the foreseeable future and in the final analysis it may be their efforts, which will have made all the difference.[94]

The members of the BMATT staff who observed the missteps of the ZNA on a daily basis did not, unfortunately, share the generally hopeful attitude of this staff officer.

Brigadier Palmer was finally able to meet with Prime Minister Mugabe on 15 October. Palmer made three very important points clear: (1) the ZNA needed to create a single and clear chain of command before any commander could be appointed; (2) if Mugabe wanted a smaller and cheaper army than the one proposed under the Ten-Year Plan, the JHC needed to know soon; and (3) the JHC needed to come up with a plan to merge any ZIPRA and ZANLA units that were to be on permanent agro-industrial work.[95] Mugabe indicated to Palmer that he had not read the JHC paper on the Ten-Year Plan, and that he felt that all the army units except the "crack troops" should rotate through agro-industrial work assignments. He also mentioned briefly that the army could be slimmed down in two to three years, but he spoke no further on the matter. Rather than focus on plans for how to bring the army together, Mugabe wanted to discuss another matter: ZIPRA. He claimed that he was not concerned about the loyalty of whites, or ZANLA. However, he suspected that ZIPRA was completely disloyal to Zimbabwe because it had lost the election.[96] Mugabe insisted that ZIPRA should disarm, putting the matter to the JHC and saying, "If the government gave orders they were to be obeyed by those concerned."[97]

Mugabe and Mujuru managed to marginalize or push out most of the ex-RSF servicemen and officers. The only remaining obstacles to complete domination of the security forces were the ZIPRA elements. The prime minister's lack of interest in the JHC proposals, his encouragement of Mujuru's side dealings, and his double-talk regarding marginalizing the ex-RSF element all indicate that Mugabe felt that the integration process was a charade. He had a completely separate agenda for the security forces that he refused to disclose to those outside of his inner circle. Whether or not Mugabe ever read the Ten-Year Plan is unclear; by December it was completely scrapped. Operation SEED was a complete failure, and it was clear from that failure that the former guerrillas could not be useful in agro-industrial work.[98]

In early December 1980, Mugabe presented a new plan to the recently promoted Major General Palmer.[99] He wanted both to speed up and extend the amalgamation process, as well as to train an additional eighteen battalions (nine were already trained). The result would be an army of roughly 60,000 trained personnel. Naturally, he wanted HMG to lead the efforts to train this much larger ZNA. Palmer and Byatt, the high commissioner, both expressed misgivings about the large size of the army, which was in sharp contrast to what they felt Zimbabwe actually needed. To put this number in perspective, the South African Defence Force (SADF) had 72,000 men serving on active duty in 1979 and was engaged in both Namibia and Angola. The Australian Army had only 31,000 men on active duty in 1979. The 60,000-strong army that Mugabe had in mind was much larger than Zimbabwe needed. Mugabe argued that the persistent security problems that the country was facing necessitated such a large force. An interesting point that Mugabe left out of the conversation was that many of the violent clashes between the police and guerrillas involved ZANLA men. Palmer and Byatt agreed that HMG would do all it could to help and sent the recommendation back to the FCO.[100] The FCO and the MOD were shaken by the brief flirtation between Nigeria and Zimbabwe. The British were extremely concerned that any hesitation on their part would lead to an introduction of communist aid to the country.

Conclusion

The first year of independence for Zimbabwe ended much as it had begun: with the security situation in the country in disarray. The ZNA was not considered a functioning element within the country. This was demonstrated in mid-December 1980 when a visit to Salisbury by President Julius Nyerere of Tanzania was planned. Major General Palmer sent an urgent request to the MOD from the Zimbabwean government. The Zimbabwean Artillery did not have ammunition for their 25-pounder guns, ammunition they would need to fire a twenty-one-gun salute for President Nyerere; nor did the Zimbabwean government have the funds necessary to purchase it. Palmer requested the MOD send a donation of ammunition to Zimbabwe within the week.[101] The British were frustrated by the request but nonetheless made sure the Zimbabwean government did not embarrass itself.

By the end of 1980, the British still felt as if they could retain control of the situation in Zimbabwe. Even though Robert Mugabe ignored British advice, demanded more money and assistance, and changed the rules of the game at every turn, British diplomats and military officers were confident in their assessment of him. The men making policy focused completely on what the communist powers would do in this situation, in a memorandum to the leadership of the FCO, Derek Day, the assistant under-secretary for African affairs, made it very clear what was at stake:

In my view, the continuation of our military assistance to Zimbabwe for the year 1981/82 is one of the most important aspects of our African policy. The continued process of integration of the three armies in Zimbabwe is a critical element in preserving political stability in that country and, more widely, in Central and Southern Africa. Mugabe wants us to continue. There are others who would only be too ready to step into our shoes (e.g., the East Germans, Cubans, etc.). It would be disastrous if we left the field open for such influences.[102]

Mugabe's mentors were the dictators of the nonaligned movement. He was determined not to fall into either the Soviet or the Western sphere of influence.[103]

The British Army, the MOD, and the FCO all wanted to accomplish the transition from Rhodesia to Zimbabwe by December 1980, and at a relatively low cost. The British aversion to long and in-depth training missions grew out of their experiences in East Africa in 1964 and in Zambia in 1970. They seemed to believe that through a small training mission and an unobtrusive approach to the formation of the army, they would be able to keep Zimbabwe in the British sphere of influence. Even so, the British Army knew that the key to creating an apolitical force was to put it through rigorous professional training and avoid the creation of a praetorian elite with a monopoly on the use of force. It was this difficult lesson that the British had ignored in their initial approach to the training mission in Zimbabwe.

As 1980 gave way to 1981, the BMATT began to face a whole new set of challenges that would test the bounds of British foreign policy. The British government faced the issues of how long they would remain in Zimbabwe and what kinds of challenges they would be willing to put up with. The introduction of communist forces in the country would be a particularly divisive issue, as would the creation of units outside the control of the JHC chain of command. Unfortunately, the events of 1981 would come to signify the eventual failure of the British mission. Over the course of 1980, the most technically skilled members of the ZNA were pushed out through intimidation or fear of the future. Many of the recruits who showed the most potential would be frightened into leaving the military in 1981 through systematic political purges within the ZNA. By the end of the year, the ZNA would fully emerge as yet another tool of the ZANU-PF regime in Zimbabwe.

The Rise of ZANLA Dominance in the ZNA and the Birth of the Fifth Brigade

By the end of 1980, a framework for the Zimbabwe National Army (ZNA) was based on the foundation provided by the Rhodesian Security Forces (RSF). In his first address of 1981, President Mugabe singled out the efforts of the British Military Advisory and Training Team (BMATT), praising its work in bringing the ZNA together as one.[1] The initial military assistance plan involved BMATT training only a portion of the former guerrilla forces. The Foreign and Commonwealth Office (FCO) projected that by 1 April 1981, the major units of the ZNA would have passed through the "sausage machine" training scheme. As 1980 gave way to 1981, however, the mission expanded and the conditions changed. Operation SEED was recognized as a failure, and Mugabe decided that all the former guerrillas needed to be brought into the ZNA. Mugabe promised that any man who wanted a place in the new army could have it, and he could ill afford to retract this promise considering the number of weapons moving freely about the country.

In 1981 the Mugabe government expected BMATT to train a sixty-five thousand-man army. As noted previously, most of these men had little military training, and even fewer had a formal education. The British government had already accepted the challenge; it intended to create an integrated, apolitical military force. This mission required significant personnel and resources in an era when fiscal constraints were paramount. British military commitments in Northern Ireland were not slackening, and the security situation in that province was getting worse with the onset of the 1981 hunger strikes. The events in Northern Ireland, NATO commitments in West Germany, and austerity measures at home were straining the Treasury. Over the course of that year, the inability of the

British to commit more trainers and funding to Zimbabwe diluted the effectiveness of the mission, as well as HMG influence in the region.

Planning for 1981

Initially, BMATT was scheduled to complete its mission in April 1981. The FCO and the Ministry of Defence (MOD) agreed that once the last ZNA battalion completed its initial training, BMATT would withdraw from Zimbabwe. They assumed that after that point the Zimbabweans would need to send only a handful of men to courses in the United Kingdom for specialized training. The British government was willing to offer up these specialty courses to the Zimbabweans because the ZNA was responsible for covering the costs. It seems that the FCO felt that by offering specialist courses and establishing ongoing foreign military sales contracts with Zimbabwe, Her Majesty's Government would be able to maintain enough influence in southern Africa to keep communist powers out, and to prevent the frontline states from invading South Africa.

Only ten days after Mugabe praised the efforts of BMATT in his New Year's Day speech, he changed the parameters of the integration process. He announced that all ex-guerrillas would participate in the integration process and join the regular army. In effect, this announcement tripled BMATT's workload. If it was to meet this new quota it had to produce no fewer than three new ZNA battalions a month, every month, until August 1981. This also meant that the size of BMATT had to increase from 134 to 161 men and remain at that level until August. Major General Patrick Palmer asserted that this additional assistance would give both Mugabe and his government confidence in the integration process and reassure them that they had the full support of the United Kingdom.[2]

From the British perspective, the Zimbabwean government was in dire need of stability and support. Shortly after Mugabe announced that the integration program was changing, he reshuffled his cabinet. Joshua Nkomo, the leader of the Zimbabwe African People's Union (ZAPU), was demoted from minister of home affairs to minister without portfolio. As minister of home affairs, Nkomo had controlled the Zimbabwe Republic Police; his removal signaled ZAPU's complete removal from national security decision-making.[3] Mugabe claimed that Nkomo would still have input regarding security issues as a member of the Cabinet Committee on

Public Security, yet it is clear from Major General Palmer's reports that Mugabe and Solomon Mujuru were quickly consolidating their power in the defense sector.[4] Yet Palmer failed to pick up on the trend that when Mujuru leaked a policy that he supported, it almost always was adopted by the Zimbabwean government. Pushing Nkomo to the side was the first sign of a concerted campaign by Mugabe and the Zimbabwe African National Union (ZANU) to wrest complete control of the national security structure and the ZNA from the settlers and ZAPU supporters.

While London considered Palmer's recommendation to increase the size of BMATT, the situation in Zimbabwe deteriorated even further. Up to this point, the British had successfully maintained exclusive control over military training in Zimbabwe. Their control was challenged during the last part of January 1981. At a meeting of the Joint High Command (JHC), Emmerson Mnangagwa, the Zimbabwean minister for state security, mentioned to Palmer the possibility of North Korean military assistance. Mnangagwa said that President Kim Il-sung offered Zimbabwe equipment for an entire armored brigade and trainers to accompany it, all without cost.[5] The proposal did not contain any details or timeline. Every member on the JHC was completely surprised by the announcement, except for Mujuru.

The possibility of a Nigerian training team had been a frustrating notion for both BMATT and the FCO, largely because of the dubious quality of the Nigerian Army.[6] The FCO and the MOD felt that they could overcome any challenges they might confront with a Nigerian training team. The Nigerian Army was modeled after the British Army and continued to receive British assistance. However, the introduction of the North Koreans into Zimbabwe had the potential to completely change the country's security dynamic. The North Korean military system was, by definition, political. Military officers underwent an extensive political education prior to receiving any military training. Additionally, the North Korean military had an entirely different military style that focused on massed armored warfare and strict adherence to orders.[7] The North Koreans were desperate both for prominence in the developing world and for hard currency. They doggedly pursued relationships with despots across Africa and partnered with countries that were close to the West and close to the Soviet bloc. By 1984 there were North Korean military training teams in eleven African nations.[8]

The British Army attempted to endow its leaders with the ability to exercise their own judgment and make the best decisions in light of any specific circumstances. The North Korean system and the British system were nothing alike; Palmer feared that Korean trainers would have a devastating effect on all the work BMATT had already done. The FCO was concerned about a situation where British trainers would work alongside soldiers from a country with which Britain had no relations.[9] From Palmer to the cabinet, everyone agreed that something had to be done to keep the North Koreans out of Zimbabwe.

Palmer met with Mnangagwa about the North Korean mission on 30 January. A North Korean delegation was already in Salisbury; it met with Mugabe and Solomon Mujuru, and made its offer. The Zimbabwean government felt that the package was too good to refuse and also pointed out that "beggars can't be choosers."[10] This comment seemed to slip past Palmer as unimportant, but it actually identifies the main complaint the Zimbabwean government had with the British military aid package. Despite the British commitment to helping Zimbabwe form its army, the Zimbabweans felt that the British should be more forthcoming with their resources. During the liberation war, ZANU relied on no-cost military support and training from China, North Korea, East Germany, and Tanzania. After independence, the British arrived to help the new government with a small training team, a limited number of courses in Britain for Zimbabwean soldiers, and an offer to sell the Zimbabweans military equipment at a discounted rate. In comparison to the other offers that Zimbabwe received, the British aid package seemed paltry. Palmer and the other members of his staff did not recognize their disadvantage in comparison with the nonaligned nations. More important, the FCO and the British prime minister's office failed to recognized that Britain was not as competitive as it believed itself to be.

Palmer did recognize that he was walking a thin line in his capacity as head of the training team. His access to the JHC and Mugabe was not something guaranteed to him by his position. On 6 February he finally had the opportunity to meet with Mugabe regarding the North Korean offer. On this occasion Mugabe was full of ideas about the military future of the country, many of which involved departing significantly from the plan the British recommended. The prime minister wanted Palmer and his men to help establish a ZANLA-only Presidential Guard to protect key points in Salisbury. Palmer did not refuse Mugabe's request but did ask that he include some ex-RSF personnel in the unit to make it more inclusive; he did not, however, go as far as to suggest the inclusion of former Zimbabwe Peoples' Revolutionary Army (ZIPRA) personnel. Mugabe did not bring up the North Korean offer, so Palmer had to broach the subject himself. The North Koreans had offered military assistance when Mugabe visited North Korea the previous year. Specifically, Kim Il-Sung offered to help equip and train a special field brigade for "counter coup and counter revolutionary" purposes.[11]

Interestingly, the idea of a counterrevolutionary brigade did not seem to concern Palmer. He pointed out to Mugabe that the inclusion of North Korean advisers could cause even further losses of white manpower and could endanger the possibility of civil aid from Western nations. Finally, Palmer made it clear that the army could not have two completely different military systems and functions. Mugabe countered that the Tanzanian Army had a mixture of military systems. Palmer responded, "Tanzania is not an example for Zimbabwe to follow."[12] The remark about Tanzania angered Mugabe; he informed Palmer that North Korea had assisted ZANU during the liberation struggle and wanted to continue to help Zimbabwe. Additionally, the prime minister did not care if the Americans or anyone else objected to this friendly gesture.

This exchange was indicative of the fine line that Palmer had to walk. While he possessed a wealth of military knowledge that he offered to Mugabe, he was also an outsider, a British officer who represented the last vestiges of the imperial world. Ronald Byatt, the high commissioner, and Palmer both felt that they had to react very carefully to the North Korean aid package. Any scaling down of the British mission or withdrawal of British troops might destroy what influence the British had left in the country.[13]

The British saw white manpower in the army as a form of influence. While these men did not necessarily represent the views and goals of the British government, they were Western-trained military professionals, something that was in increasingly short supply in Zimbabwe. On 31 December 1980, there were 686 white officers left in the ZNA; BMATT projected that by the end of April 1981 there would only be 404 white officers remaining.[14] Western influence in Zimbabwe was becoming a scarce commodity in early 1981, and the events in February of that year brought even more complicated problems to the integration process.

Chaos in Bulawayo

While there had been some interfactional disturbances in the military training program, they seemed to become less common as time passed. In November 1980 there was a minor incident in Bulawayo; fighting erupted between ex-ZANLA and ex-ZIPRA soldiers from ZNA battalions stationed there. The fighting came to an end quickly when British officers and party officials from both ZANU and ZAPU intervened. The ringleaders of the incident were rounded up and imprisoned. This incident was a setback, but since order and discipline remained intact for the army as a whole, there was no general sense of alarm among the BMATT officers.

Between November 1980 and February 1981, the situation seemed to calm. However, both ZIPRA and ZANLA troops in the ZNA, as well as unintegrated fighters, were stockpiling heavy weapons in violation of the cease-fire accords and the Lancaster House Agreement.[15] By late January it was clear that the ZNA was falling apart. While this was apparent at the lowest levels of the army, it was not clear at the ministerial level or to the BMATT staff.[16] Palmer never indicated to the FCO or the MOD that there were any serious problems in the integrated battalions. In fact, just prior to the fighting in Bulawayo, the MOD was discussing the possibility of scheduling a media visit to Zimbabwe to publicize the good work that BMATT was doing there.[17]

The major questions occupying the minds of Major General Palmer and his superiors were the possibility of North Korean intrusion and the funding situation for the upcoming year. When Joshua Nkomo was demoted in the cabinet, there was some concern about the possibility of disturbances in the ZNA. Mugabe said publicly that Nkomo would remain involved in security policy, likely to prevent the ZIPRA portion of the security forces from revolting.[18] It seems that the British were unaware of the undercurrent among rank-and-file soldiers who believed that conflict in the ZNA was inevitable.

On 9 February 1981, tense ex-ZIPRA combatants fired upon a Zimbabwe Air Force jet that flew over Chitungwiza Barracks while the soldiers there were on parade.[19] This incident is telling; these soldiers were so concerned about the possibility of attack that they carried loaded weapons on parade. Carrying loaded weapons during this type of training would never occur unless these men thought they might be attacked while they practiced in the drill square. The next day, a beer hall disagreement between former guerrillas quickly turned deadly as ex-ZIPRA and ex-ZANLA fighters opened fire on each other. Interfactional fighting quickly spread throughout the army.

The ZNA seemed to be falling apart; Mugabe called in political and military leaders from all sides to quell the violence. Since violence was spreading throughout the ZNA, none of the integrated battalions could be relied on to put down the uprising. Some of the former RSF units remained unintegrated. The First Battalion Rhodesian African Rifles (1RAR) was still led by white officers and had simply been renamed the Eleventh Infantry Battalion. This battalion, with the assistance of the unintegrated Rhodesian Armored Car Squadron, went to Bulawayo to quell the fighting.

The former RSF soldiers of the Eleventh Infantry Battalion secured Brady Barracks in Bulawayo and the nearby airfield. The Rhodesian Armored Car Squadron, along with elements of the Eleventh Infantry Battalion, stumbled upon a ZIPRA column of armored vehicles. During the battle that ensued, at least sixty ZIPRA soldiers were killed. During this time, C Company of the Eleventh Infantry Battalion withstood an assault by a numerically superior ZIPRA force on the north side of the city.[20] Throughout the rest of the country, British advisers worked to put down disturbances at their respective bases. They worked extremely closely with the Zimbabwean government and former RSF units to ensure that order was restored and mutinous elements were rounded up. However, the entirety of the British role in putting down the ZNA disturbances in 1981 remains unknown. The standard situation reports from that period are not contained in the files that cover that time frame. One file relating to the BMATT mission in Zimbabwe has been retained by the FCO beyond the standard twenty-five-year declassification period.

The complete breakdown in discipline throughout the army demonstrated the precarious point the ZNA had reached. While there were a growing number of ex-guerrillas who quickly were becoming semi-trained soldiers, there was a complete lack of corporate identity in the force. In a way, soldiers were internally resisting any unity with their former opponents by planning against them. The events in Bulawayo were far from spontaneous according to the regimental sergeant major of the Twelfth Infantry Battalion, Julius Neube. He remarked that once the fighting started, the mutinous soldiers removed their caps to differentiate friend from foe.[21] The ZNA existed on paper but not in spirit; beyond a small number of specialized units and former RSF battalions, there was no esprit de corps. When the Eleventh Infantry Battalion deployed to Bulawayo, the white officers specifically instructed their subordinates to wear the berets and insignia of their former Rhodesian Army unit.[22] While this seems like a simple adjustment on the part of officers, it was actually a much more dramatic demonstration of the fact that the Zimbabwean government had limited their control of the ZNA. The soldiers who saved the regime were representing the old Rhodesian Army and showcasing their professionalism (as compared with the ex-guerrillas).

The lack of corporate identity among the soldiers of the ZNA was a clear illustration that the short training period many of the new soldiers had experienced was insufficient to create lasting ties to their new military units. The years of conflict in the Zimbabwean wilderness ensured that the ex-guerrillas could not effectively separate their military from their political identity. BMATT, the MOD, and the FCO all realized that there was a serious and continued need for trainers to remain in the country at the same level (161 men) beyond April.[23] The training mission waited until at least September to reduce the number of British soldiers in Zimbabwe.

After the events of February, Colonel Henshaw, the British defense adviser to the High Commission, made a tour of a number of ZNA units to assess their status. His report showed the low level of readiness among Zimbabwean units and revealed some of the issues that hindered the progress of BMATT in its mission. His trip took him to three different units, the Infantry Training Depot, Grey's Scouts (the mounted infantry unit), and the First Parachute Battalion. Due to their specialized mission and skills, the Grey's Scouts had only just begun to integrate. Of the 500 men in the unit, only 105 were ex-guerrillas, most of whom had just begun their equestrian training. A group of about ten Africans were shadowing the white instructors, hoping eventually to take over their role in training. Most of the leadership in the unit at that time, including both officers and NCOs, were white. At the end of March, however, five white officers and twenty NCOs resigned from the army.[24]

The First Parachute Battalion, similarly, had only just begun to integrate. There were 1,150 men in the battalion; a former RSF officer, Lieutenant Colonel Lionel Dyke, had just recently taken command. Dyke, formerly of 1RAR, was extremely enthusiastic and not reluctant to make dramatic changes. Shortly after he took command, he fired the battalion adjutant (a white officer), the regimental sergeant major (a former ZANLA fighter), and a major in the battalion (a former ZANLA fighter).[25] Additionally, even though the men had been through a selection course, Dyke believed there were still undesirable men in the ranks. To remedy this, he decided to hold another selection course to further reduce the ranks of the battalion. Henshaw hoped that the parachute battalion and the Grey's would become two of the more effective units, largely because at least a third of the personnel in each were formerly of the RSF. Even so, neither was even close to being fully operational.

The regular units were not anywhere near the standards of the specialist units. The unit that Henshaw visited at the Infantry Training Depot was in a sorry state. Many of the soldiers were there because they had failed either parachute or commando selection. The ZIPRA and ZANLA men segregated themselves and did not interact while off duty. Worst of all, neither the battalion commander nor the second-in-command reported to the depot to attend training with the battalion; both men were former ZANLA fighters.[26] All of these units required months of training before they would approach a point where they could operate without the assistance of BMATT. The reports submitted to the FCO and the MOD were very clear; even after a year of training, the ZNA was still an embryonic organization that could fall apart at the slightest interfactional provocation. It seemed clear to the British officers working in Zimbabwe that both the former RSF men and the ex-guerrillas had the ability and potential to form an effective force. What they needed was long-term mentorship and training similar to what happened in both Kenya and Zambia. Training guerrillas to become conventional soldiers was a time-consuming task made exponentially more complicated by the need to integrate the force.

Despite these major training setbacks and the troublesome direction in which the ZNA was headed, the FCO and the MOD were intent on establishing a long-term relationship with the Zimbabwean military (but on a much more cost-effective scale). Rather than increase the size of the training mission or extend its life span, the MOD assigned an army officer to the ZNA on a loan service agreement with the purpose of serving as an adviser to the newly established ZNA Staff College.[27] Officers on loan service agreements were meant to be in country on a long-term assignment. Generally, these were multiyear assignments that would rotate in a new officer every two or three years. This arrangement, while far less comprehensive, was much more attractive to the British because it installed a British officer in the ZNA military education system for the long term, yet was comparatively inexpensive. However, the idea that the British would be able to exert any influence through a presence in ZNA staff education was shortsighted. For years both the British and the Americans had utilized their culture to win favor and influence with foreign military officers. These Western forces invited officers at all stages of their careers to attend long-duration courses in their military education systems in order to create long-lasting favorable relationships with military contacts. Although a British officer in the ZNA Staff College would give Zimbabwean officers some idea of what the British Army was like, it most likely would not convert anyone to change their view of the role of the military in the political process. The British really only needed to look to their experience in Nigeria since independence. In 1980 a British officer was still serving as an instructor in the Nigerian Staff College, but this did not seem to have any impact on military involvement in politics.

Were there no other factors distracting Zimbabwean soldiers from British influence, there may eventually have been some resonance among the ex-guerrillas. Yet this was not the case. In late May, Mnangagwa announced in the middle of a JHC meeting that three North Korean officers had arrived in Zimbabwe a few days earlier to serve as the advanced party for the North Korean training team.[28] The issue was last mentioned at a January JHC meeting; since then, there had been silence from Mugabe's office regarding the possibility of North Korean assistance.

During the same period, the Zimbabwean government concluded that all ex-guerrillas should be disarmed. This included all soldiers who were already integrated, as well as those who were awaiting training. Since the fighting in February, the government assessed that the country would be more stable if all military hardware was stored in its armories.[29] While the threat of large-scale clashes between armed camps of unintegrated men had dissipated to a certain degree, the overall security situation in Zimbabwe was not much improved. Heavy weapons and crew-served weapons were difficult to hide and thus had to be turned over to the government. However, the guerrilla armies had never cataloged small arms; there was no way of knowing how many weapons were in circulation. Men stored their rifles at home or hid them in the bush for later use. Some men who were still waiting to be integrated turned to banditry instead or used their weapons to settle old scores. Violence increased in rural areas, and murders became more and more frequent. Former guerrillas were not the only people with weapons; the civilian white population had become highly militarized and extremely well-armed. Men who had been in the Territorials kept their rifles at home. The Rhodesian government had actively encouraged whites to arm themselves and to defend their farms if attacked.

The country was awash with weapons, which posed a problem for Mugabe's government. One thing that gives governments legitimacy is a monopoly on any legal use of force. With so many weapons freely available in Zimbabwe, the government could hardly claim to have a monopoly. While not a military man himself, Mugabe understood Mao's ideology of a people's war. With weaponry widely available, any of his rivals retained the ability to wage an insurgent war against the new government. Mozambique was a living example for Mugabe of what could befall a newly independent government that faced rival armed groups at the outset of independence.[30]

Too Many Actors on the Stage

As the North Koreans arrived in Zimbabwe, BMATT leaders found themselves in the odd position of trying to justify their mission. There seemed to be a breakdown in communication between Margaret Thatcher's cabinet and Her Majesty's Treasury. The cabinet wholly agreed that the job that BMATT was doing was integral to the security of Zimbabwe and concluded that "the maintenance of law and order in Zimbabwe depended on bringing the three armies which at present existed into a new integrated national army. The presence and assistance of British officers and other ranks was essential to this process."[31] While the cabinet applauded the efforts of BMATT, the Treasury insisted that the mission was far too expensive. The Zimbabwe military mission cost £3.1 million of the £9 million UK Worldwide Military Training Scheme budget for 1981–1982.

The Thatcher government was looking to make severe reductions in defense spending. While the 1981 Defense Review made it clear that deep cuts were necessary, it focused mainly on reductions of the navy's surface fleet. However, all branches of the armed forces were hollowed out by two decades of defense cuts.[32] The priorities for the MOD were NATO, Home Defense, and the Royal Air Force, with everything else making up a distant fourth. The United States hoped that Britain would play a key role in the continued strength of the NATO alliance, as well as maintain a strong military presence in Belize.[33] There was pressure from NATO for all member nations to increase spending by 3 percent each year until 1986.[34] This increase in spending was to focus on items, personnel, and equipment that could be of use in northern Europe, and not for military assistance missions in the developing world. These commitments and the British promise to support Zimbabwe's special needs in the postconflict era did not necessarily align. The Thatcher government continued to make commitments to the Zimbabwean government. However, the amount of funding and military aid promised were nowhere near what the Zimbabweans wanted from Britain.

Britain organized a donor's conference for Zimbabwe in March 1981, in an attempt to marshal the goodwill of Western nations interested in keeping communist influence out of Zimbabwe. The conference focused on raising money for civil development in the war-ravaged nation. The British government promised a total of £30 million to the newly independent nation for land resettlement alone.[35] HMG seemed to be convinced that the most effective way to wield power in Zimbabwe was through land reform monies, and not through the military assistance fund (which amounted to a comparatively trifling £3 million). In their correspondence, Thatcher impressed upon Mugabe that the civil commitments that Britain made to Zimbabwe "demonstrate[d] the importance we attach to helping Zimbabwe in the early years of independence."[36]

The commitment of the United Kingdom to provide large amounts of money for land purchases from white farmers is an indication of the overall British goal in the country. Rather than attempt to maintain influence in the majority rule government, HMG wanted to ensure that it protected the white citizens of Zimbabwe. While this was in part an issue of race, it was also very consistent with the British policy in the 1980s to overlook racial problems in southern Africa in favor of economic opportunities. Many white Zimbabweans held dual citizenship in the United Kingdom, and in spite of the newly formed majority rule government, HMG expected whites to retain economic control of the Zimbabwean economy.

While Prime Minister Thatcher outlined the special place that Zimbabwe held in the British sphere of influence, BMATT pointed out the dramatic impact their trainers were making with the minimal resources available to them. The high commissioner in Salisbury, Robin Byatt, and the FCO were mindful of the fact that the critical issue in Zimbabwe was the security situation. If the country were not stabilized, any hope of economic recovery or renewed foreign investment would become a pipe dream. Byatt made it clear to the FCO that the end of the "sausage machine" training of the regular battalions was only the beginning of the creation of the ZNA: "Once the sausage machine project is done the papering over of the divisions will be done. But that is it. There is little point in producing an 'amalgamated' army only to watch it fall apart."[37] After the initial training of the regular battalions of the ZNA, the British planned to significantly reduce the amount of military assistance. British military influence would take the form of a single officer on loan service terms to the ZNA who was running the staff college. This officer was scheduled to begin in January 1982 and was slated to teach a series of midlevel, three-month staff courses.[38]

By the end of May 1981, British diplomats and military officers in Zimbabwe realized that they had no control over Mugabe. Byatt pointed out that "any doubts about Mugabe being in charge are gone. He has craftfully [sic] shifted the decision making power from his party's central committee to his cabinet of which he is the clear master."[39] In spite of the excellent job that BMATT was doing with the ZNA, the British found themselves more and more isolated from the military decision-making process. This became even clearer when discussions began regarding North Korean military assistance.

When the North Korean presence became a reality in May 1981, the British were flabbergasted. They had vastly overestimated their ability to scare off military assistance from other nations. Mugabe and his ministers played the fool; they claimed that the North Koreans were overzealous in their desire to help Zimbabwe, and that the ZANU-PF government was in no position to refuse.[40] The British government was caught unaware of the significance of the North Korean offer of assistance. Initially, HMG thought that the North Koreans were only planning on training a small presidential guard force. When Byatt broached the subject during a meeting, however, Mugabe made it clear that the North Korean offer of a brigade's worth of equipment was just too good to refuse. However, Mugabe indicated that the five-thousand-man unit that was to be trained would be utilized as a "special brigade" and in a "counter revolutionary role."[41] Strangely, the mention of a counterrevolutionary unit trained by the North Koreans did not raise any alarms in the High Commission or the FCO.

Since the beginning of the military mission to Zimbabwe, one of the primary goals had been the establishment of an apolitical force loyal to the Zimbabwean constitution. This North Korean issue was a warning sign of what was to come. Mugabe's government was planning on training a brigade of soldiers in a counterrevolutionary role, which is politically charged terminology. This was the first overt indication of the ZANU-PF intention of intertwining the military with the party system in Zimbabwe. If it was not clear to the public at large that Mugabe wanted to create a one-party state, the British, at least, had fair warning of what the future held.

Rather than focus on the implications of the creation of this new brigade for the internal security and political situation in Zimbabwe, the British focused on what it meant in the diplomatic world. Thatcher's hard-nosed persona was notably absent from the African continent. While she is popularly known as the consummate Cold Warrior in Europe, her toughness did not permeate the Foreign Service. Byatt did not challenge Mugabe on the subject of North Korean aid, nor did he indicate that acceptance of it would have any implications for the British relationship with Zimbabwe. Rather, he indicated that the United States would be less inclined to maintain its commitment to the pledge of civil aid to Zimbabwe if North Korean aid was accepted.[42] British officers and diplomats continued under the impression that the arrangement was forced on the Zimbabweans because of their wartime relationship with North Korea. Alternatively, white members of the ZNA seemed to view the issue as yet another in a series of problems that would degrade the professionalism of the force.[43]

The British government was content to believe that the Zimbabweans did not understand what was going on, despite the fact that Byatt had made it very clear that Mugabe knew his own mind and was firmly in control in the country. Rather than meet with the JHC first, the North

Korean officers met with Mugabe privately. The British read this as a sign that the Zimbabweans were attempting to stall the North Koreans. All the while, Solomon Mujuru freely proclaimed that the North Koreans were ready to ship the equipment necessary for a five-thousand-man heavy brigade that would not be a part of the ZNA chain of command. Instead, this unit would report directly to the minister of defense, one of the many positions that Mugabe held.[44] The US State Department was closely tracking Mugabe's relationship with all communist nations and recognized that there was close and continuing cooperation that was a troubling sign.[45]

In spite of the intelligence that the British were receiving from the JHC and Mujuru, they continued to believe that they maintained more influence in military matters than they actually did. However, Thatcher was more concerned about the issue than the FCO was. She voiced her concerns to the ministry in a memo, saying that the arrival of the North Koreans was a worrisome indication of the direction Zimbabwe was headed.[46] The concern on Thatcher's part did not translate into a policy shift regarding Zimbabwe. The FCO was convinced of the importance of BMATT in the country, in part because of Byatt's assessment of its work. The mission in Zimbabwe would continue but would be reduced in size as soon as it was feasible.[47] The "sausage machine" would continue until the end of November, when the last of the untrained battalions would graduate from basic training. After that, the British military presence in the country would be dramatically reduced.

While the British were looking at ways to reduce their presence in Zimbabwe, the North Korean government was cementing relations with the Mugabe government. The premier of North Korea, Li Jong-ok, made an unofficial visit to Salisbury in late June 1981, which concluded with a bilateral agreement between the two nations to provide £12 million worth of military equipment and 103 trainers.[48] The British government felt somewhat reassured by the fact that the North Korean advisers would only train the Fifth Brigade of the Army. This organization was intended to be entirely self-sustaining and not involved in any other part of the ZNA. Shortly, it became clear that the Fifth Brigade was to be composed entirely of former ZANLA fighters who had yet to be trained or integrated into the new ZNA.[49] The personnel of the new brigade were to undergo no British military training whatsoever and would not be assisted by any soldiers from the former RSF. Strangely, British officer diplomats in

Zimbabwe did not view this as a loss of influence. In fact, they were comforted by the fact that the North Korean government had never provided quality military training to any country.[50] This was the same position that the South Africans took. They pointed out that training an army in two incompatible systems made Zimbabwe less of a threat.

At the ministerial level, the British also overestimated the effectiveness of their "sausage machine" training program. In July, the FCO boasted to the Australians that at that point, the BMATT had already trained thirty battalions and had thirteen more to train.[51] This did not explain the level of training that the ZNA actually received. In June 1981, the British defense adviser in Zimbabwe visited three of the newly trained ZNA battalions to report on their progress. His first stop was Fourteenth Battalion (14BN) stationed in a rural area 150 kilometers north of Bulawayo. Even though 14BN completed its initial training in February, it was not a functional military unit. The unit suffered from a lack of instructors, training aids, and basic military equipment. According to the report, it had only 150 rifles to service a battalion of one thousand men. The British adviser to the unit, Major D. M. Chappel, concentrated all his time on teaching the ex-guerrillas who were now serving as officers the administrative skills necessary to keep the battalion paid and provisioned.[52] The unit was nowhere close to being able to function without a British adviser, or even move on to more advanced infantry training.

The two other battalions that Henshaw visited (the Forty-Fifth and Forty-Sixth Battalions) were not in any better shape than 14BN. Former ZIPRA fighters dominated the command team in both units. These units also suffered from a lack of equipment and training aids; they had not conducted any additional training since finishing their basic course. Although they were in better administrative shape than 14BN, it would be at least three months until a BMATT mobile training team was able to visit and conduct even rudimentary training.[53]

In the eyes of the British government, this still seemed to be progress. The units were classified as trained formations once they had passed through the "sausage machine." The level of North Korean influence became more apparent in June 1981, as former ZANLA fighters returned to Zimbabwe from their overseas training. That month, two hundred men who trained in North Korea for the previous year were set to return to Zimbabwe. This left sixty former ZANLA men in North Korea finishing up their training. The number included Perence Shiri, who was selected to serve as the commander of the Fifth Brigade. He had been in North Korea for the previous three years in an unspecified training course.[54] The men who trained in North Korea would form the core of the Fifth Brigade.[55]

North Korea was not the only nonaligned or communist state offering military training to Zimbabwe. In June 1981, an Egyptian aircraft arrived in Salisbury to pick up forty-five personnel to attend training in Egypt. Most of the men sent to Egypt were from the Central Intelligence Organization. The Chinese also offered a military aid package consisting of a number of F6 fighter jets and T59 tanks.[56] The nonaligned nations were forming close military partnerships with the Zimbabwean government. Again, it seemed that only the highest levels of the British government were concerned with the way the tide was turning in Zimbabwe. Thatcher indicated in her personal notes that the Zimbabwean move to accept aid from the North Koreans was "very worrying. It indicates the underlying attitude [of Mugabe]."[57] Still, this concern did not filter down to the men who executed policy in the FCO's Central Africa Department. The FCO and Byatt continued to believe that they would gain more ground in Zimbabwe by registering a half-hearted protest with Mugabe and then ignoring the North Korean presence altogether.

However, the British applied a very low level of pressure on Mugabe; Byatt only brought up the matter in a private meeting with Mugabe, and Mugabe's tepid response to Byatt's protestations signaled a turning point in Anglo-Zimbabwean relations. London attempted to navigate around the North Koreans altogether. The FCO wanted to foster a tripartite relationship between Britain, Kenya, and Zimbabwe. Relations between HMG and Kenya were much more cordial; the British Army maintained a training presence in the Kenya Army Staff College, as well as at a training base two hundred kilometers north of Nairobi. Kenya was the model of success that the British hoped to emulate in Zimbabwe, so the MOD believed that any influence from Kenya would be perceived as similar to British Army influence.[58]

The general impression among diplomatic and military observers was that the security situation inside Zimbabwe was improving. Officially, they called it "reasonably stable." Settler farmers were frequently targeted by the less disciplined elements of the ZNA and were subject to frequent harassment.[59] There were also an increasing number of men deserting from the ZNA; while some took to banditry, others were simply afraid for their safety after the factional fighting in February. The country was stable enough for a visit from the chief of the General Staff of the British Army, Field Marshal Sir Edwin Bramall, in mid-July 1981. London was comfortable allowing the international press to believe that he was there to challenge the Zimbabwean decision to bring in North Korean trainers.[60] However, the FCO knew what the press did not: that it was too late to challenge Mugabe on the issue of North Korean involvement in military assistance.

The infant ZNA was also forced to serve in an operational capacity long before it was ready or properly trained to do so. In 1981, Resistência Nacional Moçambicana (RENAMO) began engaging in cross-border raids into Zimbabwe with increasing frequency.[61] This was not the only border security issue that the Zimbabwean government faced. The South Africans had consistently tried to destabilize Zimbabwe since the signature of the Lancaster House Agreement. In late 1979, the South African Bureau of State Security and its descendant, the National Intelligence Service, launched Operation DRAMA, which involved recruiting Rhodesian intelligence and security personnel into South African service and then utilizing them to degrade and, at times, destroy Zimbabwean facilities.[62]

By August 1981, BMATT had trained more than thirty infantry battalions; the "sausage machine" was due to end in November, at which time all the regular units of the ZNA would be trained. Once the units were formed and had been put through training, together they would form a single corporate identity. Bonds of loyalty would begin to form, and charismatic commanders would be able to exert influence over their soldiers. In the first week in August 1981, Mnangagwa announced to the JHC a variety of new appointments in the ZNA that were effective immediately. At the same time, he announced that the JHC would be disbanded on 17 August because the new ZNA appointments effectively created a single, unified chain of command for the armed forces.[63]

The prime minister's office made these appointments abruptly, without consulting Palmer, the current ZNA commander General Sandy Maclean, or any officials from ZIPRA. Maclean, formerly the ZNA commander, was appointed the defense forces commander. Solomon Mujuru, the former ZANLA commander, took over the role of commander of the ZNA. Former ZANLA officers also occupied the other top positions in the army headquarters, the chief of staff for operations and the brigadier for equipment. Additionally, ZANLA men took command of two of the army's four brigades, as well as the Salisbury Military District.[64]

The reaction to the new appointments was further division among the factions within Zimbabwe. ZAPU/ZIPRA men were extremely unhappy about the appointments; it was clear to them that the appointments were political in nature and had little to do with skill or merit.[65] Former RSF officers were also very disturbed by the turn of events; upon the appointment of Brigadier Freddie Matanga, a particularly bombastic former ZANLA officer, to command of the Salisbury District, all the white members of his staff walked out of the headquarters. The British defense adviser described Matanga as "a volatile character who symphonizes the white fear of Africanization."[66] This comment is illustrative of the way that British observers viewed former ZANLA officers; others were described as "a disruptive influence" and "politically motivated."[67] This was true of the ZANLA men all the way up to the new ZNA commander.

London was particularly concerned about Mujuru; he was described as "uncouth but possessed of an innate animal cunning[;] he is anti-British and would like to see BMATT removed."[68] However, just as Palmer and Byatt had underestimated Mugabe, they also underestimated Mujuru. The British officials thought that once Mujuru "learned his job," he would change his mind about the need for BMATT.[69] They made this assumption, however, with no knowledge of the extent of the cooperation between the Zimbabwean government and other nonaligned powers. In the short term, Palmer and Byatt were comforted by the fact that Mujuru was scheduled to attend a yearlong staff college course in Pakistan.

In the days and weeks following the announcement, London waited with anticipation to learn how these changes would impact the effectiveness of its mission in Zimbabwe. Interestingly, London felt that the new single chain of command would actually damage Palmer's ability to influence. Under the JHC model, Palmer had a seat at the table where all the commanders met; additionally, he had direct access to the prime minister on a biweekly basis. All this came to an end with the disbandment of the JHC. MOD planners were particularly concerned about the impact that the new appointments had on the white officers who remained in the ZNA. Initially, officials in London were reassured by the fact that Maclean was appointed defense forces commander. This was the first time the position was filled since General Walls had retired from the army. Even so, Palmer was not impressed with Maclean's record. Maclean was a very negative person who had done little to reassure the white officers of the army since Zimbabwe's independence.[70] The British realized that they might find themselves frozen out of the Zimbabwean command structure, and therefore unable to influence policy.

On 14 August 1981, Colonel Henshaw sent a report on the stability of the Zimbabwean military to the British defense adviser in Pretoria. At this point, BMATT had produced a total of thirty-six infantry battalions, all of which were 50 percent ZIPRA and 50 percent ZANLA. There were three additional infantry battalions that were composed of ZIPRA/ZANLA/ RSF troops. The former Rhodesian African Rifles battalions all remained unintegrated. The last three units were scheduled to finish training in mid-November. Henshaw claimed that factionalism was at an all-time low and that morale and overall enthusiasm in the units were high, though this was balanced out by the fact that the standard of training in the units was extremely low.[71] The officer corps seemed to be the foundation of the issue. The standards among the former guerrilla officers were low; Henshaw specifically commented that they "lack[ed] a sense of responsibility to their men: a gulf therefore exists between officers and men which was borne out in the mutinies in February when the officers tended to be unaware of what was going on."[72] As had been the case in Kenya and Zambia, the level of training and professionalism was the bedrock of an effective military organization.

Lack of knowledge on the part of former guerrilla officers, as well as the exodus of white officers from the ZNA, began to take a dramatic toll on the ability of the ZNA to function. The army had swelled to such a size that the Zimbabwe Army Service Corps was no longer able to provide effective, or even minimal, logistical support to the force. The significant body of equipment that the guerrilla armies brought into the country was suffering. The guerrillas had not maintained the equipment well, and the Service Corps did not have the technical knowledge necessary to keep it running.[73]

The situation was further complicated by Zimbabwe's difficult relationship with South Africa. South African agents were responsible for no fewer than four sabotage operations in 1980, from the theft of weapons to blowing up army vehicles. In August 1981, South African operatives set off an explosion at Inkomo Barracks near Bulawayo that destroyed $50 million worth of weapons.[74] The man who orchestrated the operation was the white commander of the Zimbabwe Army Corps of Engineers. He later escaped from prison with the help of South African agents and went on to join the South African Army. This further damaged Mugabe and Mujuru's view of the 320 settlers who remained in the ZNA. While the British were concerned about these incidents, they did not have any impact on British plans in Zimbabwe.

Officials in London were convinced that the authorities in Zimbabwe had no idea what to do with the North Korean military assistance. The North Korean training team, led by a lieutenant general, arrived in Zimbabwe on 13 August 1981 and immediately began their work. Only then did Mugabe unveil the details of the training plan to his senior military officers. Two thousand men were selected from the ZANLA-only battalions that had already been trained; an additional one thousand men were selected from the unintegrated ZANLA camp, and a further thousand men were to be brought in from an unspecified source.[75] This last group ended up being fighters who had returned from training in North Korea and elsewhere. The FCO said that it was not a surprise that this brigade was entirely ZANLA. Even so, no one in the chain of command raised the alarm. By this point in 1981, Mugabe had told Palmer on numerous occasions that the unit trained by North Korea would be a countercoup force. The fact that it was entirely composed on ZANLA men, as well as the continued efforts by Mugabe's regime to marginalize both ZIPRA and ZAPU, were open indicators that the military was intended to be a political force and a full partner in a one-party state.

By the end of August, the full impact of the new appointments had begun to sink in to both BMATT and ZIPRA. Palmer and Henshaw both realized that there would soon be a mass exodus of those whites still remaining in the ZNA. Many of these men were commanders, at least until the new political appointees had replaced them. Palmer fully expected most of the remaining settlers to leave the army by April 1982.[76] This situation was paired with the sweeping Africanization of the army staff or, more accurately, the ZANLA-ization. ZANLA men who had little experience or training in staff work were tapped to replace experienced staff officers, European and African alike.[77] While it was possible that the lack of experience among staff officers could have led to further dependence on BMATT, Henshaw correctly predicted otherwise. It was the opinion of the British officers in the country that the appointments, combined with the creation of the Fifth Brigade, would only exacerbate tension between Mugabe and Nkomo and increase the possibility of a repeat of the events of February 1981, only on a larger scale.[78]

This was not an opinion held solely by the British. Joshua Nkomo frequently spoke out in parliament and in ministerial meetings against the establishment of the Fifth Brigade. Later, he even claimed that the Fifth Brigade reported directly to the ZANU Central Committee rather than to any part of the Zimbabwean government.[79] Even *The Times* reported that the Fifth Brigade trained for an abnormal purpose that could threaten the balance of power in Zimbabwe.[80] As August gave way to September, the specter of a one-party state increased. Mugabe began to include the notion in public speeches. The minister of youth, sport, and recreation, Ernest Kadungure, organized large youth demonstrations advocating a one-party state led by ZANU.[81] At the same time, Mugabe began to make references to youth military training programs. His intention was for ZANU to establish military training centers across Zimbabwe, ostensibly to keep the youth occupied.[82]

This was a troublesome prospect for the British, who felt the program was analogous to those found in Cuba, the USSR, and East Germany. However, the Zimbabweans very easily could have framed it as a revival of the army cadet programs that had been present in Rhodesia prior to independence. The key difference for both Mugabe and London was that ZANU ran the program, rather than the Zimbabwean government. This is an excellent example of the fundamental misunderstanding by the British of what had occurred in Zimbabwe at this juncture. By this point, Mugabe and ZANU had dispensed with the trappings of a unified government; the de facto condition for Zimbabwe at this point was that it had become a one-party state.

Fifth Brigade Takes Shape

As personnel of the North Korean training team continued to arrive in Zimbabwe, the British tried to understand what Pyongyang stood to gain. Colonel Henshaw informally consulted with the Chinese diplomatic mission in an attempt to gain some sort of insight into the intentions of the

North Koreans. Sun Guotung, the deputy chief of mission, told Henshaw that the Chinese had no knowledge of Kim Il-sung's plans in Zimbabwe. However, Guotung did say that if the Fifth Brigade was made up entirely of ZANLA men (as was currently planned), it would have "sinister implication[s]."[83] In spite of the warning provided by this Chinese diplomat, Henshaw and the rest of the British mission failed to recognize the seriousness of the situation.

The Fifth Brigade began to absorb many of the highly trained ZANLA specialists previously integrated into the ZNA service units. The brigade was 3,100-men strong by the end of September 1981. At the same time, Mugabe began a demobilization program. The ZNA had grown far too large and had absorbed almost a third of the government's budget.[84] By September 1981, 9,000 former guerrillas had volunteered to leave the army as part of a demobilization scheme.[85] A further 2,763 men were involuntarily demobilized; of this number, 2,432 were former ZIPRA fighters.[86] The new ZNA command structure actively encouraged ZIPRA men and RSF soldiers to leave the army, claiming, "They had [already] served for so many years."[87] Only six months earlier, Mugabe had argued that Zimbabwe needed to maintain a large army to counter the possibility of a South African invasion. However, it seems that what he really meant was that Zimbabwe needed a large army of soldiers loyal to ZANU to consolidate power inside the country and then face off with South Africa. As the ZNA units passed through their training program and the integration exercise continued, the army became more and more partisan.

Matters at the Defense Forces headquarters did not improve with the rearrangement of the command structure. Even though Sandy Maclean was the titular defense force commander, he had little real power. He had set up a small headquarters staff inside the Zimbabwe MOD; however, his duties and powers still were not defined by the prime minister's office.[88] While Maclean was slipping into irrelevance, Mujuru was quickly becoming more and more dominant inside the Zimbabwean Security Forces. Mugabe and ZANU were satisfied with the progress of the ZNA; however, the Air Force of Zimbabwe (AFZ) was far from satisfactory. Almost all the African pilots who trained in the Eastern Bloc nations had failed all the initial tests to serve as pilots in the AFZ. At that point the AFZ maintained the same training standards as the Royal Air Force. Western military flight training was completely different than the approach taken

by Eastern Bloc nations. Whereas Western pilots were supposed to exercise initiative and independently adjust plans during missions, Eastern
Bloc pilots took centralized direction from ground flight controllers who
were responsible for tactical decision-making. These two systems were
fundamentally at odds and likely contributed to the failure of the students
who trained in Eastern Europe. The other significant factor was also likely
racial prejudice on the part of the white AFZ instructional staff.

All the officers and pilots in the AFZ were white, except for a handful
of administrative officers who trained in Nigeria.[89] The commander of the
AFZ, Air Marshall Norman Walsh, who had served in the Rhodesian Air
Force since 1949, hoped to maintain its high educational standards. As
had previously been the case in Zambia and Kenya, the maintenance of
educational standards had been the thinly veiled racism that was present
throughout the colonial world.

Mujuru was behaving more like the commander of defense forces than
the commander of the ZNA. He insisted that the AFZ make immediate
changes. Particularly in terms of the chain of command, it would not do
for the air force to remain a bastion of white control in an independent
Zimbabwe. Particularly since the AFZ was the component of the security forces that the South Africans were most concerned about, it was the
most modern force on the continent (second only to the South African Air
Force). While Mujuru did not immediately insist that an African replace
Walsh, he did request that an African serve as deputy commander of the
AFZ.[90] Palmer feared that Mujuru's insistence and the overall lowering of
the educational standards in the AFZ would lead to more resignations by
white officers from the service. Even members of the Non-Aligned Movement were concerned about the direction the Zimbabwean services were
taking. The Egyptians approached Byatt to discuss his concerns about the
AFZ. The Egyptian ambassador to Zimbabwe, Mohamed El-Farnawany,
felt that the air force was the perfect place for the USSR to insert itself
into Zimbabwean affairs. Mugabe had already approached the Egyptians,
Pakistanis, and Chinese with a request to train Zimbabwean pilots, but
they had all declined, claiming that the cost was too high to provide these
services for free. The USSR was the only country willing to offer pilot
training at no cost. The British government insisted that the Zimbabweans share the costs of the two flying instructors who were training the
forty-two air cadets in Zimbabwe.[91] The British solution to this problem

was to attempt to get other parties to pay for the training. As was the case with the ZNA, London was simply unable to fund a large technical training mission for the AFZ that would prevent it from seeking assistance elsewhere.

In October 1981, the last three ZNA battalions began training, and BMATT was scheduled to start reducing its strength by the end of the month. Rather than solidifying the defense relationship between Britain and Zimbabwe, Mugabe had opened up the country to any nation wanting to be involved in southern Africa. A team from Pakistan had arrived in Salisbury to determine how best to provide military assistance. The French were actively looking to sell arms to the newly independent nation, and Mugabe sent a delegation to Bulgaria to solicit military assistance.[92] Affairs had come a long way from the point when Mugabe had sat in Thatcher's office and insisted that he wanted Britain to be Zimbabwe's only military assistance provider.

The Fifth Brigade was quickly growing into something much larger and more complex than anticipated. The ZNA possessed only one field artillery regiment in October 1981. However, the British learned that the Fifth Brigade would have its own artillery regiment and had already absorbed a large number of other specialists.[93] Even so, Palmer and Byatt seemed to be comfortable with the apparent lack of progress the North Korean trainers were making. As of October, the Fifth Brigade's training was confined to political indoctrination. With the stated British goal of ensuring that the military was a force that stayed out of domestic politics, it was curious that a heavy regimen of political indoctrination did not concern them.[94]

The hastily planned demobilization scheme seemed to be unraveling before it even got started. As a test for the system, five hundred men were scheduled for demobilization in November; however, the sparsely staffed Ministry of Social Services did not have the resources to manage the plan properly. The desire to discharge two thousand men from the army every month, with benefits, was unattainable at the time.[95] It was more likely that the former ZIPRA men were simply going to be discharged without ceremony and forced to fend for themselves.

It was also becoming more technically challenging for the British to train the ZNA. In October, the rest of the ZNA was brought into line with the Fifth Brigade when the decision was made to equip the army

with AK-47 assault rifles and Chinese Type 56 light machine guns, as opposed to the FN FAL battle rifle and the FN general purpose machine
guns that had been used by the Rhodesian Army.[96] The FN FAL was a
Belgian designation for the rifle used by the British Army at the time,
the L1A1. The FN and the AK-47 used completely incompatible ammunition, 7.62mm NATO and 7.62x39mm, respectively. The Fifth Brigade
was equipped with these weapons, and the rest of the army followed suit.
This decision brought an end to any real possibility of a sale of British- or
Western-manufactured equipment to the army. This meant major supply
chain changes for the army and a complete reorientation of the acquisition
system from the West to the East. BMATT had already had some difficulty
with attempting to train ZNA personnel on Eastern Bloc equipment with
which they were unfamiliar; now all the standard-issue equipment was
to be Eastern Bloc in origin. The British approached the Egyptians and
requested their assistance in training the ZNA on this type of equipment.
The Egyptian Army was trained along British lines but utilized Soviet-
supplied equipment. The Egyptian government agreed to provide places
in some training courses but not a mobile training team.

Offers of military assistance from other nations continued. The Pakistanis offered pilot training and places for Zimbabweans at their staff
college. The Bulgarians promised they would provide some military equipment. As these offers trickled, in fresh delegations went to Algeria and
East Germany, also seeking military aid.[97] The Zimbabweans were shop-
ping around among the communist and nonaligned nations. They were
making no effort to seek aid from Western nations other than the United
Kingdom. However, it is unlikely that this was because of any dramatic
ideological differences between ZANU and the West. Military assistance
from Western nations came at a much higher monetary price, and frankly
Zimbabwe was not strategically important enough to countries like the
United States, France, or Israel to warrant cost-free aid grants. Additionally, all the aforementioned countries were far too invested in the maintenance of the status quo in southern Africa to give Zimbabwe any tools that
could possibly lead to a larger regional confrontation with South Africa.
The United States provided covert aid to União Nacional para a Inde-
pendência Total de Angola in Angola, whose forces were openly operating
with the South Africans in their campaign against the Movimento Popular de Libertação de Angola (MPLA). The French had sold Mirage III
fighter aircraft to the South Africans, along with other advanced military

aircraft and weapons systems. The Israelis supplied arms to both sides in the African liberation wars; they provided Uzi submachine guns and UH-1 helicopters to the Rhodesians, as well as officer training to various African liberation forces and newly independent armies. However, all this assistance came at a price; these were never free grants of arms or training. Western nations generally sold weapons and training for money as well as favors, but not simply to expand their influence.

The Zimbabweans were beginning to sense that the South Africans were behind the growing number of security incidents in the country. After the arrest of the white officer in charge of the Zimbabwe Engineer Corps, Mugabe's government suspected the South Africans were responsible for almost every report of sabotage and violence. To a degree they were right; in November 1981, RENAMO fighters destroyed a hundred-meter span of bridge inside Zimbabwe.[98] While RENAMO forces were certainly behind this action, after the fall of the Smith regime, the Central Intelligence Organization passed off support and direction of RENAMO sabotage operations to the South Africans.[99] Operation DRAMA was also becoming much more active. As more and more disgruntled ZIPRA men left or were forced out of the ZNA, the South Africans recruited them for their effort to destabilize Zimbabwe.[100]

BMATT Moves into a New Phase

Officially, the integration process ended on 11 November 1981, sixteen years after the Unilateral Declaration of Independence. The ZNA's officer corps was understrength by 205 officers; the army was authorized for 2,341 officer positions and had only 2,136 men in uniform. However, the force was drastically overstrength in other ranks; 39,496 were authorized, but as of 11 November there were 55,449 men serving.[101] This number also did not include the 3,000 men serving in the Fifth Brigade. This excessively large number of troops made the ZNA one of the largest armies in Africa, far larger than a country of its size required or could afford.

The British government had come to terms with the necessity of continuing the military mission in Zimbabwe. Thatcher and Mugabe spoke on 6 October 1981 about the internal situation in Zimbabwe. In their conversation, Mugabe appealed to Thatcher to continue British training support for the army after the end of the integration exercise, although he stated that the army needed to develop "a single allegiance to the government in power."[102] He was very specific when he chose his terms; the implication was that the army should be loyal to the ZANU government, not necessarily the Zimbabwean constitution. This was an important distinction about which Mugabe was quite clear. At the end of October 1981, Mugabe presented the First Commando Battalion with its colors, making it the first unit in the ZNA to receive the Zimbabwean colors. In his remarks at the parade, he emphasized the duty the men had to remain loyal to the nation and the government.[103] In any other circumstances this speech would have sounded the same as any other given by an elected official at a military event, yet the implication was clear: loyalty to the government meant loyalty to ZANU. The ministers in Mugabe's government had openly campaigned for and were in the process of creating a one-party state. In January 1981, the Zimbabwean government created the Mass Media Trust and purchased all the major newspapers in the country including the *Herald*. Throughout the course of 1981, the paper and its editorial board extolled the virtues of a one-party state for the betterment of the future of the country.[104] ZANU was the government; the two were inseparable, and so by design the ZNA would also have to be loyal to ZANU.

The end of the integration exercise passed unceremoniously in November 1981. The last of the ZNA battalions graduated from basic training during the first week of November. There was no mention of the graduation in the *Herald*; the first report of the end of the exercise was an article that announced that both the British and Korean military training teams would remain in Zimbabwe past integration.[105] However, the article was far from flattering; it exposed the financial commitment made by each country in the military training process:

> Mr. Mugabe has several times praised the British for their help in training the four infantry brigades, and the Koreans for their willingness to equip and train the fifth brigade. About 160 British instructors had come to Zimbabwe and a little over 100 Koreans. The British were paid by the United Kingdom government while the Koreans were paid by Zimbabwe in return for having supplied several million dollars' worth of arms.[106]

This attempt to demonstrate the high level of commitment that North Korea had made to Zimbabwe was not the first time that the Zimbabwean government called out the decline in British aid. In the "Army Review" series of articles in the *Herald* dated 6 October, the article on BMATT were lukewarm in tone. It pointed out that while the British had sponsored a number of Zimbabwean soldiers in courses in Britain, this number had dramatically declined over the past year and would continue to do so.[107] The language of reconciliation that had been the order of the day only a year ago had simply fallen away. Mugabe and his ministers spoke plainly in public about their intentions for a one-party state, as well as the need of the army to be loyal to that state. Concurrently, government ministers and the state-controlled media slowly began to expose the lack of support from Britain in the areas of military assistance and funds for land reform.

By November 1981, however, Margaret Thatcher's government decided that military aid was not the best way to gain influence in Zimbabwe. In a letter to Mugabe at the beginning of November, Thatcher outlined the level of commitment that the British government displayed in support of the reconstruction in Zimbabwe. The focus of her comments was the £20 million the British pledged to Zimbabwe to support land resettlement.[108] She made it very clear to Mugabe that this was the largest British aid program in Africa, and that it demonstrated a very firm British commitment to the future of Zimbabwe. Mugabe, the consummate politician, made sure that he thanked Thatcher for her support of Zimbabwe. Yet he did not muzzle his ministers or the newspapers in their criticism of the British, and by extension the whites who remained in Zimbabwe.[109] As Mugabe had played political games with Palmer, Byatt, and Walls when he denied being able to control the inflammatory partisan statements of his ministers; he played the same game with the Iron Lady.

Only a week after *The Times* reported that the military integration exercise was completed, the government announced that the ZNA would shrink by twenty thousand soldiers over the course of the next year.[110] Interestingly enough, this move by the ZANU government passed unnoticed in the government-controlled press in Salisbury. While *The Times* reported that the men who were demobilized were volunteers, the reality was far different. While some ZANLA men were forced out of the army, for the most part it was former ZIPRA fighters who received involuntary discharges. Joshua Nkomo recounted one incident where he was asked to go and speak to a group of ZNA soldiers who had been selected for discharge but had refused to leave their posts.[111] Nkomo was able to convince the men to lay down their arms and accept that they were to be discharged. However, as he was driving away, he saw that the men were being told to take off their army uniforms and change into civilian clothes on the public road at the front gate. The men not only were targeted because of their political affiliation during the war but also were publicly humiliated. This intentionally emasculated these men by indicating publicly that they did not possess the same martial spirit that ZANLA men did, and were not allowed to wear their uniforms on their return trip home (which was com-, mon practice at the time).[112]

These incidents focused on undermining the position of ZAPU supporters (mostly Ndebele's people) in Zimbabwe. Such practices became more and more common in 1983 when the Fifth Brigade was committed to Matabeleland. Since there were British officers attached to most of the ZNA battalions, these events were reported to the BMATT headquarters. After the end of the initial training phase of the integration exercise, the FCO and the MOD needed to reevaluate what kind of role they were playing in Zimbabwe, particularly considering Thatcher's decision to focus on civil aid. In doing so, they needed to consider the situation in Zimbabwe as it stood in December 1981.

The fissures in the ZNA were increasingly problematic. While fewer and fewer white officers remained in the army, racial problems were still cause for concern. In mid-November Captain Frank Gericke, the man responsible for the destruction of the ZNA armory, escaped from prison with the assistance of a senior officer of the Zimbabwe Republic Police Criminal Investigation Division.[113] This type of subversion from within one of the most elite organizations in the Zimbabwean Security Forces worried Mugabe and his government and made them increasingly suspicious of whites. On 5 December 1981, an odd event occurred at the officers' mess at the ZNA headquarters. Some white officers attempted to hold two events, and black officers were invited to both; however, none of the black officers who were invited decided to attend. General Mujuru caught wind of these events and personally intervened, claiming that "relics of colonialism were on display."[114] The European mess officer was arrested, and the rest of the group was detained overnight on charges that they were involved in subversive activities.

As the racial tensions in the army grew, the white officers who remained seemed simply to be waiting until they could qualify for their pensions.[115] Very few were committed to the task of training the ZNA to a high standard. However, a small number of European officers committed themselves to the future of the Zimbabwean regime. Colonel Lionel Dyck commanded a company of the Rhodesian African Rifles in 1980 and went on to command the Zimbabwe Parachute Battalion. He continued to serve in the Zimbabwe National Army well into the late 1980s and was implicated in the atrocities committed by the Mugabe regime in Matabeleland throughout the decade.[116] Some white personnel remained in the special units of the ZNA into the 1990s.[117]

The Fifth Brigade had been relatively well concealed from the Zimbabwean public until December 1981, when news of tourists being harassed by members of the unit surfaced.[118] Four British tourists accidentally drove into a restricted area, where they were accosted by a group of soldiers from the Fifth Brigade. The soldiers ransacked the car the tourists were traveling in and then assaulted them. Only direct intervention by Colonel Prentice Shiri kept the situation from getting any more out of hand.[119] This was an early sign of the type of problems stemming from lack of discipline from which the brigade suffered. However, it is not surprising considering the level and quality of training the soldiers received from the North Koreans. The Zimbabweans themselves complained about the unprofessional conduct of the Korean trainers, who insisted that the Zimbabwean government pay for their expensive liquor-fueled outings.[120] There also were continuous problems because of the language barrier between the Zimbabwean soldiers and the Korean trainers. Yet, these issues were not unusual; the Australians had come to the conclusion as early as July 1981 that the North Korean foray into Zimbabwe would be militarily counterproductive. The Australian Office of National Assessments (ONA) concluded that the creation of the Fifth Brigade would only further destabilize the country. Additionally, the ONA asserted that the only real utility of the Fifth Brigade was as ZANU's "private army and a counter-weight to the British trained ZNA.[121] Even so, this assessment was not passed along to the British government because it was classified as for "Australian Eyes Only."

The British government continued along the path it set well over a year before with its military assistance plan. British officers remained as advisers with the ZNA battalions in an attempt to set them on the proper path in the areas of training and administration. As had been the case in

June, BMATT officers posted to battalions quickly realized that most of the ZNA battalions were incapable of operating as military units.[122] Even though these units needed advanced training, most of the ZANLA officers had no interest in following BMATT's recommendations.

The security situation in Zimbabwe became more tense in the first months of 1982. While racial tensions had escalated in the army in December 1981 and continued into January, factional tensions in Zimbabwe as a whole became the leading cause for concern in February 1982.[123] Early in the month, Mugabe's government announced that it found no fewer than thirty-five arms caches on property either controlled by ZAPU or owned by party leaders.[124] Mugabe claimed that ZAPU's leadership was planning a military coup in concert with the remaining whites in the country.[125] Nkomo and other ZANU leaders denied any connection to the caches and pointed out that weapons stores had been discovered all over the country, and no one had even bothered to find out to whom they belonged.[126]

Even though there was no concrete evidence linking ZAPU with a planned military coup, the die was cast. ZANU used these arms caches as ammunition to destroy its rival party. In December 1981, ZANU, and by extension the Zimbabwean government, made a very simple case to the public that the party was under attack. South African agents exacerbated the situation when they planted a bomb at the ZANU party headquarters in Salisbury.[127]

Nkomo was dismissed from the cabinet on 18 February.[128] The deputy commander of the ZNA, Lieutenant General Lookout Masuku, was arrested, along with other high-ranking ZAPU army officers, for allegedly plotting against the government. However, this was only the beginning; at the time, former ZIPRA men made up roughly 30 percent of the officer corps in the army. Many ZIPRA officers were battalion commanders, deputy brigade commanders, or chiefs of staff. While not at the highest levels of command, these positions held significant influence over the daily operations of the army. The Central Intelligence Organization and the Special Branch targeted midlevel and low-level officers for both arrest and harassment. Publicly, the government made statements that there would be no retribution against former ZIPRA men in the security forces; however, the reality was far different. In September 1982, the Mechanized Battalion of the Second Brigade was purged of all ZIPRA men. The unit had equal thirds RSF, ZIPRA, and ZANLA soldiers. More than 250 soldiers were sent elsewhere in the ZNA; many ended up being discharged. The Mechanized Battalion functioned well up until that point, but its readiness dropped dramatically after the ZIPRA purge.[129]

This became common practice in the army; even ZIPRA men who were not personally attacked or harassed saw what was happening around them and simply left the army. Unfortunately, there are no statistics available that shed light on how many ZIPRA men deserted. By the end of 1983 the ZNA reduced its size from almost sixty-five thousand to fifty thousand soldiers. Based on the accounts available from ZNA soldiers at the time, it seems that the vast majority of those who left were ZIPRA men.[130] This is not to say that there was a Soviet-style purge of the army. The intimidation was localized and kept out of the media, but it was not hidden from BMATT. British officers were well aware of what was occurring, but they often felt that all they could do was attempt to keep the situation from getting worse. Major General Colin Shortis, who commanded BMATT from January 1982 until June 1983, commented that BMATT continued to encourage Mujuru and the ZNA to pursue their demobilization plan more vigorously. Mujuru's solution was to "parade all officers and demob all the ZIPRA officers. We can reduce the army and solve the ZIPRA problem."[131] Shortis was able to convince the defense minister that the army would be far worse off than it already was if it lost that many officers. Yet this attitude toward ZIPRA had become an institutional norm in the ZANLA-controlled ZNA. During this same period, Mugabe met with Thatcher in London. At their meeting she restated the British commitment to Zimbabwe and promised that her government intended to continue supporting Mugabe's government with both military and civil aid.[132] By December 1981, BMATT was down to seventy-three soldiers; in light of the rising factionalism in the army and the renewed commitment by Thatcher, thirty-four more advisers were dispatched from Britain in October 1982.[133]

ZANU supporters in the army were not the only targets of the Mugabe regime; civilians also suffered for their political associations. On 26 July 1982, South African agents infiltrated Thornhill Airbase and destroyed ten AFZ planes, including four newly arrived BAE Hawk jet aircraft.[134] The destruction of these aircraft and six Hawker Hunter fighters was a huge blow to the AFZ. This led to a loss in confidence in white officers in the AFZ. The commander, Air Marshal Norman Walsh, and other senior white officers were arrested and imprisoned for more than a year before the Mugabe government released them.

In July 1982, the Mugabe government claimed it had to reinstate the Emergency Powers Act because there was such a dramatic increase in sabotage, banditry, and other violent acts committed by ZAPU dissidents.[135] The act protected members of the security forces from any form of prosecution for acts committed combating dissident forces.[136] In a way, Mugabe was correct. There had been a rise in the activities of the South African–trained fighters, known at the time as Super ZIPRA.[137] Of course, all the operations involving Super ZIPRA were part of Operation DRAMA. Even so, there were never more than about 120 men active in the Super ZIPRA program. Still, for the most part, ZIPRA men who had fled the army or simply taken their demobilization settlement returned to their homes. Since ZAPU largely represented those who either were Ndebele men or had aligned themselves politically with the Ndebele group, the bastion of ZAPU supporters resided in the southern part of the country known as Matabeleland.

In order for Mugabe to secure power in the country and accomplish his goal of a one-party state, he needed to break this region of opposition. The dismissal of Nkomo from the cabinet and the arrest of high-level ZAPU military leaders helped criminalize the leadership element of the party. Now, he had to deal with the rank and file. The true purpose of the Fifth Brigade finally materialized in December 1982; after the brigade graduated from its training program, it deployed to Matabeleland North the following month.[138] A number of other ZNA units also deployed in a supporting role. Counting South African–trained Super ZIPRA, there were never more than roughly two hundred dissidents operating in the Matabeleland area.[139] The Fifth Brigade embarked on a campaign of rape, murder, pillage, and a variety of other shameful acts over the course of the next year. During the first six weeks of the Fifth Brigade's time in Matabeleland, its soldiers killed roughly two thousand civilians.[140] Publicly, the British played down these incidents. When a crew from the British TV show *Panorama* interviewed Colonel Charles Ivey, he addressed the stories of the atrocities by casting doubt on the reports, saying, "There are stories in Matabeleland and there are stories in Ireland and you want to believe who writes what story?"[141] The British commander was doing his best to turn a blind eye to the excesses that occurred in Matabeleland, in order to preserve a tenuous diplomatic and military relationship with the Mugabe government.

Conclusion

The atrocities that occurred throughout Matabeleland over the course of the next decade killed somewhere between ten thousand and twenty thousand people.[142] Mugabe's knowledge of what occurred in the area is also quite certain. Not only did the Fifth Brigade get its orders directly from the prime minister's office, but a former ZNA officer, Lieutenant Colonel Esau Sibanda, confirmed that Mugabe received a daily briefing of the brigade's activities throughout its deployment.[143] Other units of the ZNA also participated in the atrocities, some in a supporting role, others in a much more direct manner. From the beginning of the atrocities in Matabeleland, both the British government and the US government were aware of the excesses of Mugabe's troops.[144] The Fifth Brigade deployment and the aftermath were the point at which it became clear that the British had failed in their military mission. The goal from the beginning had been to secure British influence in the Zimbabwean security apparatus and create a military force divorced from political parties and domestic politics. In fact, what had occurred over the course of the first three years of independence was that a completely politicized military force had been created that acted as the military arm of the party in power.

The British government prioritized military assistance in its 1981 Defence Statement. The government considered assistance requests based on the following considerations: "the United Kingdom's strategic interests, the nature of our defense relationship with the country concerned, and whether their armed forces operate similarly to our own and use British equipment."[145] In mid-1983, Zimbabwe met only the first of the four criteria. By this point, the defense relationship between Britain and Zimbabwe was growing tense. The Zimbabweans seemed to know they needed the British for their technical proficiency but wanted none of their policy advice. The ZNA was leaning closer and closer to operating like a communist-style force, with its introduction of political commissars into the military, the prevalence of party membership being connected to promotion prospects, and the rigidity of the command structure. In the Soviet Army officer corps, there was an intimate connection to the party that prevented the officer corps from being a professional organization, in part because it lacked the autonomy to maintain its own standards. By this point, the same can be said of the ZNA. Since officers who were not members of ZANU could not rise beyond the rank of colonel, it was almost impossible for the army to be professional.[146]

During Operation AGILA in 1979, the British had high hopes that Zimbabwe would be an African success story. They imagined that the existing infrastructure could create a professional force that stayed out of domestic politics. The training that they conducted gave the Zimbabweans a framework for a military force, but it had not made any significant impact on the culture of the Zimbabwean military. The ZNA culture resembled the revolutionary guerrilla forces that preceded it, more than a professional military force. Promotion, posting, and other benefits came from political patronage and proximity to the ruling elite in ZANU, rather than to any sort of professional excellence.

In both Kenya and Zambia, the British recognized that the officers most willing to work with them were men whom they brought to the United Kingdom and trained in British military institutions. The connections these men had to the traditions instilled in them at Sandhurst and Mons were not easily broken. These officers not only were more likely to work with the British but also were better trained than those who underwent brief commissioning courses in their own country. Finally, many of the African officers in both Kenya and Zambia who trained at Sandhurst were firmly committed to remaining aloof from domestic politics. This was one of the many hard lessons the British Army, the FCO, and the MOD had learned since 1945 in training African armies. Yet in spite of this knowledge, BMATT, the FCO, and the MOD overestimated their ability to project training power in Zimbabwe, with only thin resources. Relying on influence that it did not have, the British government felt confident that it would be able to curry favor with the new Zimbabwean government through only minimal military assistance.

Britain's failure in Zimbabwe was clear to many observers by 1983. While the British managed to place British officers as the army commanders in both Kenya and Zambia, they were not able to do so in Zimbabwe. After the arrest of Air Marshal Walsh, the Zimbabwean government replaced him with a Pakistani officer, Air Marshal Mohammed Azim Daudpota. The British government was no longer the primary resource for military training and resources for the Zimbabwean government. The North Koreans and the Chinese were the major arms suppliers; the Pakistanis provided a significant amount of professional education to Zimbabwean senior leaders.

Even though much of the world protested the actions of the Mugabe government in Matabeleland by February 1983, the British refused to retract their military assistance program. In September 1983, Margaret Thatcher told the US ambassador to London that even though Britain was not pleased with Mugabe, it would not cut off military aid unless the situation got much more out of hand.[147] That day did not come until 2001, when the Mugabe government seized land from white farmers and began cracking down on Western journalists.[148] The 1981 Defence Statement made it very clear that the British government provided military assistance only to those nations where there were British strategic interests at stake. The displacement of much of the remaining white population seemed to be the last of any lingering strategic interests in Zimbabwe.

Conclusion: Military Assistance as a Diplomatic Weapon

The process of transition from colony to independent nation is fraught with difficulty. One of the biggest challenges is filling the void left by the colonial power in the military and civil administration. This transition is even more difficult when the colonial power leaves, but its progeny remain. Minority settler communities complicate the transition because they are seldom willing to give up their place of privilege in society or government. In Africa, race exacerbated the difficulties. White settlers in African nations maintained power even after the end of colonialism; often it was the type of power that changed. Political power gave way to economic power, and even though many settlers left their African homes after independence, it was the protection of those who remained that became a cornerstone of British strategy in these former colonies.

The relationships developed in Kenya and Zambia, while strained at times, persisted throughout the twentieth century. While both Kenya and Zambia had relationships with the Eastern Bloc and at times built military ties that temporarily supplanted their relationship with the West, British influence persisted in the military sphere. The Kenya Army continues to send selected officer cadets to Sandhurst even though it has its own military academy. Between independence and 2009, Kenya sent 103 and Zambia sent 43 officers to Sandhurst for training.[1] These numbers do not include officers sent to Britain for staff college or other specialist courses. However influential senior or specialist courses are, they seldom leave the same impression as the foundational military experience that these cadets had at Sandhurst. These training links are the bedrock of the British military-to-military influence in both Zambia and Kenya and have helped sustain relationships in periods of tension. The 1980s were a period of grave tension between Britain and many African nations. This was in no small part due to Thatcher's lack of interest Africa, and her callousness in the face African complaints about apartheid.

As the 1980s continued, British strategic interests in Zimbabwe quickly faded away. By 1990, China was both Zimbabwe's largest arms supplier and the largest supplier of weapons to the third world.[2] BMATT remained in Zimbabwe, but its role dramatically changed by the late 1980s and early 1990s. The difference for the British came in April 1982 when the Argentines invaded the Falkland Islands. The entire military focus of Margret Thatcher's government shifted from Northern Ireland and military assistance around the world to meeting a military challenge in the South Atlantic. This massive military effort pulled resources from across the MOD to liberate the islands. While the Falklands War brought a military victory and was an example of the value of a well-established logistical system, it also exposed some grave weaknesses in British defense. The British government saw the shortcomings of its land, air, and sea systems on the battlefield. The war also refocused the British government's objectives and priorities such as the NATO commitment, independent nuclear deterrents, and out-of-area operations. The defense budget did rise during the remainder of the 1980s; however, the additional funds were to make up for war losses and to address communication, equipment, and training issues that were discovered during the conflict. The British Army refocused itself on the continental commitment, home defense, and contingency operations outside of the NATO area.[3]

All this meant that Britain was even less focused on military assistance missions than it had been in 1980. After the departure of Major General Shortis as BMATT commander in June 1983, the mission was downgraded. His replacement was a brigadier whose primary focus was staff training.[4] The mission continued well into the 1990s, while the quality of the Zimbabwean forces continued to deteriorate. By the early 1990s, the once-skilled AFZ and Zimbabwean Parachute Battalion were shadows of their former selves, no longer having the skills and capacity to train their own parachute jump instructors) or pathfinders. American Special Forces trainers provided this training to the ZNA and AFZ. One American soldier recounted that the Zimbabwean Special Air Service was quite skilled and professional, but the parachute battalion was at a very low state of readiness. While US soldiers conducted a jump with the Parachute

Battalion, both the pilot and the Zimbabwean pathfinder on the ground miscalculated, and the troopers were dropped on the Harare International Airport parking lot rather than the military drop zone.[5]

The ZNA deployed on active service against RENAMO in Mozambique throughout the 1980s, which took a tremendous toll on the force itself and its feeble logistical system.[6] Zimbabwean forces also deployed on a number of UN missions throughout Africa, including Somalia, South Sudan, and Liberia. In 1998, Mugabe committed himself and his army to support Laurent Kabila, the president of the Democratic Republic of the Congo. The Second Congo War was a tremendous drain on Zimbabwean resources. Government ministers made financial deals with the Kabila government for both land and diamond mining claims.[7] The five-year conflict drained the resources of the cash-poor nation at a time when Zimbabwe was in a difficult economic situation. Zimbabwean special operations forces and the AFZ were a tremendous asset in the conflict, but the Mugabe government could not sustain the $15 million monthly expense.[8] The experience wore down the ZNA and had a dramatic impact on its readiness.

The position of the military in Africa has been the source of volumes of research over the course of the last fifty years. Claude Welch separated military involvement in Africa into three broad categories: the nonpolitical army, resentment against neocolonialism, and coups d'état.[9] Interestingly, the ZNA does not fall precisely into any of these categories. The ZNA was completely politicized by the mid-1980s and never feared neocolonialism because the former colonial masters did not exert real influence in Zimbabwe. Of course, the political nature of the ZNA made sure that until 2017 there was no attempted coup d'état against the government. In November 2017 the Zimbabwean military vehicles rolled through the streets of Harare, seizing the facilities of the state broadcast corporation. While the military leaders insisted that what they were doing was explicitly not a coup d'état, it very closely resemble one. The military did not seize power, but it facilitated Mugabe's removal and the installation of Emmerson Mnangagwa as president.[10] Mnangagwa, one of Mugabe's closest confidants since the liberation war, was not a soldier but a politician who worked closely with the military and security services for years. While the coup did remove Mugabe from power, military officers were motivated to do so to reassert the status quo ante prior to the emergence of younger political leaders who lacked roots in the liberation war. The military wanted to preserve its privileged place in Zimbabwean society and remain firmly ensconced in the political future of the nation.[11]

One issue that feeds military involvement in domestic politics is a lack of professionalism. A high level of professionalism generally is one of the primary barriers for military involvement in democratic states. Herbert Howe points out that unprofessional forces have a far greater tendency to become involved in domestic politics or to be the enforcement arm of a repressive regime.[12] Zimbabwe, like many other African nations, was guilty of exhibiting many of the factors that Howe highlights as preventing professionalism in the military: the ethnicization of the military, domestic deployments, a lack of foreign threats, and the advent of personal rule of the country.[13]

Mugabe's personal rule in Zimbabwe broke down one of the key components of military professionalism, the partition of civil and military affairs. From the beginning of the integration exercise, the military was involved in civil affairs. Operation SEED put soldiers to work in the exclusively civilian world of economic development. The use of ZNA in fighting dissidents and putting down domestic political opposition in Matabeleland blurred the line forever for Zimbabwean soldiers. By the mid-1980s, the majority of the soldiers in the ZNA had received some form of political indoctrination designed by the ZANU leadership. The ZNA lacked an external perspective; its focus was on both internal politics and internal threats to the regime. This outlook created further problems within the military system. As one British officer put it, Western commanders work through their staffs, relying on their staff officers to keep them informed so they can make the best decisions possible. However, he noted that in Zimbabwe, knowledge is power; therefore, giving up knowledge is ceding power. Zimbabwean commanders hoarded knowledge and kept it from their staff officers and other commanders.[14] This created endemic problems within the military system that, at times, had the potential to bring the entire machine to a standstill.

This was most apparent in the support services; the Zimbabweans were unable to provide sufficient logistical support for the ZNA. At the outset of independence, officers from the settler community kept the logistical system functioning. However, as the army swelled to a size that was well beyond what the ZNA logistical system was designed to support, the quality of support services dropped dramatically. This issue was inflamed by the loss of knowledge possessed by European officers who left the army. By the early 1990s, the main priority for BMATT was to help fix the logistical system.[15] ZNA officers who were focused on advancing their careers through political appointments to higher command were not interested in professional development in support areas. These types of jobs required significant technical expertise and education, whereas command in line units did not. So even though the British were expending a great deal of time developing support officers, the investment did not come with much of a return. Officers in the support services were not likely to rise to positions of influence in the Zimbabwean security services. Therefore, those who spent the most time with British officers or on British courses were likely to be the least influential on a national scale.

This raises an important questions regarding the use of military assistance programs overseas by countries like the United Kingdom and the United States. What is the real purpose, and how comprehensive do these programs have to be in order to be effective? There are different sets of goals at each level of government. In each case examined in this study, ministries seemed to have the same basic goal: to buy British influence with military assistance. The MOD sought currency in the military-to-military sphere, and the FCO in the international relations realm. However, for those at the country level or the military training team level, the goal was to create a stable environment, while also achieving British influence. HMG intended to establish functioning democracies out of the former African colonies. In a democracy, military professionalism and noninvolvement in the political process are key components in maintaining civilian control of security forces. In the eyes of those British officers on the ground, it was imperative to ingrain professionalism into the officers of the African forces, as was demonstrated by the British teams in all three examples in this study.

Zimbabwean officers who exhibited the most professionalism in all these cases were also the men who received the most substantive and professional training. What constitutes professional training? Oftentimes it is outside of the control of the beneficiary government, as was the case in Zimbabwe when BMATT wanted to implement a staff training program for all officers, including senior officers. However, the intervention of Zimbabwean political leaders kept the most senior guerrilla officers (who were politically appointed) from any sort of training or evaluation program. Officer training in Zimbabwe was conducted under the supervision of the Mugabe government, and therefore officers were susceptible to the political pressures at play throughout the training. Yet in both Kenya and Zambia, the British removed officer candidates from the country and brought them to the United Kingdom for training at either Mons or Sandhurst. These courses, which were either six months or twenty-four months, indoctrinated students into the Western view of military professionalism, which encouraged an aloofness from domestic politics and a focus on technical skill. Additionally, African officers in Kenya and Zambia were given progressively higher levels of responsibility at an accelerated rate, from the lowest officer rank up to higher levels of command. This phase of training and development was absent in Zimbabwe. Those who had achieved senior rank in guerrilla armies through political maneuvering maintained that rank in the ZNA. The carryover and continuation of a politicized officer corps in Zimbabwe directly affected the ability of the British trainers to carry out their mission of professionalizing the force and establishing British influence.

Did policy makers in London recognize that they needed to instill professionalism in an officer corps in order for it to function as a subordinate element to the elected civilian government? The Colonial Office considered establishing a military academy to train officers in Kenya in 1960, as Ghana had done. However, it decided against this plan because it felt that an academy in Kenya would not meet the high standard of training that cadets received at either Mons or Sandhurst. Additionally, those in the MOD and the Colonial Office recognized that those African officers who trained at Sandhurst often attempted to replicate their experience in their home nation. So, if the first several cohorts of Kenyan or Zambian officers trained in the United Kingdom, they would return to their home countries and attempt to replicate their time at Sandhurst in their own officer training programs. As discussed in chapters 1 and 2, the MOD and the Colonial Office preferred that African officers undergo extensive training rather than short training courses that accelerated Africanization.

In 1964, however, the British learned that longer training courses and slow Africanization had certain shortcomings. The East African mutinies of 1964 were, in part, caused by the continued presence of British officers in command roles in the independent armies. If the soldiers did not see change after independence, they tended to believe that colonialism had simply continued. British intervention in East Africa had significant monetary and political costs. The MOD, Colonial Office, and Foreign Office did not want to repeat the events of 1964 in any other African country. The result was an increased focus on Africanization over professionalization. The desire to decrease the likelihood that British forces would need to intervene in Africa also ensured that the British were less committed to leaving their colonies with an officer corps that was able to separate military from civil affairs.

In many ways the training missions in both Kenya and Zambia were successful. The British were able to maintain a significant amount of influence, as well as supply both countries with a wide variety of military weapons. In comparison to places like Uganda and Nigeria, the military has remained largely removed from domestic politics. In fact, on numerous occasions the Zambia Army has put down coup attempts that originated from within its own ranks.[16] The British continue to enjoy a fruitful military relationship with both countries, Kenya in particular. The British Army Training Unit Kenya trains thousands of British soldiers every year in battalion-size live fire exercises. In 2021 the British government committed to building a £70 million headquarters, as well as new accommodations.[17] Kenya has also developed into a critical counterterrorism partner in East Africa. Kenyan troops work with both British and American forces trying to counter violent extremist threats in the region.

However, Zimbabwe took a wildly different course than either of the other two examples discussed here. The focus of policy makers at the time was how to reconcile these former enemies into one army. While this was a concern, the primary goal of the military mission was to create a functional and professional army that gave the British a modicum of influence inside Zimbabwe. In the planning stages, the FCO and the MOD looked at the examples of both Kenya and Zambia and discounted them because they lacked the integration of an opposing force. Yet in doing so the British government turned a blind eye to all the lessons learned in these training missions. The fact that opposing forces were integrated in Zimbabwe overshadowed the many similarities to previous British training missions in Africa. In my interviews, various military officers who have knowledge of the subject and even some scholars, insisted that the integration aspect of the Zimbabwean mission makes the experience without comparison.

However, the similarities of the situations in the three examples described in this study have more than merited the comparison of these cases. More specifically, while there were differences in Zimbabwe in the collective training of the forces involved, the British ignored all the lessons they learned about the individual training of officers and technical personnel.

The importance of professional training for African officers was subjugated to the desire by the British to extricate themselves from Zimbabwe as quickly and cheaply as possible. Rather than relying on a comprehensive military mission with officers on loan service and extensive training programs in the United Kingdom, the British government attempted to execute a similar mission to those in Kenya and Zambia at a fraction of the cost and time required. Instead of trying to buy influence with an extensive aid package, the British government relied on buying influence with prestige and the continued presence of the settler community. The offer of a small military training team and limited arms sales to Zimbabwe did not create the type of dependence that the British needed to create in order to wield the political influence they desired.

During her ministry, Margaret Thatcher intended for Britain to be a bastion of strength against communism. She valued three things above all others in foreign affairs: increased respect for Britain as a leading power, a close alliance with the United States, and skepticism about closer ties with Europe.[18] The partnership with the United States and the maintenance of an independent nuclear deterrent were important components of Thatcher's policy to fight the influence of communism in the world. However, the United Kingdom was not a superpower like the United States or the Soviet Union. Military aid packages from one of these superpowers created dependency that bought compliance, to a degree. US military aid to the Shah in Iran, the Saigon government until 1975, and Manuel Noriega in Panama all produced results for a time. Soviet military aid created an even higher degree of dependence. For example, in Ethiopia the government was unable to afford any other supplier because of the reasonable grant conditions and the variety of equipment available.[19] The downfall was that there were no maintenance packages, and the Soviets dictated what equipment the Ethiopians received, which was not necessarily what they needed. The Ethiopian Army had far too many tanks and interceptor aircraft and not enough counterinsurgency equipment.

As demonstrated in Kenya and Zambia, effective military assistance programs were expensive long-term commitments. British officers serving on loan service to both armies were present almost a decade after independence. In Kenya, British officers continue to serve on loan service at the Kenya Army Staff College. As the empire fell away, so did a great deal of Britain's ability to project power; as this waned, an exclusive military partnership with Britain carried little weight. The United Kingdom simply could not compete with the Chinese or the Soviets by 1980 as a purveyor of military hardware and training. HMG and Thatcher did not recognize this reality, particularly with regard to Zimbabwe. The goals of the British government in Zimbabwe outmatched what was possible to achieve with the scant resources allocated. Even though London had significant policy goals when they sent BMATT to Zimbabwe, the officers on the ground treaded lightly with the party in power.

The British government never directly confronted Mugabe regarding the atrocities in Matabeleland. The high commissioner at the time said that it would be counterproductive to push Mugabe on the issue of the activities of the Fifth Brigade: "I think to have protested to Mugabe or to have gone on record as not liking what was going on there would not have been helpful. Mugabe would have resented it very acutely."[20] The guidance from the government was simply to look the other way. Even the US government was concerned about the atrocities that occurred in Matabeleland. However, when the US ambassador to the United Kingdom broached the issue with Thatcher, he discovered that the British were not planning on leaving Zimbabwe unless things got much worse.[21]

Interestingly enough, the British government felt comfortable applying pressure at all levels when white AFZ officers were imprisoned after the sabotage of the Hawkes in 1983. Not only did Thatcher write directly to Mugabe asking him to release these men, but the British government also threatened to cut off military assistance if he did not comply. After divesting themselves of responsibility for Zimbabwe as a colonial relic, the British government's true interests in the region were extremely limited. On the surface it would seem that the British wanted to keep communism and other bad actors out of southern Africa. However, as time went by, the British were less and less committed to this goal. It was common knowledge that the North Koreans trained the Fifth Brigade; however, their training mission expanded beyond this single unit. In June 1982, the North Korean training team assisted in the establishment of the Zimbabwe

People's Militia.[22] The stated goal of the organization was to "mobilize all Zimbabweans to be loyal to the ruling party and Government."[23] The Zimbabwe People's Militia formed the reserve component of the ZNA. By the end of 1983, the North Korean Military Training Mission was responsible for training a far higher percentage of ZNA than was BMATT.

By the middle of the 1980s, communist nations in East Asia had overtaken Britain as the primary purveyors of military hardware and training. In spite of this development, the British government remained committed to a presence in Zimbabwe in the security sector. Even though the Thatcher government threatened to withdraw military assistance in 1984, such a plan did not come to fruition. The threat of the withdrawal of aid did not deter Mugabe's actions in Matabeleland in 1984, nor did the final withdrawal of British trainers in 2001 stop the land occupations that displaced most of the remaining white farmers in Zimbabwe. Even though the British demonstrated their military power in the Falklands in 1982, it was clear to many observers that the British government was not capable of that kind of unilateral intervention on a regular basis. The British government had been unable to support the movement of the Commonwealth Monitoring Force to Zimbabwe and had to ask the United States to provide airlift assets. Most British military operations since the Falklands War have been multinational efforts under the banner of the United Nations, the European Union, or NATO.

Unilateral deployments of forces outside of the United Kingdom have been limited in both scale and scope; Operation PALLISER in Sierra Leone involved one battalion from the Parachute Regiment and a Special Air Service squadron. Operation PALLISER assisted the United Nations mission in Sierra Leon. The Parachute Regiment deployed to cover the evacuation of civilians from the capital. British politicians in the 1980s behaved as if they had the ability to replicate the Falklands operation at a moment's notice. However, other nations, such as Zimbabwe, recognized that British power had long since faded. The embarrassment of Suez in 1957 was a stain on British legitimacy in the world. Nations like Zimbabwe were in a position to accept aid from Britain and the nonaligned powers as long as they kept clear of the conflict between the United States and the Soviet Union. Mugabe's decision to avoid the USSR and Cuba as sources of military training and aid was a shrewd political move that kept him from attracting the ire of the United States. Additionally, his maintenance of the status quo with South Africa kept both Britain and the United States from being in an awkward position in their very delicate dealings with Pretoria.

Prime Minister Thatcher and the diplomats in the Foreign Service grew up in an era when British forces were able to extinguish security threats that flared up across a vast empire. Operations in Palestine, Malaya, Kenya, Oman, Belize, and many other places were commonplace throughout the 1950s and 1960s. The 1970s and 1980s were an era of security stagnation for Britain; the forces focused on operations in Northern Ireland and commitments to NATO on the Continent. The international prestige of British power decayed right alongside the declining British economy and defense budgets. The British desire to remain a prominent player on the world's stage outpaced the country's military capability in the late 1980s and 1990s. After the 1981 Defense Review, the House of Commons did not examine security policy until the end of the Cold War. The 1990 *Options for Change* report came at the insistence of the service chiefs who were looking for cost-saving measures.[24] The continental commitment and the overall size of the army were targets for reduction. Even so, requests for British military trainers in southern Africa continued. British teams traveled to both Namibia and South Africa, in 1990 and 1994, respectively. The teams in both of these instances were only a fraction of the size of what BMATT Zimbabwe had been.[25] However, in both cases British officers served in more of a supervisory role than an actual training role. The next time the British government undertook a training mission as ambitious as the one in Zimbabwe was in Afghanistan in 2002 in coordination with the United States; it required the deployment of 10 percent of the army.

The tragedies that occurred in Zimbabwe from 1965 to 1987 were an early indication of the decline of British power in the world. Whereas London previously was able to use military assistance as a weapon in the Cold War, economic decline and an unwillingness to spend limited defense funds on assistance programs sterilized the effectiveness of the programs. In a world where the coffers of rogue states were open to those willing to flout the designs of the West, trainers who did not bring money and equipment with them were simply an opportunity to exploit. In Zimbabwe the British hoped that the military would remain uninvolved in domestic politics but supported a democratic system. However, what they enabled was a politicized military force that supported the foundation of Mugabe's authoritarian state. The British idea of democratizing through military professionalism worked in a European context; it was far less effective when those whom the British intended to influence were not overpowered by British culture. As in many cases, the most effective tool that the British government could bring to bear in a military assistance scheme was the weight of hundreds of years of military history and culture, reaching all the way back to Oliver Cromwell's reforms of his army.

NOTES

INTRODUCTION

1. Luise White, "'Whoever Saw a Country with Four Armies?': The Battle of Bulawayo Revisited," *Journal of Southern African Studies* 33 (September 2007): 619–631.

2. Daniel Compagnon, *A Predictable Tragedy: Robert Mugabe and the Collapse of Zimbabwe* (Philadelphia: University of Pennsylvania Press, 2011), 24–25.

3. Martin Meredith, *The Fate of Africa from the Hopes of Freedom to the Heart of Despair: A History of 50 Years of Independence* (New York: Public Affairs, 2005), 622–624; Hazel Cameron, "The Matabeleland Massacres: Britain's Wilful Blindness," *International History Review* 40 (2017): 1–19.

4. Ashley Jackson, "British-African Defence and Security Concerns," *Defence Studies* 6 (September 2006): 351–376.

5. Timothy Parsons, *The African Rank-and-File: Social Implications of Colonial Military Service in the King's African Rifles, 1902–1964* (Portsmouth, NH: Heinemann, 1999).

6. Ian Smith, *The Great Betrayal: The Memoirs of Ian Douglas Smith* (London: Blake Publishing, 1997), 3.

7. Anthony Clayton and David Killingray, *Khaki and Blue: Military and Police in British Colonial Africa* (Athens: Ohio University Center for International Studies, 1989).

8. Anthony Clayton, *France, Soldiers and Africa* (London: Brassey's Defence Publishers, 1988); Myron Echenberg, *Colonial Conscripts: The Tirailleurs Senegalais in French West Africa, 1857–1960* (Portsmouth, NH: Heinemann, 1990); Nancy Lawler, *Soldiers of Misfortune: Ivoirien Tirailleurs of World War II* (Athens: Ohio University Press, 1992); Charles J. Balesi, *From Adversaries to Comrades-in-Arms: West Africans and the French Military, 1885–1918* (Waltham, MA: Crossroads Press, 1979).

9. Heather Streets, *Martial Races: The Military, Race and Masculinity in British Imperial Culture, 1857–1914* (Manchester: Manchester University Press, 2005); Timothy Parsons, "'Wakamba Warriors Are Soldiers of the Queen': The Evolution of the Kamba as a Martial Race, 1890–1970," *Ethnohistory* 46 (1999): 671–701; Parsons, *African Rank-and-File*; Timothy Parsons, *The 1964 Army Mutinies and the Making of Modern East Africa* (Westport, CT: Praeger, 2003).

10. Parsons, *The 1964 Army Mutinies*.

11. Kenneth Grundy, *Soldiers without Politics: Blacks in the South African Armed Forces* (Berkeley: University of California Press, 1983); Gavin Cawthra, *Brutal Force: The Apartheid War Machine* (London: International Defence and Aid Fund for Southern Africa, 1986); Cynthia Enloe, *Ethnic Soldiers: State Security in Divided Societies* (Athens: University of Georgia Press, 1980).

12. Grundy, *Soldiers without Politics*, 14.

13. P. McLaughlin, "Collaborators, Mercenaries or Patriots? The 'Problem' of

African Troops in Southern Rhodesia during the First and Second World Wars," *Zimbabwean History* 10 (1979): 21–50; P. McLaughlin, "Victims as Defenders: African Troops in the Rhodesian Defence System 1890–1980," *Small Wars and Insurgencies* 2 (1991), 240–275; Paul Moorcraft and Peter McLaughlin, *The Rhodesian War: A Military History* (Johannesburg: Jonathan Ball, 2008); White, "'Whoever Saw a Country with Four Armies?,'" 619–631.

14. Peter Hennessy and Anthony Seldon, "The Attlee Government, 1945–1951," in *Ruling Performance: British Governments from Attlee to Thatcher*, ed. Peter Hennessy and Anthony Seldon (Oxford: Blackwell, 1987), 28–62.

15. David Percox, *Britain, Kenya and the Cold War: Imperial Defence, Colonial Security and Decolonisation* (New York: Tauris Academic Studies, 2004), 22.

16. For an examination of the military campaign in Kenya, see Anthony Clayton, *Counter-insurgency in Kenya: A Study of Military Operations against Mau Mau* (London: Frank Cass, 1976); David Anderson, *Histories of the Hanged: The Dirty War in Kenya and the End of Empire* (New York: W. W. Norton, 2005). Some of the most recent works on Mau Mau are Huw C. Bennett, *Fighting the Mau Mau: The British Army and Counter-insurgency in the Kenya Emergency* (London: Cambridge University Press, 2012), and Daniel Branch, *Defeating Mau Mau, Creating Kenya: Counterinsurgency, Civil War and Decolonization* (London: Cambridge University Press, 2009).

17. Jan Pettman, *Zambia: Security and Conflict* (New York: St. Martin's Press, 1974), 12.

18. L. J. Butler, "The Central African Federation and Britain's Post-war Nuclear Programme: Reconsidering the Connections," *Journal of Imperial and Commonwealth History* 36 (September 2008): 509–525.

19. Donal Lowry, *Oxford Dictionary of National Biography—Welensky, Sir Ronald [Roy] (1907–1991), Prime Minister of the Federation of Rhodesia and Nyasaland*, November 2004, http://www.oxforddnb.com/view/printable/50688.

20. Philip E. Hemming, "Macmillan and the End of the British Empire in Africa," in *Harold Macmillan and Britain's World Role*, ed. Richard Aldous and Sabine Lee (London: Macmillan, 1996), 98.

21. Richard Lamb, *The Macmillan Years, 1957–1963: The Emerging Truth* (London: John Murray, 1995), 246.

22. Lamb, 253.

23. Hemming, "Macmillan and the End of the British Empire in Africa," 100.

24. Hemming, 111.

25. Elaine Windrich, *Britain and the Politics of Rhodesian Independence* (London: Croom Helm, 1978), 16.

26. Pettman, *Zambia*, 107.

27. Pettman, 102.

28. Pettman, 103.

29. Clayton and Killingray, *Khaki and Blue*; Hemming, "Macmillan and the End of the British Empire in Africa"; Robert B. Edgerton, *Africa's Armies from Honor to Infamy: A History from 1791 to the Present* (Cambridge, MA: Westview Press, 2002).

30. Brian Roberts, *Cecil Rhodes: Flawed Colossus* (New York: W. W. Norton, 1987), 39.
31. Robert Blake, *A History of Rhodesia* (New York: Alfred A. Knopf, 1977), 39.
32. Blake, 46.
33. Blake, 46. For a more in-depth look at the early history of Rhodesia and the chartered company, see D. C. De Waal, *With Rhodes in Mashonaland* (Bulawayo: Books of Rhodesia, 1974); John S. Galbraith, *Crown and Charter: The Early Years of the British South Africa Company* (Berkeley: University of California Press, 1974); and Arthur Keppel-Jones, *Rhodes and Rhodesia: The White Conquest of Zimbabwe 1884–1902* (Kingston, ON: McGill-Queen's University Press, 1983).
34. Timothy Stapleton, *No Insignificant Part: The Rhodesian Native Regiment and the East Africa Campaign of the First World War* (Waterloo, ON: Wilfrid Laurier University Press, 2006), 135.
35. Timothy Stapleton, *African Police and Soldiers in Colonial Zimbabwe, 1923–80* (Rochester, NY: University of Rochester Press, 2011), 7–8.
36. McLaughlin, "Collaborators, Mercenaries or Patriots?," 37.
37. Windrich, *Britain and the Politics of Rhodesian Independence.*
38. South Africa, *Truth and Reconciliation Commission (South Africa) Report*, vol. 2 (Pretoria, 1998), 86–88.
39. Moorcraft and McLaughlin, *Rhodesian War*, 51.
40. Luise White, "Civic Virtue, Young Men, and the Family: Conscription in Rhodesia, 1974–1980," *International Journal of African Historical Studies* 37 (2004): 105.
41. Jeffrey Davidow, *Peace in Southern Africa: The Lancaster House Conference on Rhodesia, 1979* (Boulder, CO: Westview Press, 1984), 14.
42. Brian Raftopoulos and Alois Mlambo, eds., *Becoming Zimbabwe* (Harare: Weaver, 2009), 164.
43. Anthony King, *Frontline: Combat and Cohesion in the Twenty-First Century* (Oxford: Oxford University Press, 2015), 10–11.
44. Hew Strachan, "Training, Morale and Modern War," *Journal of Contemporary History* 41, no. 2 (April 2006): 211–227.
45. Sarah Stockwell, "'Losing an Empire and Winning Friends': Sandhurst and British Decolonization," in *The British End of the British Empire* (Cambridge: Cambridge University Press, 2018), 234–285.
46. Edward Burke, *An Army of Tribes: British Army Cohesion, Deviancy, and Murder in Northern Ireland* (Liverpool: Liverpool University Press, 2018), 40.

1. THE KING'S AFRICAN RIFLES, INDEPENDENCE, AND MUTINY

1. John MacKenzie, *Propaganda and Empire: The Manipulation of British Public Opinion, 1880–1960* (Manchester: Manchester University Press, 1984).
2. Timothy Parsons, *The 1964 Army Mutinies and the Making of Modern East Africa* (Westport, CT: Praeger, 2003), 67.
3. Timothy Parsons, *The African Rank-and-File: Social Implications of Colonial Military Service in the King's African Rifles, 1902–1964* (Portsmouth, NH: Heinemann, 1999), 15.

4. Parsons, 15.
5. Hubert Moyse Bartlett, *The King's African Rifles: A Study in the Military History of East and Central Africa 1890–1945* (Aldershot: Gale & Polden, 1956), 75; Arthur Hardinge, *A Diplomat in the East* (London: Jonathan Cape, 1928), 164.
6. Hardinge, *Diplomat in the East*, 129.
7. Parsons, *African Rank-and-File*, 19.
8. Guy Campbell, *The Charging Buffalo: A History of the Kenya Regiment, 1937–1963* (London: Leo Cooper, 1986); Leonard Gill, *Remembering the Regiment* (Victoria, BC: Trafford, 2004).
9. Parsons, *African Rank-and-File*, 27–29.
10. Parsons, 34; Byron Farwell, *Armies of the Raj: From the Great Indian Mutiny to Independence, 1858–1947* (New York: Norton, 1989), 299–301.
11. Waruhiu Itote, *"Mau Mau" General* (Nairobi: East African Publishing House, 1967), 10–15.
12. Hal Brands, "Wartime Recruiting Practices, Martial Identity and Post–World War II Demobilization in Colonial Kenya," *Journal of African History* 46 (2005): 103–125.
13. Brands, 107.
14. Ian Spencer, "Settler Dominance, Agricultural Production and the Second World War in Kenya," *Journal of African History* 21 (1980): 497–514.
15. Spencer, 507; "Technical College on Non-racial Lines," *Kenya Daily Mail*, 1 March 1946.
16. Brands, "Wartime Recruiting Practices," 119.
17. David Percox, *Britain, Kenya and the Cold War: Imperial Defence, Colonial Security and Decolonisation* (New York: Tauris Academic Studies, 2004), 20.
18. Keith Kyle, *The Politics of the Independence of Kenya* (New York: St. Martin's Press, 1999), 43.
19. Wm. Roger Louis, "Britannia's Mau Mau," in *Penultimate Adventures with Britannia: Personalities, Politics and Culture in Britain*, ed. Wm. Roger Louis (London: I. B. Tauris, 2008), 259–274; Thomas R. Metcalf, *Imperial Connections: India in the Indian Ocean Arena, 1860–1920* (Berkeley: University of California Press, 2007).
20. Wm. Roger Louis and Roger Owens, eds., *Suez 1956: The Crisis and Its Consequences* (Oxford: Clarendon Paperbacks, 1989).
21. David Percox, "Mau Mau and the Arming of the State," in *Mau Mau and Nationhood: Arms, Authority and Narration*, ed. E. S. Atieno Odhiambo and John Lonsdale (Oxford: James Currey, 2003), 121–155.
22. The National Archives (TNA), Public Record Office (PRO), WO 276/76 f. 2, "Third Meeting of the East Africa High Commission Held in Nairobi on Tuesday and Wednesday 8th and 9th March, 1949."
23. Percox, *Britain, Kenya and the Cold War*, 125; Campbell, *Charging Buffalo*, 1.
24. Campbell, *Charging Buffalo*, 2; Gill, *Remembering the Regiment*.
25. Great Britain, Colonial Office, *Colonial Office Report on the Colony and Protectorate of Kenya for the Year 1951* (London: HMSO, 1952), 76–89.

26. Richard Vinen, *National Service: Conscription in Britain, 1945–1963* (New York: Allen Lane, 2014), 336.
27. Daniel Branch, *Defeating Mau Mau, Creating Kenya: Counterinsurgency, Civil War and Decolonization* (London: Cambridge University Press, 2009), 5.
28. David Anderson, *Histories of the Hanged: The Dirty War in Kenya and the End of Empire* (New York: W. W. Norton, 2005), 26.
29. Itote, *"Mau Mau" General*, 50.
30. Benjamin Grob Fitzgibbon, *Imperial Endgame: Britain's Dirty Wars and the End of Empire* (New York: Palgrave Macmillan, 2011), 214; Caroline Elkins, *Imperial Reckoning: The Untold Story of Britain's Gulag in Kenya* (New York: Henry Holt, 2005), 28.
31. Branch, *Defeating Mau Mau*, 8.
32. Parsons, *African Rank-and-File*, 95.
33. Anthony Clayton and David Killingray, *Khaki and Blue: Military and Police in British Colonial Africa* (Athens: Ohio University Center for International Studies, 1989), 244.
34. Clayton and Killingray, 244.
35. Itote, *"Mau Mau" General*, 105.
36. Itote, 106.
37. Parsons, *African Rank-and-File*, 192–193.
38. Campbell, *Charging Buffalo*, 100.
39. Stephen Luscombe, "The Kenya Police: A Living History Written by Those Who Served: Volumes 1, 2 and 3," accessed 26 January 2021, https://www.brit ishempire.co.uk/library/kenyapolice.htm.
40. Percox, *Britain, Kenya and the Cold War*, 61.
41. Great Britain, Colonial Office, *Colonial Office Report on the Colony and Protectorate of Kenya for the Year 1956* (London: HMSO, 1957), 114.
42. Parsons, *The 1964 Army Mutinies*, 60.
43. TNA, PRO, CAB 126/76, "Security in the Colonies," 30.
44. TNA, PRO, CAB 126/76, "Security in the Colonies," 47.
45. Office Great Britain, Colonial Office, *Colonial Office Report on the Colony and Protectorate of Kenya for the Year 1957* (London: HMSO, 1958), 124.
46. Great Britain, Colonial Office, 124.
47. TNA, PRO, WO 968/791, f. 1, "Africanization of the East African Land Forces, Chart of Cadets Sent to RMA from East Africa since 1957."
48. Kenya, *Kenya National Assembly Official Record (Hansard)*, vol. 90 (Nairobi, 1962), 498.
49. Great Britain, Colonial Office, *Colonial Office Report on the Colony and Protectorate of Kenya for the Year 1958* (London: HMSO, 1959), 91.
50. Great Britain, Colonial Office, *Colonial Office Report on the Colony and Protectorate of Kenya for the Year 1959* (London: HMSO, 1960), 91.
51. TNA, PRO, CAB 129/100, "The Future of the East Africa Land Forces," 2.
52. TNA, PRO, CAB 129/100, "The Future of the East Africa Land Forces," 2.
53. Great Britain, Colonial Office, *Colonial Office Annual Report on the East Africa High Commission, 1959* (London: HMSO, 1960), 81.

54. Great Britain, Colonial Office, 81.
55. TNA, PRO, WO 968/791, f. 1, "Africanisation of the East African Land Forces, Request for Information about the Ghana Military Academy."
56. Jon Kraus, "The Men in Charge," *Africa Report* 11 (April 1966): 17.
57. Kisangani Emizet, "Explaining the Rise and Fall of Military Regimes: Civil-Military Relations in the Congo," *Armed Forces and Society* 26 (Winter 2000): 207.
58. Claude Welch, "Praetorianism in Commonwealth West Africa," *Journal of Modern African Studies* 10 (July 1972): 207.
59. Percox, *Britain, Kenya and the Cold War*, 160.
60. TNA, PRO, CO 968/791, 14A, "Africanisation of the East African Land Forces."
61. TNA, PRO, WO 32/20382, 8A, "Establishing a Viable Force in East Africa."
62. TNA, PRO, WO 32/20382, 8A, "Establishing a Viable Force in East Africa."
63. TNA, PRO, CO 968/723, "Africanisation of the East African Land Forces 1960–1962," 16, letter dated 8 November 1961.
64. D. W. Throup, "Renison, Sir Patrick Muir (1911–1965)," in *Oxford Dictionary of National Biography*, ed. Lawrence Goldman (Oxford: Oxford University Press), accessed 3 April 2020, http://www.oxforddnb.com.lib-ezproxy.tamu.edu:2048/view/article/38476.
65. TNA, PRO, WO 32/20382, 8A, "Establishing a Viable Force in East Africa."
66. TNA, PRO, WO 32/20382, 8A, "Establishing a Viable Force in East Africa."
67. TNA, PRO, WO 32/20382, 8A, "Establishing a Viable Force in East Africa," 3.
68. "Kenya Becomes Aware of Need to Train African Officers," *The Times*, 13 December 1961, 10.
69. "Major General William Dimoline, Letter to the Editor," *The Times*, 29 December 1961.
70. TNA, PRO, WO 32/20382, 8A, "Establishing a Viable Force in East Africa," 2.
71. TNA, PRO, CO 968/723, 16, "Africanisation of the East African Land Forces 1960–1962," 16.
72. TNA, PRO, WO 305/1653, Anx. C, "KAR Course Wing 1961–1963."
73. TNA, PRO, CO 968/723, "Africanisation of the East African Land Forces 1960–1962," 60.
74. TNA, PRO, CO 968/723, 14A, "Africanisation of the East African Land Forces 1960–1962."
75. TNA, PRO, CO 968/723, E16, "Africanisation of the East African Land Forces 1960–1962."
76. TNA, PRO, CO 968/723, "Africanisation of the East African Land Forces 1960–1962," 60.
77. Kenya, *Kenya National Assembly Official Record (Hansard)*, 498.
78. Kenya, 499.
79. TNA, PRO, CO 968/723, E59, "Africanisation of the East African Land Forces 1960–1962."
80. TNA, PRO, CO 968/791, "Africanisation of the East African Land Forces," 1.
81. Great Britain, Colonial Office, *Colonial Office Report on the Colony and Protectorate of Kenya for the Year 1962* (London: HMSO, 1964), 105.

82. Great Britain, Colonial Office, 106.
83. William Dimoline to M. F. Fitzalan-Howard, 30 May 1963, William Dimoline Papers, Liddell Hart Centre for Military Archives, King's College, London, UK.
84. TNA, PRO, CO 968/791, "Africanisation of the East African Land Forces," 4, letter dated 29 July 1963.
85. TNA, PRO, CO 968/791, 5/7, "Africanisation of the East African Land Forces," letter dated 4 September 1963.
86. TNA, PRO, CO 968/791, "Africanisation of the East African Land Forces," 8, letter dated 17 October 1963.
87. TNA, PRO, CO 968/791, "Africanisation of the East African Land Forces," 8, letter dated 17 October 1963.
88. TNA, PRO, CO 968/791, "Africanisation of the East African Land Forces," 3.
89. TNA, PRO, CO 968/791, "Africanisation of the East African Land Forces," 3.
90. John Lee, *African Armies and Civil Order* (New York: Praeger, 1969), 44.
91. Parsons, *The 1964 Army Mutinies*, 65.
92. Parsons, 67.
93. Abel Jacob, "Israel's Military Aid to Africa, 1960–66," *Journal of Modern African Studies* 9, no. 2 (1971): 165–187.
94. Parsons, *The 1964 Army Mutinies*, 104.
95. TNA, PRO, DO 213/54, 6A, "Causes of the East African Mutinies during January 1964," dispatch No. 1 dated 31 January 1964.
96. TNA, PRO, DO 213/54, 6A, "Causes of the East African Mutinies during January 1964," 2.
97. TNA, PRO, ADM 202/509, "45 Commando Operational Notes East Africa," 1.
98. TNA, PRO, DO 213/54, 11, "Causes of the East African Mutinies during January 1964," 2, dispatch dated 1 February 1964.
99. TNA, PRO, DO 213/54, 11, "Causes of the East African Mutinies during January 1964," 6.
100. *Daily Nation*, 23 January 1964; Parsons, *The 1964 Army Mutinies*, 118.
101. "BRITISH AID KENYA AS HER SOLDIERS MUTINY OVER PAY; Third Army Revolt in Week Occurs in East Africa—Nairobi Asks Help; TROOPS CLASH AT CAMP; London Sends Commandos—Also Lands Forces in Tanganyika after Plea," *New York Times*, 25 January 1964, sec. Archives, https://www.nytimes.com/1964/01/25/archives/british-aid-kenya-as-her-soldiers-mutiny-over-pay-third-army-revolt.html.
102. "BRITISH PUT DOWN AFRICAN MUTINIES IN THREE NATIONS; London Sends Troops after Calls from Tanganyika, Kenya and Uganda; 3 DIE AT DAR ES SALAAM; Action Lasts 40 Minutes—Warships in Indian Ocean Fire Blank Ammunition," *New York Times*, 26 January 1964, sec. Archives, https://www.nytimes.com/1964/01/26/archives/british-put-down-african-mutinies-in-three-nations-london-sends.html.
103. TNA, PRO, DO 213/54, 11, "Causes of the East African Mutinies during January 1964," 2, dispatch dated 1 April 1964.
104. Jacob, "Israel's Military Aid to Africa, 1960–66."

105. Lee, *African Armies and Civil Order*, 123, 149.

106. Clayton and Killingray, *Khaki and Blue*, 265.

107. Lee, *African Armies and Civil Order*, 79.

108. Kenya, *Kenya National Assembly Official Record*, 4th ser. (Nairobi, 1966), vol. 10, cols. 2897–2898.

109. Lee, *African Armies and Civil Order*, 126.

110. TNA, PRO, FCO 16/152, E1B, "Armed Forces Personnel Training Teams Senior Appointments Kenya."

111. Thomas Stubbs, "Ethnopolitics and the Military in Kenya," in *Forging Military Identity in Culturally Pluralistic Societies: Quasi-Ethnicity*, ed. D. Zirker (Lanham, MD: Lexington Books, 2015), 71.

112. Stubbs, 72–73.

113. Lee, *African Armies and Civil Order*, 44.

114. *Kenya National Assembly Official Record*, 4th ser., vol. 10, cols. 2897–2898.

115. Charles Hornsby, *Kenya: A History since Independence* (London: I. B. Tauris, 2012), 99.

116. Njagi Munene, "The Colonial Legacy in Kenya-British Military Relations: 1963–2005" (PhD diss., Kenyatta University, 2013).

117. Munene, 85.

118. British Army, "Africa," accessed 2 February 2021, https://www.army.mod.uk /deployments/africa/.

2. THE ZAMBIA ARMY AND THE CONSEQUENCES OF POOR POLICY

1. Rosaleen Smyth, "War Propaganda during the Second World War in Northern Rhodesia," *African Affairs* 83 (July 1984): 345.

2. W. V. Brelsford, ed., *The Story of the Northern Rhodesia Regiment* (Lusaka, Northern Rhodesia: Government Printer, 1954). Chapters 1 and 2 cover the early days of the NRP through the course of the First World War.

3. Brelsford, chap. 6.

4. TNA, PRO, WO 100/548, "General Service Medal with clasp Palestine, 1945–1948," 1.

5. Great Britain, Colonial Office, *Colonial Reports: Northern Rhodesia, 1957* (Lusaka, Northern Rhodesia: Government Printer, 1958), 121.

6. Rhodesia and Nyasaland Army, *Ceremonial Parade: Farewell to the Federal Prime Minister the Right Honorable Sir Roy Welensky, KCMG, MP* (Salisbury: Government Printer, 1963), 15–16.

7. TNA, PRO, DEFE 25/127, "Notes on the Armed Forces of Rhodesia and Nyasaland," 2.

8. TNA, PRO, CAB 195/15, "Cabinet Secretary's Notebook, 5 July 1956," 54.

9. TNA, PRO, DEFE 25/127, "Notes on the Armed Forces of Rhodesia and Nyasaland," 6.

10. TNA, PRO, DEFE 25/127, "Notes on the Armed Forces of Rhodesia and Nyasaland," 25.

11. Richard Whiting, "The Empire in British Politics," in *Britain's Experience of Empire in the Twentieth Century*, ed. Andrew S. Thompson (Oxford: Oxford University Press, 2012), 189.

12. Federation of Rhodesia and Nyasaland, *Debates of the Federal Assembly, Second Session, Second Parliament, 28th March to 19th July 1960* (Salisbury: Parliamentary Printer, 1961), 1445.

13. Federation of Rhodesia and Nyasaland, *Debates of the Federal Assembly, Second Session, Second Parliament*, 1460.

14. Rhodesia and Nyasaland Army, *Ceremonial Parade*, 12.

15. Benjamin Grob Fitzgibbon, *Imperial Endgame: Britain's Dirty Wars and the End of Empire* (New York: Palgrave Macmillan, 2011), 145.

16. Fitzgibbon, 15.

17. TNA, PRO, DO 123/25, "Rhodesia and Nyasaland Administrative Reports 1961," 4. The total number of Europeans in the RF in 1960 was 1,054, which included officers. The total of Europeans in the RF by the end of 1961 was 1,878.

18. Federation of Rhodesia and Nyasaland, *Annual Report of the Secretary for Defense and the Chief of General Staff and of the Chief of Air Staff for the Year Ended 31st December, 1960*, 1.

19. Federation of Rhodesia and Nyasaland, *Debates of the Federal Assembly, Second Session, Second Parliament*, 1486.

20. TNA, PRO, DO 123/25, "Rhodesia and Nyasaland Administrative Reports 1961," 4.

21. TNA, PRO, DO 123/27, "Rhodesia and Nyasaland Administrative Reports 1962," 3.

22. Federation of Rhodesia and Nyasaland, *Annual Report of the Secretary for Defense and the Chief of General Staff and of the Chief of Air Staff for the Year Ended 31st December, 1960*, 9.

23. TNA, PRO, DO 123/27, "Rhodesia and Nyasaland Administrative Reports 1962," 4.

24. Robert I. Rotberg, *The Rise of Nationalism in Central Africa: The Making of Malawi and Zambia, 1873–1946* (Cambridge, MA: Harvard University Press, 1965), 258.

25. Rotberg, 282.

26. Rotberg, 293.

27. Jan Pettman, *Zambia: Security and Conflict* (New York: St. Martin's Press, 1974), 16–18.

28. Robert Blake, *A History of Rhodesia* (New York: Alfred A. Knopf, 1977), 342.

29. Blake, 347.

30. TNA, PRO, DEFE 25/127, "Notes on the Armed Forces of Rhodesia and Nyasaland," 29.

31. International Institute for Strategic Studies, "Part III: Non-aligned Countries," *Military Balance* 65, no. 1 (January 1965): 34–39.

32. TNA, PRO, DO 183/153, "Defense Aspects of Nyasaland's Withdrawal from the Federation," 16.

33. TNA, PRO, DO 183/252, "Certain Defense Considerations," 5.

34. TNA, PRO, DO 183/252, "Certain Defense Considerations," 7–8.

35. TNA, PRO, DO 183/153, "Defense Aspects of Nyasaland's Withdrawal from the Federation," 13.

36. TNA, PRO, DO 183/153, "Defense Aspects of Nyasaland's Withdrawal from the Federation," 14.
37. TNA, PRO, DO 183/153, "Defense Aspects of Nyasaland's Withdrawal from the Federation," 16, Annex to COS.116/63, 2.
38. Dudley Cowderoy and Roy Nesbit, *War in the Air: Rhodesian Air Force, 1935–1980* (Alberton, South Africa: Galago Books, 1987), 31.
39. TNA, PRO, DO 183/153, "Defense Aspects of Nyasaland's Withdrawal from the Federation," 2, Annex to COS.1446/8/3/63.
40. Elaine Windrich, *Britain and the Politics of Rhodesian Independence* (London: Croom Helm, 1978), 14–15.
41. Windrich, 16.
42. Federation of Rhodesia and Nyasaland, *Debates of the Federal Assembly, Second Session, Third Parliament* (Salisbury: Parliamentary Printer, 1963), 1490.
43. Federation of Rhodesia and Nyasaland, 1494.
44. Rhodesia and Nyasaland Army, *Dissolution of the Federation of Rhodesia and Nyasaland: Options Available to Officers and European Members* (Salisbury: Government Printer, 1963), 1–2.
45. Rhodesia and Nyasaland Army, 4.
46. Rhodesia and Nyasaland Army, 40.
47. TNA, PRO, DEFE 25/127, "Notes on the Armed Forces of Rhodesia and Nyasaland," 16; Rhodesia and Nyasaland Army, *Dissolution of the Federation of Rhodesia and Nyasaland*, 47.
48. TNA, PRO, DEFE 25/127, "Notes on the Armed Forces of Rhodesia and Nyasaland," 16.
49. TNA, PRO, DEFE 25/127, "Notes on the Armed Forces of Rhodesia and Nyasaland," 16.
50. TNA, PRO, DEFE 25/127, "Notes on the Armed Forces of Rhodesia and Nyasaland," 17.
51. Bizeck Jube Phiri, *A Political History of Zambia: From Colonial Rule to the Third Republic, 1890–2001* (Trenton, NJ: Africa World Press, 2006), 116.
52. TNA, PRO, FCO 371/176575, "Africanisation of the Northern Rhodesia and Nyasaland Armies," 2.
53. TNA, PRO, DO 183/155, "The Effects of the Tanganyika and Uganda Mutinies on the Situation and the Troops in N. Rhodesia, Nyasaland and Southern Rhodesia," 2, 1964.
54. TNA, PRO, DO 183/155, "The Effects of the Tanganyika and Uganda Mutinies on the Situation and the Troops in N. Rhodesia, Nyasaland and Southern Rhodesia," 6.
55. TNA, PRO, DO 183/155, "The Effects of the Tanganyika and Uganda Mutinies on the Situation and the Troops in N. Rhodesia, Nyasaland and Southern Rhodesia," 12.
56. TNA, PRO, DO 183/155, "The Effects of the Tanganyika and Uganda Mutinies on the Situation and the Troops in N. Rhodesia, Nyasaland and Southern Rhodesia," 13.
57. TNA, PRO, DEFE 25/127, "Notes on the Armed Forces of Rhodesia and Nyasaland," p. 3 of Annex to COS.178/64.

58. TNA, PRO, DEFE 25/127, "Notes on the Armed Forces of Rhodesia and Nyasaland," 3.

59. TNA, PRO, DEFE 25/127, "Notes on the Armed Forces of Rhodesia and Nyasaland," 4.

60. TNA, PRO, DEFE 25/127, "Notes on the Armed Forces of Rhodesia and Nyasaland," 7. Upon the dissolution of the federation, 2KAR became the Second Battalion of the Northern Rhodesia Regiment.

61. TNA, PRO, DEFE 25/127, "Notes on the Armed Forces of Rhodesia and Nyasaland," p. 2 of "Annex 'A' to DP.56/64(Final)."

62. TNA, PRO, DEFE 25/127, "Notes on the Armed Forces of Rhodesia and Nyasaland," 2.

63. Phiri, *Political History of Zambia*, 131.

64. Rhodesia, Northern. *Report of the Commission Appointed to Review the Salaries and Conditions of Service of the Northern Rhodesia Public and Teaching Services and of the Northern Rhodesia Army and Air Force* (Lusaka, Northern Rhodesia: Government Printer, 1964), 4.

65. Francis Gershom Sibamba, *The Zambia Army and I: Autobiography of a Former Army Commander* (Ndola, Zambia: Mission Press, 2010), 34.

66. Claude E. Welch, "Civil-Military Relations in Newer Commonwealth States: The Transfer and Transformation of British Models," *Journal of Developing Areas* 12, no. 2 (1978): 153–170.

67. Welch, 160.

68. Welch, 162.

69. Sibamba, *The Zambia Army and I*, 71.

70. Welch, 164.

71. "Rhodesia Discussions Break Down," *The Times*, 9 October 1965, 10.

72. "Announcement of Unilateral Declaration of Independence," *East Africa and Rhodesia*, 18 November 1965, 204–205.

73. TNA, PRO, CAB 128/46, "Cabinet Conclusion, 31 October 1966," "using force to bring an end to the rebellion in Rhodesia"; Carl Watts, "Killing Kith and Kin: The Viability of British Military Intervention in Rhodesia, 1964–5," *Twentieth Century British History* 16 (2005): 382–415.

74. Andrew DeRoche, "'You Can't Fight Guns with Knives': National Security and Zambian Responses to UDI, 1965–1973," in *One Zambia, Many Histories: Towards a History of Post-colonial Zambia*, ed. Jan-Bart Gewald and Marja Hinfelaar (Boston: Brill, 2008), 80.

75. "Cabinet Faces Crisis on Zambia Troops," *The Times*, 27 November 1965, 8.

76. TNA, PRO, DEFE 70/320, "Staff Requirements for Rhodesia and Zambia," "OP Amberley, 22 December 1965," 19.

77. TNA, PRO, DEFE 5/165, "The Rapid Introduction of a Battalion Group into Zambia or Rhodesia. 12 January 1966," 5.

78. DeRoche, "'You Can't Fight Guns with Knives,'" 81.

79. TNA, PRO, DEFE 70/320, 15A, "Staff Requirements for Rhodesia and Zambia," "Second Report on Zambia, December 1965."

80. "Mr. Kaunda to Build Up Forces Swiftly," *The Times*, 10 December 1965, 10.

81. Sibamba, *The Zambia Army and I*, 71.

82. Blake, *History of Rhodesia*, 396.
83. TNA, PRO, DEFE 5/165, "British Military Intervention in Rhodesia 12 January 1966," 6.
84. Paul Moorcraft and Peter McLaughlin, *The Rhodesian War: A Military History* (Johannesburg: Jonathan Ball, 2008), 32. For a firsthand account of this mission from the perspective of an ANC fighter, see Thula Bopela and Daluxolo Luthuli, *Umkhonto we Sizwe: Fighting for a Divided People* (Alberton, South Africa: Galago Books, 2005).
85. TNA, PRO, DEFE 11/619, "Central Africa," "Defense Advisor Zambia, Quarterly Report 1 August 1968."
86. TNA, PRO, DEFE 11/619, "Central Africa," "Defense Advisor Zambia, Quarterly Report 3 May 1968."
87. TNA, PRO, WO 32/21128, E29, "Service Personnel on Loan to Zambian Armed Forces 1967."
88. TNA, PRO, DEFE 11/619, "Central Africa," "Defense Advisor Zambia, Quarterly Report 3 May 1968," 9.
89. TNA, PRO, WO 32/21128, E48, "Service Personnel on Loan to Zambian Armed Forces 1967."
90. TNA, PRO, WO 32/21128, E48, letter dated 15 August 1967 from Harold Davies of the MOD to R. C. Shaw from the Commonwealth Office.
91. TNA, PRO, WO 32/21128, E48, cable from Lusaka to the Commonwealth Office dated 2 November 1967.
92. TNA, PRO, WO 32/21128, E48, draft letter from DS 6a to DS 11 dated 20 November 1967.
93. Zambia, *Report of the Commission Appointed to Review the Grading Structure of the Civil Service, the Salary Scales of the Civil Service, the Teaching Service, the Zambian Police and the Prison Service. The Salary Scales and Wages of Non–Civil Service (Industrial) Employees of the Government and the Pay Scales and Conditions of Service of the Zambia Defense Forces* (Lusaka, Zambia: Government Printer, 1966); TNA, PRO, WO 32/21128, E57, "Service Personnel on Loan to Zambian Armed Forces 1967."
94. TNA, PRO, WO 32/21128, E48, "Service Personnel on Loan to Zambian Armed Forces 1967."
95. TNA, PRO, WO 32/21128, E58, "Service Personnel on Loan to Zambian Armed Forces 1967."
96. TNA, PRO, WO 32/21128, E60, "Service Personnel on Loan to Zambian Armed Forces 1967," cable from Lusaka to the Commonwealth Office dated 6 December 1967.
97. TNA, PRO, WO 32/21128, E73, "Service Personnel on Loan to Zambian Armed Forces 1967," letter from the High Commission, Lusaka, to the Zambia Department of the Commonwealth Office dated 2 February 1968.
98. TNA, PRO, WO 32/21128, E78, "Service Personnel on Loan to Zambian Armed Forces 1967," letter from DS 6 to DS15 dated 27 March 1968.
99. TNA, PRO, WO 32/21128, E81, "Service Personnel on Loan to Zambian Armed Forces 1967," "Anglo-Zambian Joint Services Training Team Agreement," 4.

100. TNA, PRO, DEFE 11/619, "Central Africa," "Defense Advisor Zambia, Quarterly Report 3 May 1968," para. 16–17.
101. TNA, PRO, DEFE 11/619, "Central Africa," "Defense Advisor Zambia, Quarterly Report 3 May 1968," para. 24.
102. TNA, PRO, DEFE 11/619, "Central Africa," "Defense Advisor Zambia, Quarterly Report 3 May 1968," para. 27.
103. TNA, PRO, DEFE 11/619, "Central Africa," "Defense Advisor Zambia, Quarterly Report 3 May 1968," para. 31.
104. Information Service, Zambia, "Wings Awarded to first Zambian Pilots," *Zambia*, December 1966, 21.
105. TNA, PRO, DEFE 11/619, "Central Africa," "Defense Advisor Zambia, Quarterly Report 1 August 1968," para. 6.
106. Phiri, *Political History of Zambia*, 141.
107. TNA, PRO, DEFE 11/619, "Central Africa," "Defense Advisor Zambia, Quarterly Report 1 August 1968," "Central Africa," "Defense Advisor Zambia, Quarterly Report 1 August 1968," para. 8–9.
108. TNA, PRO, DEFE 11/619, "Central Africa," "Defense Advisor Zambia, Quarterly Report 1 August 1968," para. 18–19.
109. TNA, PRO, DEFE 11/619, "Central Africa," "Defense Advisor Zambia, Quarterly Report 1 August 1968," para. 17.
110. TNA, PRO, FCO 45/582, CS1, "Effects on Zambia of the Withdrawal of British Joint Services Training Team," "Despatch, Zambian Defense Forces on the Departure of the British Joint Services Training Team," 1.
111. TNA, PRO, FCO 45/582, CS1, "Effects on Zambia of the Withdrawal of British Joint Services Training Team," "Despatch, Zambian Defense Forces on the Departure of the British Joint Services Training Team," 1.
112. TNA, PRO, FCO 45/582, CS1, "Effects on Zambia of the Withdrawal of British Joint Services Training Team," "Despatch, Zambian Defense Forces on the Departure of the British Joint Services Training Team," 4.
113. TNA, PRO, FCO 45/582, CS1, "Effects on Zambia of the Withdrawal of British Joint Services Training Team," letter from M. B. Mbozi, Permanent Secretary, Minister of Foreign Affairs dated 14 February 1970.
114. Winston Brent, *Rhodesian Air Force: A Brief History 1947–1980* (Kwambonambi, South Africa: Freeworld Publications, 1987), 5.
115. TNA, PRO, FCO 45/582, CS1, "Effects on Zambia of the Withdrawal of British Joint Services Training Team," "Despatch, Zambian Defense Forces on the Departure of the British Joint Services Training Team," 2.
116. TNA, PRO, FCO 45/582, CS1, "Effects on Zambia of the Withdrawal of British Joint Services Training Team," "Despatch, Zambian Defense Forces on the Departure of the British Joint Services Training Team," 7.
117. TNA, PRO, FCO 45/582, CS1, "Effects on Zambia of the Withdrawal of British Joint Services Training Team," "Despatch, Zambian Defense Forces on the Departure of the British Joint Services Training Team," 7–8. Patrick Shovelton, "Sir Laurence Pumphrey: Diplomat Decorated for Wartime Bravery Who Later Served as Ambassador to Pakistan," *Independent*, 4 February 2010.

118. Sibamba, *The Zambia Army and I*, 87; Information Service, Zambia, "Marshal of Zambia," *Zambia*, November 1966, 21.
119. Sibamba, *The Zambia Army and I*, 199.
120. Sibamba, 200; Pettman, *Zambia*, 108.
121. TNA, PRO, FCO 45/906, "Military Training for Zambians in the UK 1971," letter to Sir Alec Douglas-Home from Christopher E. Diggines, Deputy High Commissioner of Zambia, dated 28 May 1971, 3.
122. TNA, PRO, FCO 45/906, Military Training for Zambians in the UK 1971," 4; TNA, PRO, FCO 45/582, CS1, "Effects on Zambia of the Withdrawal of British Joint Services Training Team," "Despatch, Zambian Defense Forces on the Departure of the British Joint Services Training Team," 2.
123. TNA, PRO, FCO 45/906, "Military Training for Zambians in the UK 1971," letter to Sir Alec Douglas-Home from Christopher E. Diggines, Deputy High Commissioner of Zambia, dated 28 May 1971, 10.
124. TNA, PRO, FCO 45/906, "Military Training for Zambians in the UK 1971," 1, letter from A. R. Kettles to ACDS(POLS) dated 7 May 1971.
125. TNA, PRO, FCO 45/906, "Military Training for Zambians in the UK 1971," 6, letter to Sir Alec Douglas-Home from Christopher E. Diggines, Deputy High Commissioner of Zambia, dated 28 May 1971.
126. TNA, PRO, FCO 45/906, "Military Training for Zambians in the UK 1971," 11.
127. Vladimir Shubin, "Unsung Heroes: The Soviet Military and the Liberation of Southern Africa," *Cold War History* 7, no. 2 (May 2007): 251–262.
128. TNA, PRO, FCO 45/906, "Military Training for Zambians in the UK 1971," letter from C. M. Rose to Mr. Fingland dated 17 June 1971.
129. For a complete accounting of Soviet plans and actions in southern Africa from the 1950s until the fall of the Soviet Union, see Vladimir Shubin, *The Hot "Cold War": The USSR in Southern Africa* (Scottsville, South Africa: University of KwaZulu-Natal Press, 2008).
130. TNA, PRO, FCO 45/906, "Military Training for Zambians in the UK 1971," 5, letter to Sir Alec Douglas-Home from Christopher E. Diggines, Deputy High Commissioner of Zambia, dated 28 May 1971.
131. Sibamba, *The Zambia Army and I*, 100.
132. Sibamba, 98.
133. Sibamba, 178.
134. Hanania Lungu and Naison Ngoma, "The Zambian Military—Trials, Tribulations and Hope," in *Evolutions and Revolutions: A Contemporary History of Militaries in Southern Africa*, ed. Martin Rupiya (Pretoria: Institute for Security Studies, 2005), 322.
135. Sibamba, *The Zambia Army and I*, 100.
136. Richard J. Reid, *Warfare in African History* (Cambridge: Cambridge University Press, 2012).

3. THE RHODESIAN ARMY AND THE LIBERATION FORCES

1. Timothy Stapleton, *No Insignificant Part: The Rhodesian Native Regiment and the East Africa Campaign of the First World War* (Waterloo, ON: Wilfrid Laurier University Press, 2006), 31.

2. Paul Moorcraft, *Mugabe's War Machine: Saving or Savaging Zimbabwe?* (Barnsley, UK: Pen & Sword Military, 2011), 28.

3. Rhodesia, Southern. *Report of the Commander Military Forces for the Year Ended 31st December, 1950* (Salisbury: Government Printer, 1951), 5.

4. TNA, PRO, DEFE 25/126, "Rhodesian SAS Training," 4, cable from MIDEAST HQ to MOD London, dated 3 August 1962.

5. TNA, PRO, DO 123/25, "Rhodesia and Nyasaland Administrative Reports," "Annual Reports of the Secretary for Defense, Chief of General Staff and the Chief of Air Staff, for the Year Ended 31st December 1961," 5.

6. TNA, PRO, DEFE 25/127, "Notes on the Armed Forces of Rhodesia and Nyasaland," 6.

7. TNA, PRO, DO 123/27, "Rhodesia and Nyasaland Administrative Reports," "Annual Reports of the Secretary for Defense, Chief of General Staff and the Chief of Air Staff, for the Year Ended 31st December 1962," 3.

8. Timothy Stapleton, "'Bad Boys': Infiltration and Sedition in the African Military Units of the Central African Federation (Malawi, Zambia and Zimbabwe) 1953–63," *Journal of Military History* 73 (October 2009): 1190.

9. TNA, PRO, DO 64/94, "Southern Rhodesia Administration Reports, 1964 v.3," "Ministry of Defense, Southern Rhodesia Army, Royal Rhodesia Air Force, Annual Reports for the Year Ended 31st December 1964," 6.

10. TNA, PRO, DO 64/94, "Southern Rhodesia Administration Reports, 1964 v.3," "Ministry of Defense, Southern Rhodesia Army, Royal Rhodesia Air Force, Annual Reports for the Year Ended 31st December 1964," 3.

11. Paul Moorcraft and Peter McLaughlin, *The Rhodesian War: A Military History* (Johannesburg: Jonathan Ball, 2008), 52.

12. Stapleton, "'Bad Boys,'" 1190; TNA, PRO, DO 64/94, "Southern Rhodesia Administration Reports, 1964 v.3," "Ministry of Defense, Southern Rhodesia Army, Royal Rhodesia Air Force, Annual Reports for the Year Ended 31st December 1964," 6.

13. Lt. Col. (Ret.) Ronald Marillier, BCR, email message to author, 17 January 2011.

14. Marillier, email to author, 17 January 2011.

15. TNA, PRO, DEFE 25/126, "Rhodesian SAS Training, Etc.," 62.

16. TNA, PRO, DEFE 25/126, A106/02, "Rhodesian SAS Training, Etc." All of the Rhodesians who asked to be returned to the colony were flown back before the end of November 1965.

17. William Minter and Elizabeth Schmidt, "When Sanctions Worked: The Case of Rhodesia Reexamined," *African Affairs* 87, no. 347 (1988): 207–237.

18. Moorcraft, *Mugabe's War Machine*, 34–35.

19. Terence Ranger, "Violence Variously Remembered: The Killing of Pieter Oberholzer in July 1964," *History in Africa* 24 (1997): 273–286.

20. Peter Godwin, *Mukiwa: A White Boy in Africa* (New York: Grove Press, 1996), 3.

21. TNA, PRO, FCO 36/260, "Rhodesian Army and Air Force," 8, letter dated 12 April 1967 from Col. PH Moir to KJ Neale.

22. TNA, PRO, FCO 36/260, "Rhodesian Army and Air Force," "The Anti-Regime Group."

23. TNA, PRO, FCO 36/24, "Rhodesian Armed Forces Loyalty," 3.
24. TNA, PRO, FCO 36/260, "Rhodesian Army and Air Force," "The Rhodesian Army: Views of LtCol. R Wilson," 1–2.
25. Faan Martin, *James and the Duck: Tales of the Rhodesian Bush War (1964–1980)* (Bloomington, IN: Authorhouse, 2007), 47.
26. TNA, PRO, FCO 36/260, "Rhodesian Army and Air Force," 35, letter from Wg Cmd. Theo Kearton to Maj. G. L. Olley dated 16 December 1967.
27. TNA, PRO, FCO 36/260, "Rhodesian Army and Air Force," 30, telegram from Interests Section Salisbury to Commonwealth Office dated 12 September 1967.
28. Martin, *James and the Duck*, 137.
29. Lt. Col. (Ret.) Ronald Marillier, BCR, email to author, 25 July 2021.
30. Moorcraft and McLaughlin, *Rhodesian War*, 33.
31. TNA, PRO, FCO 36/260, "Rhodesian Army and Air Force," 40, letter from High Commission in Botswana to the Commonwealth Office dated 7 March 1968.
32. Imperial War Museum, interview with Peter McAleese (1995), Catalogue No. 15433.
33. Marillier, email to author, 21 February 2011.
34. Ken Flower, *Serving Secretly: An Intelligence Chief on Record, Rhodesia into Zimbabwe, 1964 to 1981* (London: John Murray, 1987), 94.
35. Flower, 94.
36. Flower, 95.
37. Great Britain, Colonial Office, *Rhodesia, Report of the Commission on Rhodesian Opinion under the Chairmanship of the Right Honorable Lord Pearce, Presented to Parliament by the Secretary of State for Foreign and Commonwealth Affairs by Command of Her Majesty, May 1972* (London: HMSO, 1972), 59.
38. TNA, PRO, FCO 36/1035, "Security Situation in Rhodesia 1972," 1.
39. Moorcraft and McLaughlin, *Rhodesian War*, 37.
40. Luise White, "Civic Virtue, Young Men, and the Family: Conscription in Rhodesia, 1974–1980," *International Journal of African Historical Studies* 37 (2004), 105.
41. J. K. Cilliers, *Counter-insurgency in Rhodesia* (London: Croom Helm, 1985), 17.
42. A. K. H. Weinrich, "Strategic Resettlement in Rhodesia," *Journal of Southern African Studies* 3 (April 1977): 210.
43. Weinrich, 207.
44. Moorcraft and McLaughlin, *Rhodesian War*, 104.
45. Charles Melson, "Top Secret War: Rhodesian Special Operations," *Small Wars and Insurgencies* 16 (March 2005): 63. For a complete examination of the history of this notorious unit, see Peter Stiff and Ron Reid-Daly, *Selous Scouts: Top Secret War* (Alberton, South Africa: Galago Books, 1982).
46. South Africa, Truth and Reconciliation Commission, *Truth and Reconciliation Commission of South Africa Report* (Cape Town: Truth and Reconciliation Commission, 1999), 86. This was a part of the testimony of Colonel Craig Williamson.

47. Rhodesian Broadcasting Corporation, *Selous Scouts* (1978; Memories of Rhodesia, 2003).
48. John Cann, *Counterinsurgency in Africa: The Portuguese Way of War 1961–1974* (London: Greenwood Press, 1997), 56–59.
49. Director of Security Manpower, *National Service Information Sheet* (Salisbury: Director of Security Manpower, 1977), 2.
50. Zimbabwe African National Union, "Smith's Troops Are Murderers," *Zimbabwe News* 9 (July 1978): 36–37.
51. Peter McAleese, *No Mean Soldier: The Autobiography of a Professional Fighting Man* (London: Orion, 1993), 94–95.
52. McAleese, 90.
53. Anti-Apartheid Movement, *Fire Force Exposed: The Rhodesian Security Forces and Their Role in Defending White Supremacy*, Anti-Apartheid Movement Collection (Anti-Apartheid Movement, November 1979), Bodleian Library, University of Oxford, 13.
54. Anti-Apartheid Movement, 17.
55. Imperial War Museum, interview with H. A. Berriff (1973), Catalogue No. (98/16/1).
56. J. K. Seirlis, "Undoing the United Front? Coloured Soldiers in Rhodesia 1939–1980," *African Studies* 63 (July 2004): 87.
57. Seirlis, 88.
58. Ibbo Day Joseph Mandaza, "White Settler Ideology, African Nationalism and the 'Coloured' Question in Southern Africa: Southern Rhodesia/Zimbabwe, Northern Rhodesia/Zambia, and Nyasaland/Malawi, 1900–1976" (PhD diss., University of York, 1979), 1040.
59. Brian Raftopoulos and Alois Mlambo, eds., *Becoming Zimbabwe* (Harare: Weaver, 2009), 162.
60. South Africa, Truth and Reconciliation Commission, *Truth and Reconciliation Commission of South Africa Report*, 86.
61. Peter Godwin and Ian Hancock, *"Rhodesians Never Die": The Impact of War and Political Change on White Rhodesia, 1970–1980* (Oxford: Oxford University Press, 1993), 212.
62. Flower, *Serving Secretly*, 194.
63. Raftopoulos and Mlambo, *Becoming Zimbabwe*, 183.
64. Nicholas Ashford, "Missile Brought Down Rhodesian Airliner," *The Times*, 8 September 1978, 1.
65. Godwin and Hancock, *"Rhodesians Never Die,"* 232.
66. TNA, PRO, FCO 36/2279, "Rhodesian Armed Forces," 8.
67. TNA, PRO, FCO 36/2580, "Rhodesian Armed Forces," 1.
68. "Intake 183," *Assegai: The Magazine of the Rhodesian Army*, February 1979, 12–13.
69. Alexandre Binda, *Masodja: The History of the Rhodesian African Rifles and Its Forerunner the Rhodesian Native Regiment* (Johannesburg: 30 Degrees South Publishers, 2007), 314.
70. D. Gray, "Commissioning of African Officers at the School of Infantry, Gwelo," *Assegai: The Magazine of the Rhodesian Army*, July 1977, 19–20.
71. Rhodesian Army recruiting posters from the period demonstrate this idea. One

popular poster showed a white soldier and an African soldier on patrol together with a caption that read, "Terrorism Stops Here!"

72. "Presentation of Kim Rule's Sword," *Assegai: The Magazine of the Rhodesian Army*, September 1977, 19–20.

73. "Integrated Training at Depot, Rhodesia Regiment," *Assegai: The Magazine of the Rhodesian Army*, December 1977, 17–18.

74. "Officers Commissioned at Inkomo Garrison," *Assegai: The Magazine of the Rhodesian Army*, March 1978, 17–20.

75. Rhodesia, House of Assembly, *Parliamentary Debates, House of Assembly, Fourth Session, Thirteenth Parliament Comprising Period from 21st June, 1977 to 15th July 1977* (Salisbury: Government Printer, 1977), 726.

76. TNA, PRO, FCO 36/2580, "Rhodesian Armed Forces," 3, "Private Armies," dated 23 January 1978, 1.

77. Anti-Apartheid Movement, *Fire Force Exposed*, 44.

78. Anti-Apartheid Movement, 35; TNA, PRO, FCO 36/2580, "Rhodesian Armed Forces," 3, "Private Armies," dated 23 January 1978, 3. This document also confirms the use of the SFA to convince people to vote.

79. TNA, PRO, FCO 36/2580, "Rhodesian Armed Forces," from Mirimba House Salisbury to the Rhodesia Department FCO, dated 23 January 1978.

80. McAleese, *No Mean Soldier*, 151.

81. TNA, PRO, FCO 36/2279, "Rhodesian Armed Forces," 2.

82. John Keegan, *World Armies* (New York: Facts on File, 1979), 587.

83. Robert Barnes, "Vigilante! Anti-Stock Theft Force on a Rhodesian Ranch," *Soldier of Fortune*, April 1979, 54–59.

84. Rory Pilossof, *The Unbearable Whiteness of Being: Farmers' Voices from Zimbabwe* (Harare: Weaver, 2012), 25.

85. Imperial War Museum, interview with Major General Sir John Acland (1990), Catalogue No. 11753.

86. Imperial War Museum, interview with Major General Sir John Acland.

87. Moorcraft and McLaughlin, *Rhodesian War*, 69.

88. Luise White, "'Heading for the Gun': Skills and Sophistication in an African Guerrilla War," *Comparative Studies in Society and History* 51 (2009), 244.

89. White, 244.

90. "People's Army," *Zimbabwe Review*, February 1977, 6–7.

91. Liberation Support Movement, *Zimbabwe: The Final Advance, Documents on the Zimbabwe Liberation Movement* (Oakland, CA: Liberation Support Movement Press, 1978), 26.

92. At this time the Chinese were actually training both ZANLA and ZIPRA fighters in Tanzania. However, ZIPRA was under significant pressure from its major supplier, the USSR, to break ties with China, and by 1971 it refused Chinese help altogether.

93. John Woodmansee, "Mao's Protracted War: Theory vs. Practice," *Parameters* 3 (1973): 30–45.

94. Terence Ranger and Ngwabi Bhebe, *Soldiers in Zimbabwe's Liberation War* (Harare: University of Zimbabwe Publications, 1995), 40–41.

95. Moorcraft and McLaughlin, *Rhodesian War*, 72.

96. Moorcraft and McLaughlin, 77.
97. Liberation Support Movement, *Zimbabwe*, 34.
98. Norma Kriger, *Guerrilla Veterans in Post-war Zimbabwe: Symbolic and Violent Politics, 1980–1987* (Cambridge: Cambridge University Press, 2003), 28.
99. Stiff and Reid-Daly, *Selous Scouts*, 710–713.
100. Kriger, *Guerrilla Veterans in Post-war Zimbabwe*, 27.
101. Zvakanyorwa Wilbert Sadomba, *War Veterans in Zimbabwe's Revolution: Challenging Neo-colonialism and Settler and International Capital* (Suffolk: James Currey, 2011), 36.
102. Kriger, *Guerrilla Veterans in Post-war Zimbabwe*, 27.

4. HOW DO YOU CREATE AN ARMY? BRITISH
POSTCONFLICT PLANNING

1. Phillip Whitehead, "The Labour Governments, 1974–1979," in *Ruling Performance: British Governments from Attlee to Thatcher*, ed. Peter Hennessy and Anthony Seldon (Oxford: Basil Blackwell, 1989), 248.
2. TNA, PRO, CAB 129/181/21, "Statement on the Defense Estimates 1975." Priority 1 and Priority 2 were the MOD's designations for military commitments in the Defense Estimates.
3. The size of the army in 1974 was 338,000 soldiers.
4. TNA, PRO, DEFE 68/295 Policy Including the Integration of the Armed Forces (Rhodesia), "Rhodesia: HMG's Attitude Following a Settlement, 10 NOV 1976," 2.
5. TNA, PRO, DEFE 68/295 Policy Including the Integration of the Armed Forces (Rhodesia), "Record of a Meeting Held in the Secretary of State's Office on 28 July 1976."
6. TNA, PRO, DEFE 68/295 Policy Including the Integration of the Armed Forces (Rhodesia), "Brief for the Secretary of State for Defense, 22 NOV 1976, Rhodesia: The British Role during the Interim Period, Appendix C."
7. TNA, PRO, DEFE 68/295 Policy Including the Integration of the Armed Forces (Rhodesia), "Rhodesia: HMG's Attitude Following a Settlement, 10 NOV 1976," 2.
8. TNA, PRO, DEFE 68/295 Policy Including the Integration of the Armed Forces (Rhodesia), "Rhodesia: Security and Integration of Armed Forces, 9 DEC 1976."
9. TNA, PRO, DEFE 68/295 Policy Including the Integration of the Armed Forces (Rhodesia), "Rhodesia: Security and Integration of Armed Forces, First Draft," 4.
10. Annette Seegers, "Revolutionary Armies of Africa: Mozambique and Zimbabwe," in *Military Power and Politics in Black Africa*, ed. Simon Baynham (London: Croom Helm, 1986), 129–165.
11. "Interview with Rhodesian Army Recruiting Officer," *Soldier of Fortune*, Spring 1977, 14–16.
12. TNA, PRO, DEFE 68/295 Policy Including the Integration of the Armed Forces (Rhodesia), "Rhodesia: The Armed Forces and Public Service Interim Administration."

13. TNA, PRO, DEFE 68/295 Policy Including the Integration of the Armed Forces (Rhodesia), "Final Draft of the Working Groups Report, 20 December 1976," 1.

14. TNA, PRO, DEFE 68/295, Policy Including the Integration of the Armed Forces (Rhodesia), "Final Draft of the Working Groups Report, 20 December 1976," 4.

15. TNA, PRO, DEFE 68/295, Policy Including the Integration of the Armed Forces (Rhodesia), "Final Draft of the Working Groups Report, 20 December 1976," 16.

16. TNA, PRO, DEFE 68/295, Policy Including the Integration of the Armed Forces (Rhodesia), "Final Draft of the Working Groups Report, 20 December 1976," 17.

17. TNA, PRO, DEFE 68/296 Rhodesia Policy, Memo from Gp Capt. H. Davidson Air Staff to Head of DS11, 2.

18. TNA, PRO, DEFE 68/296, Rhodesia Policy, Memo from Gp Capt. H. Davidson Air Staff to Head of DS11, 5.

19. TNA, PRO, FCO 36/1877 Future Defence and Law and Order Ministries and Personnel (1976), "How Did the Transition Work in Mozambique."

20. TNA, PRO, FCO 36/2065 Military and Police Forces of Rhodesia (1977), "Mr. Richards Trip to Africa," 1.

21. TNA, PRO, FCO 36/2065, Military and Police Forces of Rhodesia (1977), "Mr. Richards Trip to Africa," 3.

22. TNA, PRO, DEFE 11/858 Talks about the Future of Rhodesia, cable from Salisbury to FCO 3 NOV 1977.

23. TNA, PRO, FCO 36/2278 Zimbabwe National Army (1977), letter from C. W. Squire, British Embassy Washington, D.C. to James Allan, Rhodesia Department FCO, 14 JAN 1978.

24. TNA, PRO, FCO 36/2278 Zimbabwe National Army (1977), letter to Col. Reilly from W. E. Rous, 16 MAY 1978.

25. TNA, PRO, FCO 36/2278 Zimbabwe National Army (1977), Lord Carver's proposal for the formation of the ZNA, 1.

26. TNA, PRO, FCO 36/2278, Zimbabwe National Army (1977), Lord Carver's proposal for the formation of the ZNA, 3.

27. TNA, PRO, FCO 36/2278, Zimbabwe National Army (1977), Lord Carver's proposal for the formation of the ZNA, 5.

28. Hugh Beach, "Carver, (Richard) Michael Power, Baron Carver (1915–2001),", in *Oxford Dictionary of National Biography*, ed. Lawrence Goldman (Oxford: Oxford University Press, January 2011), accessed 24 July 2013, http://www .oxforddnb.com.lib-ezproxy.tamu.edu:2048/view/article/76553.

29. TNA, PRO, FCO 36/2278 Zimbabwe National Army (1977).

30. Imperial War Museum, interview with Major General Sir John Acland (1990), Catalogue No. 11753.

31. J. H. Learmont, "Reflections from Rhodesia," *RUSI: Royal United Services Institute for Defense Studies, Journal* 125 (December 1980): 50.

32. Learmont, 52.

33. Norma Kriger, *Guerrilla Veterans in Post-war Zimbabwe: Symbolic and Violent Politics, 1980–1987* (Cambridge: Cambridge University Press, 2003), 59.
34. Imperial War Museum, interview with Major General Sir John Acland.
35. TNA, PRO, DEFE 13/1415 Defense Policy Rhodesia/Zimbabwe, cable from MG Acland to MOD, SITREP for 24 JAN 1980.
36. "Operation Quartz—Rhodesia 1980," accessed 23 March 2021, http://www.rhodesia.nl/quartz.htm.
37. TNA, PRO, DEFE 13/1415 Defense Policy Rhodesia/Zimbabwe, cable from MG Acland to MOD, SITREP for 24 JAN 1980.
38. *The Times* (London), 4 January 1980.
39. *The Times* (London), 30 January 1980.
40. TNA, PRO, FCO 36/2805 Military Assistance Programme 1980/81 Part A.
41. TNA, PRO, FCO 36/2801 Zimbabwe Military Policy General Walls Part B, 31 July 1980 from British High Commission Salisbury to FCO "Zimbabwe Military Assistance."
42. TNA, PRO, FCO 36/2805 Military Assistance Programme 1980/81 Part A, 17 MAR 1980 Visit of ACDS(OPS) MG Perkins to Rhodesia.
43. TNA, PRO, FCO 36/2805 Military Assistance Programme 1980/81 Part A, 14 MAR 1980 from Salisbury to FCO No. 1059 "Rhodesia Military Assistance."
44. TNA, PRO, FCO 36/2805 Military Assistance Programme 1980/81 Part A, 24 MAR 1980 from A. Godson to the FCO Defense Department.
45. TNA, PRO, DEFE 68/295 Policy Including the Integration of the Armed Forces (Rhodesia), "Rhodesia: Security and Integration of Armed Forces, 9 DEC 1976."
46. TNA, PRO, FCO 36/2805 Military Assistance Programme 1980/81 Part A, 14 MAR 1980 from Salisbury to FCO No. 1059 "Rhodesia Military Assistance."
47. TNA, PRO, FCO 36/2805 Military Assistance Programme 1980/81 Part A, 14 MAR 1980 from Salisbury to FCO No. 1059 "Rhodesia Military Assistance."
48. TNA, PRO, FCO 36/2805 Military Assistance Programme 1980/81 Part A, 17 MAR 1980 from MG Acland to Lord Soames.
49. TNA, PRO, FCO 36/2805 Military Assistance Programme 1980/81 Part A, 17 MAR 1980 Visit of ACDS(OPS) MG Perkins, to Rhodesia.
50. Peter McAleese, *No Mean Soldier: The Autobiography of a Professional Fighting Man* (London: Orion, 1993), 170.
51. Timothy Bax, *Three Sips of Gin: Dominating the Battlespace with Rhodesia's Elite Selous Scouts* (London: Helion, 2013), 449.
52. TNA, PRO, FCO 36/2805 Military Assistance Programme 1980/81 Part A, 17 MAR 1980 memo from the Defense Department FCO on the "Military Assistance Programme 1980/81."
53. TNA, PRO, FCO 36/2805 Military Assistance Programme 1980/81 Part A, 31 MAR 1980 from MG Fusdon to MOD No. 13D/Z7A.
54. TNA, PRO, FCO 36/2805 Military Assistance Programme 1980/81 Part A, 11 APR 1980 Minutes of an MOD Meeting on Military Assistance.
55. TNA, PRO, FCO 36/2805 Military Assistance Programme 1980/81 Part A, 18 APR 1980 from Lord Soames to the FCO.

56. TNA, PRO, FCO 36/2805 Military Assistance Programme 1980/81 Part A, 20 APR 1980 from MG Fursdon to FCO.

57. TNA, PRO, DEFE 13/1415 Defense Policy Rhodesia/Zimbabwe, "Memo from Private Secretary PMs Office, 9 MAY 1980 on the meeting with Robert Mugabe."

58. David Albright, "South Africa's Nuclear Weapons Program," MIT Security Studies Program, March 2001, http://web.mit.edu/ssp/seminars/wed_archives 01spring/albright.htm.

59. TNA, PRO, DEFE 13/1415 Defense Policy Rhodesia/Zimbabwe, "Loose Minute, 22 May 1980 written by the Vice Chief of the General Staff to BMATT(Zimbabwe)."

60. TNA, PRO, DEFE 13/1415 Defense Policy Rhodesia/Zimbabwe, "Loose Minute, 22 May 1980 written by the Vice Chief of the General Staff to BMATT(Zimbabwe)."

61. TNA, PRO, DEFE 13/1415 Defense Policy Rhodesia/Zimbabwe, From Lord Carrington to SoS for Defense, "Zimbabwe: Command of the Armed Forces," 18 July 1980.

62. TNA, PRO, DEFE 13/1415 Defense Policy Rhodesia/Zimbabwe, From Lord Carrington to SoS for Defense, "Zimbabwe: Command of the Armed Forces," 18 July 1980.

63. TNA, PRO, DEFE 13/1415 Defense Policy Rhodesia/Zimbabwe, From MOD to FCO 21 July 1980, "Zimbabwe: Command of the Armed Forces."

64. TNA, PRO, FCO 36/2801 Zimbabwe Military Policy General Walls Part B, 31 JUL 1980 From Salisbury to FCO "Zimbabwe Military Integration."

65. TNA, PRO, FCO 36/2801 Zimbabwe Military Policy General Walls Part B, 12 AUG 1980 Memo to Sir L. Allison "Replacement of Gen. Walls."

66. TNA, PRO, FCO 36/2801 Zimbabwe Military Policy General Walls Part B, 19 AUG 1980 BMATT to MOD Cable No. 1355.

67. TNA, PRO, FCO 36/2807 Military Assistance to Zimbabwe Part C, from British High Commissioner Lagos to FCO, 29 July 1980.

68. TNA, PRO, FCO 36/2807 Military Assistance to Zimbabwe Part C, "Report of Military Delegation to Zimbabwe, 5 June 1980," by Brig. IA Bako, Nigerian Army.

69. Nicholas Ashford, "Creation of Zimbabwe Army Held Up," The Times, 6 June 1980.

70. A British instructor quoted in Kriger, Guerrilla Veterans in Post-war Zimbabwe, 106.

71. R. A. Boys, "BMATT Zimbabwe," Journal of the Royal Artillery 109 (1982): 22.

72. TNA, PRO, FCO 36/2807 Military Assistance to Zimbabwe Part C, from British Defense Advisor Salisbury to British Defense Advisor Lagos, "Training of ZNA Personnel in Nigeria."

73. TNA, PRO, FCO 36/2807 Military Assistance to Zimbabwe Part C, from Lagos to BRITDEF ZIM, 1 Sept. 1980.

74. TNA, PRO, FCO 36/2808 Military Assistance to Zimbabwe Part D, from BRITDEF Lagos to MOD, 27 Oct. 1980.

75. TNA, PRO, FCO 36/2808 Military Assistance to Zimbabwe Part D, "Application for Permission to Release Classified Information to Another Country, 22 Oct. 1980."
76. TNA, PRO, FCO 36/2807 Military Assistance to Zimbabwe Part C, From BRITDEF Salisbury to MODUK 29 AUG 1980, SITREP No. 23 (23–30 AUG).
77. TNA, PRO, FCO 36/2807 SITREP No. 23 (23–30 AUG).
78. TNA, PRO, FCO 36/2807 SITREP No. 23 (23–30 AUG).
79. Boys, "BMATT Zimbabwe," 23.
80. TNA, PRO, FCO 36/2808 Military Assistance to Zimbabwe Part D, From BRITDEF Salisbury to MODUK SITREP No. 24 (31 AUG–12 SEP80).
81. TNA, PRO, FCO 36/2808 Military Assistance to Zimbabwe Part D, From Brig. Palmer to Gen. Bramall, "Report on the Future of BMATT, 5 SEP 1980," 2.
82. TNA, PRO, FCO 36/2808 Military Assistance to Zimbabwe Part D, From Brig. Palmer to Gen. Bramall, "Report on the Future of BMATT, 5 SEP 1980," 1.
83. TNA, PRO, FCO 36/2808 Military Assistance to Zimbabwe Part D, From Brig. Palmer to Gen. Bramall, "Report on the Future of BMATT, 5 SEP 1980," 2.
84. TNA, PRO, FCO 36/2808 Military Assistance to Zimbabwe Part D, From Brig. Palmer to Gen. Bramall, "Report on the Future of BMATT, 5 SEP 1980," 2.
85. TNA, PRO, FCO 36/2808 Military Assistance to Zimbabwe Part D, From British High Commission Salisbury to Derick Day FCO, "Future of BMATT."
86. TNA, PRO, FCO 36/2808 Military Assistance to Zimbabwe Part D, From Brig. Palmer to Gen. Bramall, "Report on the Future of BMATT, 5 SEP 1980," 3.
87. TNA, PRO, FCO 36/2808, Military Assistance to Zimbabwe Part D, From Brig. Palmer to Gen. Bramall, "Report on the Future of BMATT, 5 SEP 1980," 3.
88. TNA, PRO, FCO 36/2808 Military Assistance to Zimbabwe Part D, From Brig. Palmer to Gen. Bramall, "Report on the Future of BMATT, 5 SEP 1980," Annex A, 3.
89. TNA, PRO, FCO 36/2808 Military Assistance to Zimbabwe Part D, From BRITDEF Salisbury to MODUK SITREP No. (13–25SEP80).
90. TNA, PRO, FCO 36/2808 Military Assistance to Zimbabwe Part D, From BRITDEF Salisbury to MODUK SITREP No. (13–25SEP80); Brian Streak, "Farewell to the RLI," Cheetah: The Magazine of the RLI Association, October 1980, 1–2.
91. TNA, PRO, FCO 36/2808 Military Assistance to Zimbabwe Part D, Report on the Visit of Officer from GS MO2 to Zimbabwe from 27 SEP to 2 OCT80.
92. TNA, PRO, FCO 36/2808 Military Assistance to Zimbabwe Part D, Minutes of a Meeting Held in the MOD by All Staff Sections Concerned with Zimbabwe, 13 OCT 80; "Whites Quit Police and Army in Zimbabwe," The Times, 30 April 1980.
93. TNA, PRO, FCO 36/2808 Military Assistance to Zimbabwe Part D, Report on the visit of Officer from GS MO2 to Zimbabwe from 27 SEP to 2 OCT80.
94. TNA, PRO, FCO 36/2808 Military Assistance to Zimbabwe Part D, Report on the visit of Officer from GS MO2 to Zimbabwe from 27 SEP to 2 OCT80.
95. TNA, PRO, FCO 36/2808 Military Assistance to Zimbabwe Part D, Record of Discussion with the Prime Minister, Mr. Mugabe on 15 October 1980.

96. TNA, PRO, FCO 36/2808 Military Assistance to Zimbabwe Part D, Record of Discussion with the Prime Minister, Mr. Mugabe on 15 October 1980.

97. TNA, PRO, FCO 36/2809 Military Assistance to Zimbabwe Part E, From Palmer to Col. Guthrie, MOD 27 NOV 1980.

98. TNA, PRO, FCO 36/2809 Military Assistance to Zimbabwe Part E, From British High Commissioner Zimbabwe to FCO 27 NOV 1980.

99. The MOD decided that Brigadier Palmer would be more effective as a general officer, so he was given the local rank of major general.

100. TNA, PRO, FCO 36/2809 Military Assistance to Zimbabwe Part E, From RT Jacking to Permanent Undersecretary for Defense 5 DEC 1980.

101. TNA, PRO, FCO 36/2809 Military Assistance to Zimbabwe Part E, From BMATT to MODUK 10 DEC 1980.

102. TNA, PRO, FCO 36/2808 Military Assistance to Zimbabwe Part D, Memo from Assistant Under-Secretary for African Affairs, Derek M Day dated 29 OCT 1980.

103. Stephen Chan, *Robert Mugabe: A Life of Power and Violence* (Ann Arbor: University of Michigan Press, 2003), 113.

5. THE RISE OF ZANLA DOMINANCE IN THE ZNA AND THE BIRTH OF THE FIFTH BRIGADE

1. TNA, PRO, FCO 106/461, Cable from BMATT to MOD, 12 JAN 1981.

2. TNA, PRO, FCO 106/461, from BMATT to MOD, "Revised BMATT Manning Recommendation for 81/82," 10JAN81.

3. Stephen Taylor, "Nkomo Men Take Stock of Mugabe Snub," *The Times*, 12 January 1981, 4.

4. TNA, PRO, FCO 106/461, From Salisbury to FCO, "North Korean Military Assistance," 22JAN81.

5. TNA, PRO, FCO 106/461, From Salisbury to FCO, "North Korean Military Assistance," 22JAN81.

6. A. R. Luckham, "Institutional Transfer and Breakdown in a New Nation: The Nigerian Military," *Administrative Science Quarterly* 16, no. 4 (1971): 387–406.

7. James Minnich, *The North Korean People's Army: Origins and Current Tactics* (Annapolis, MD: Naval Institute Press, 2005), 30.

8. Benjamin Young, *Guns, Guerillas, and the Great Leader: North Korea and the Third World* (Stanford, CA: Stanford University Press, 2021), 129.

9. TNA, PRO, FCO 106/461, From Salisbury to FCO, "North Korean Military Assistance," 22JAN81.

10. TNA, PRO, FCO 106/461, from Salisbury to FCO, "Meeting with Mnangagwa," 30JAN81.

11. TNA, PRO, FCO 106/461, from British High Commission Salisbury to JA Sankey, Central Africa Department.

12. TNA, PRO, FCO 106/461, from British High Commission Salisbury to JA Sankey, Central Africa Department.

13. TNA, PRO, FCO 106/461, from British High Commission Salisbury to JA Sankey, Central Africa Department.

14. TNA, PRO, FCO 106/461, Report on Military Budget.
15. Luise White, "'Whoever Saw a Country with Four Armies?': The Battle of Bulawayo Revisited," *Journal of Southern African Studies* 33 (September 2007): 624.
16. White, 624.
17. TNA, PRO, FCO 106/461, From Brigadier GH Watkins, DPR(A) to Permanent Under Secretary of State for the Army, 18FEB81.
18. Stephen Taylor, "Mr. Nkomo Takes on New Cabinet Tasks in Salisbury Compromise," *The Times*, 28 January 1981.
19. White, "'Whoever Saw a Country with Four Armies?,'" 624.
20. Alexandre Binda, *Masodja: The History of the Rhodesian African Rifles and Its Forerunner the Rhodesian Native Regiment* (Johannesburg: 30 Degrees South Publishers, 2007), 300; White, "'Whoever Saw a Country with Four Armies?,'" 626; "Uneasy Calm Established in Bulawayo," *Herald*, 13 February 1981, 1.
21. "Camp Fighting Caught RSM by Surprise," *Herald*, 6 March 1981, 3.
22. White, "'Whoever Saw a Country with Four Armies?,'" 631.
23. TNA, PRO, FCO 106/461, From John Sankey, Central Africa Department, 3 March 1981.
24. TNA, PRO, FCO 106/461, Col. CLG Henshaw, Defense Advisor, "Report on Visit to Inkomo Garrison," 3 April 1981.
25. TNA, PRO, FCO 106/461, Col. CLG Henshaw, Defense Advisor, "Report on Visit to Inkomo Garrison," 3 April 1981.
26. TNA, PRO, FCO 106/461, Col. CLG Henshaw, Defense Advisor, "Report on Visit to Inkomo Garrison," 3 April 1981.
27. TNA, PRO, FCO 106/461, From P. Kemp, Defense Department FCO to Central Africa Department, 15 May 1981.
28. TNA, PRO, FCO 106/461, From Defense Advisor Salisbury to MOD, "North Korean Military Assistance," 20 May 1981.
29. Nicholas Ashford, "Zimbabwe to Disarm Both Guerrilla Factions," *The Times*, 18 February 1981, 7.
30. Ken Flower, *Serving Secretly: An Intelligence Chief on Record, Rhodesia into Zimbabwe, 1964 to 1981* (London: John Murray, 1987), 300–302; Colin Legum, *The Battlefronts of Southern Africa* (New York: Africana Publishing Company, 1988), 216.
31. TNA, PRO, CAB 128/70/14 "Conclusions of a Meeting of the Cabinet Held in the Prime Minister's Room, House of Commons, on 2 April 1981," 2.
32. Margaret Thatcher, *The Downing Street Years* (New York: HarperCollins, 1993), 249–250.
33. Thatcher, 248.
34. TNA, PRO, PREM 19/161 f126, "Pym Minute to MT" ("The Defense Budget and Cash Limit").
35. Churchill Archive Centre, Thatcher MSS THCR 3/2/73 f133, Margaret Thatcher letter to Prime Minister Mugabe of Zimbabwe (aid for Zimbabwe) *[land resettlement, fees for students from Zimbabwe in the United Kingdom]*.
36. Churchill Archive Centre, Thatcher MSS THCR 3/2/73 f133, Margaret

Thatcher letter to Prime Minister Mugabe of Zimbabwe (aid for Zimbabwe) *[land resettlement, fees for students from Zimbabwe in the United Kingdom]*, 2.

37. TNA, PRO, FCO 106/461, From Byatt to Central Africa Department, 28 MAY 1981.
38. TNA, PRO, FCO 106/461, From Byatt to Central Africa Department, 28 MAY 1981.
39. TNA, PRO, FCO 106/461, Report by the High Commissioner at Salisbury to the Secretary of State for Foreign and Commonwealth Affairs, 14 May 1981.
40. TNA, PRO, FCO 106/464, From Salisbury to FCO, 29 MAY 1981.
41. TNA, PRO, FCO 106/464, From Salisbury to FCO, 29 MAY 1981.
42. TNA, PRO, FCO 106/464, From Salisbury to FCO, "Meeting Between High Commissioner (Byatt) and Mugabe," 1 June 1981.
43. TNA, PRO, FCO 106/464, From Salisbury to FCO, "North Korean Military Assistance," 1 June 1981.
44. TNA, PRO, FCO 106/464, From BMATT to MOD, 1 June 1981.
45. US Department of State, Foreign Service, US Embassy Salisbury, Cable SALISB 06118, Zimbabwe, 07 DEC 1981.
46. TNA, PRO, FCO 106/464, Memo from 10 Downing St. to FCO, 10 June 1981.
47. TNA, PRO, FCO 106/461, Memo from Anthony Acland to Mr. Day, Central African Department.
48. TNA, PRO, FCO 106/464, From Salisbury to FCO, "North Korean Military Assistance," 26 June 1981.
49. TNA, PRO, FCO 106/464, From Salisbury to FCO, 17 July 1981.
50. TNA, PRO, FCO 106/464, Memo to Mr. McLaren from Mr. B. England, "North Korean Military Assistance to Zimbabwe," 4 June 1981.
51. TNA, PRO, FCO 106/464, From FCO to Canberra, 20 July 1981.
52. TNA, PRO, FCO 106/461, Report by Col. CLG Henshaw, Defense Advisor, 5 June 1981.
53. TNA, PRO, FCO 106/461, Report by Col. CLG Henshaw, Defense Advisor, 5 June 1981.
54. TNA, PRO, FCO 106/461, Report by Col. CLG Henshaw, Defense Advisor, 5 June 1981; Paul Moorcraft, *Mugabe's War Machine: Saving or Savaging Zimbabwe?* (Barnsley, UK: Pen & Sword Military, 2011), 105.
55. TNA, PRO, FCO 106/461, From Col. Henshaw to MOD, "Military Situation Report as of 17 JUN," 17 June 1981.
56. TNA, PRO, FCO 106/461, From Col. Henshaw to MOD, "Military Situation Report as of 17 JUN," 17 June 1981.
57. TNA, PRO, PREM 19/606 f17, FCO Letter to No. 10, "North Korean Military Assistance to Zimbabwe," 3 June 1981.
58. TNA, PRO, PREM 19/606 f17, FCO Letter to No. 10, "North Korean Military Assistance to Zimbabwe," 3 June 1981.
59. TNA, PRO, FCO 106/464, Military SITREP 30 June 1981.
60. Stephen Taylor, "British Hope to Keep Up the Good Work in Zimbabwe," *The Times*, 25 July 1981.
61. Taylor, "British Hope to Keep Up the Good Work in Zimbabwe."

62. South Africa, Truth and Reconciliation Commission South Africa, *Truth and Reconciliation Commission of South Africa Report* (Cape Town: Truth and Reconciliation Commission, 1999), 90.
63. TNA, PRO, FCO 106/466, From BRITDEF Salisbury to MOD, ZNA Senior Appointments, 10 AUG 1981.
64. TNA, PRO, FCO 106/466, From BRITDEF Salisbury to MOD, ZNA Senior Appointments, 10 AUG 1981.
65. TNA, PRO, FCO 106/466, From BRITDEF Salisbury to MOD, ZNA Senior Appointments, 10 AUG 1981.
66. TNA, PRO, FCO 106/466, New ZNA Senior Appointments, 28 August 1981, 4.
67. TNA, PRO, FCO 106/466, New ZNA Senior Appointments, 28 August 1981, 4.
68. TNA, PRO, FCO 106/466, New ZNA Senior Appointments, 28 August 1981, 2.
69. TNA, PRO, FCO 106/466, New ZNA Senior Appointments, 28 August 1981, 2.
70. TNA, PRO, FCO 106/466, From Fuller, Central Africa Department, to Sir Allison, "Zimbabwe: Senior Military Appointments," 11 August 1981.
71. TNA, PRO, FCO 106/466, From Col. Henshaw to Col. Jav De Candole, Pretoria, "Stability of Zimbabwe Military," 14 August 1981.
72. TNA, PRO, FCO 106/466, From Col. Henshaw to Col. Jav De Candole, Pretoria, "Stability of Zimbabwe Military," 14 August 1981.
73. TNA, PRO, FCO 106/466, From Col. Henshaw to Col. Jav De Candole, Pretoria, "Stability of Zimbabwe Military," 14 August 1981.
74. South Africa, Truth and Reconciliation Commission South Africa, *Truth and Reconciliation Commission of South Africa Report*, 155.
75. TNA, PRO, FCO 106/466, Military SITREP for 31 JUL to 14 AUG 1981, "Military Assistance from Overseas."
76. TNA, PRO, FCO 106/466, From Salisbury to FCO and MOD, "Zimbabwe Army Senior Appointments," 28 August 1981.
77. TNA, PRO, FCO 106/466, From Salisbury to FCO and MOD, "Zimbabwe Army Senior Appointments," 28 August 1981.
78. TNA, PRO, FCO 106/466, From Salisbury to FCO and MOD, "Zimbabwe Army Senior Appointments," 28 August 1981.
79. Joshua Nkomo, *Nkomo; The Story of My Life* (London: Methuen, 1984), 222–223.
80. Stephen Taylor, "White Officer to Lead Zimbabwe Forces," *The Times*, 8 August 1981, 4.
81. Stephen Taylor, "Zimbabwe Youth March to Back One-Party State," *The Times*, 22 September 1981, 2.
82. TNA, PRO, FCO 106/466, From DL McMillian (Salisbury) to FCO, Military Training of Zimbabwe's Youth, 11 September 1981.
83. TNA, PRO, FCO 106/464, Discussion between DA Salisbury and Mr. Sun Guotong, Chinese Embassy, September 1981.
84. "South Africa Invasion Threat Must Be Countered," *Herald*, 29 January 1981.
85. Zvakanyorwa Wilbert Sadomba, *War Veterans in Zimbabwe's Revolution: Challenging Neo-colonialism and Settler and International Capital* (Suffolk: James Currey, 2011), 68.

86. TNA, PRO, FCO 106/466, BMATT to MOD Military SITREP, 15 August to 24 September 1981.
87. TNA, PRO, FCO 106/466, BMATT to MOD Military SITREP, 15 August to 24 September 1981.
88. TNA, PRO, FCO 106/466, BMATT to MOD Military SITREP, 15 August to 24 September 1981.
89. TNA, PRO, FCO 106/466, BMATT to MOD Military SITREP, 15 August to 24 September 1981.
90. TNA, PRO, FCO 106/466, BMATT to MOD Military SITREP, 15 August to 24 September 1981.
91. TNA, PRO, FCO 106/465, "Zimbabwe Air Force Pilot Training and Egyptian Military Assistance," 1.
92. TNA, PRO, FCO 106/466, BMATT to MOD Military SITREP 25 September to 8 October 1981.
93. TNA, PRO, FCO 106/466, BMATT to MOD Military SITREP 25 September to 8 October 1981.
94. TNA, PRO, FCO 106/466, BMATT to MOD Military SITREP 25 September to 8 October 1981.
95. TNA, PRO, FCO 106/466, BMATT to MOD Military SITREP 25 September to 8 October 1981.
96. TNA, PRO, FCO 106/466, BMATT to MOD Military SITREP 25 September to 8 October 1981.
97. TNA, PRO, FCO 106/466, BMATT to MOD Military SITREP 23 October to 13 November 1981.
98. TNA, PRO, FCO 106/466, BMATT to MOD Military SITREP 23 October to 13 November 1981.
99. Flower, *Serving Secretly*, 300–302.
100. South Africa, Truth and Reconciliation Commission South Africa, *Truth and Reconciliation Commission of South Africa Report*, 89.
101. TNA, PRO, FCO 106/466, BMATT to MOD Military SITREP 23 October to 13 November 1981.
102. TNA, PRO, PREM19/606 f12, Zimbabwe: No. 10 record of conversation (MT-Prime Minister Mugabe of Zimbabwe).
103. "Loyalty Is All, PM Tells Army," *Herald*, 31 October 1981, 1.
104. "Western Democracy May Not Be the Answer," *Herald*, 7 April 1981, 1; "Unity of the Party and the State Our Objective," *Herald*, 2 November 1981, 1.
105. "Military Teams from Britain and Korea Here to Stay," *The Herald*, 13 November 1981.
106. "Military Teams from Britain and Korea Here to Stay," *Herald*, 13 November 1981.
107. "No Blueprint for Success," *Herald*, 6 October 1981.
108. Churchill Archive Centre, Thatcher MSS THCR 3/2/73 f133, Margaret Thatcher letter to Prime Minister Mugabe of Zimbabwe (aid for Zimbabwe) *[land resettlement, fees for students from Zimbabwe in the United Kingdom]*.
109. "Unity of the Party and the State Our Objective."
110. Stephen Taylor, "Mugabe Slashes His Army," *The Times*, 27 November 1981.
111. Nkomo, *Nkomo the Story of My Life*, 225.

112. Nkomo, 225.
113. "Detective Helps SA Spy Escape," *Herald*, 19 November 1981, 1.
114. TNA, PRO, FCO 106/466, BMATT to MOD Military SITREP No. 59, 20 NOV to 16 DEC 81.
115. Norma Kriger, *Guerrilla Veterans in Post-war Zimbabwe: Symbolic and Violent Politics, 1980–1987* (Cambridge: Cambridge University Press, 2003), 130.
116. "Zimbabwe: Operation Glossary—A Guide to Zimbabwe's Internal Campaigns," *IRIN Humanitarian News and Analysis*, 1 May 2008, http://www .irinnews.org/report/78003/zimbabwe-operation-glossary-a-guide-to-zimba bwe-s-internal-campaigns.
117. Curt Harig, interview, 5 August 2013. Chief Warrant Officer Harig, USA (ret.), was a Special Forces officer who participated in military training missions to Zimbabwe in 1993.
118. "Soldiers Harass Tourists Near Inyanga," *Herald*, 12 December 1981.
119. "Soldiers Harass Tourists Near Inyanga."
120. TNA, PRO, FCO 106/466, BMATT to MOD Military SITREP No. 59, 20 NOV to 16 DEC 81.
121. National Archives of Australia (NAA): A13952, 13, ONA Weekly Summary 28/81 Zimbabwe Military Assistance.
122. Kriger, *Guerrilla Veterans in Post-war Zimbabwe*, 132.
123. "Three White Security Men Arrested in Zimbabwe," *The Times*, 8 January 1982, 4.
124. Eliakim Sibanda, *The Zimbabwe African People's Union, 1961–87: A Political History of Insurgency in Southern Rhodesia* (Trenton, NJ: Africa World Press, 2005), 249.
125. *The Chronicle*, 8 February 1982.
126. Catholic Commission for Justice and Peace inside Zimbabwe, *Gukurahundi in Zimbabwe: A Report on the Disturbances in Matabeleland and the Midlands 1980–1988* (New York: Columbia University Press, 2008), 66.
127. "Killer Bomb at ZANU(PF) Headquarters," *Herald*, 19 December 1981, 1.
128. "Zimbabwe Fears Backlash by Nkomo's Men," *The Times*, 18 February 1982, 6.
129. Kriger, *Guerrilla Veterans in Post-war Zimbabwe*, 135.
130. Kriger, 135; Sadomba, *War Veterans in Zimbabwe's Revolution*, 80.
131. Kriger, *Guerrilla Veterans in Post-war Zimbabwe*, 137.
132. "Thatcher Pledge on Aid to Zimbabwe," *The Times*, 20 May 1982, 8.
133. Stephen Taylor, "British Team Reinforced in Zimbabwe," *The Times*, 27 October 1982, 8.
134. Stephen Taylor, "Zimbabwe Jets Destroyed," *The Times*, 26 July 1982, 1.
135. These were the same emergency powers that the Smith regime had used to oppress Africans during the colonial period.
136. Catholic Commission for Justice and Peace inside Zimbabwe, *Gukurahundi in Zimbabwe*, 71.
137. South Africa, Truth and Reconciliation Commission South Africa, *Truth and Reconciliation Commission of South Africa Report*, 90.
138. Catholic Commission for Justice and Peace inside Zimbabwe, *Gukurahundi in Zimbabwe*, 71.

139. Catholic Commission for Justice and Peace inside Zimbabwe, 76.
140. Catholic Commission for Justice and Peace inside Zimbabwe, 77.
141. "The Price of Silence," *Panorama*, BBC1, 10 March 2002.
142. Catholic Commission for Justice and Peace inside Zimbabwe, *Gukurahundi in Zimbabwe*; "Survivors Tell of Slaughter by Zimbabwe Army," *The Times*, 26 February 1983, 24.
143. "The Price of Silence."
144. Hazel Cameron, "The Matabeleland Massacres: Britain's Wilful Blindness," *International History Review* 40 (2017): 1–19.
145. TNA, PRO, CAB 129/211/11, "Statement on the Defense Estimates 1981," 70.
146. Roger Reese, *Red Commanders: A Social History of the Soviet Army Officer Corps, 1918–1991* (Lawrence: University Press of Kansas, 2005).
147. Reagan Library: European and Soviet Directorate NSC (Thatcher Visit—Dec 84 [4] Box 90902).
148. Tim Butcher, "Britain Will Pull Military Trainers Out of Zimbabwe," *Telegraph*, 20 February 2001.

CONCLUSION: MILITARY ASSISTANCE AS A DIPLOMATIC WEAPON
 1. Sarah Stockwell, "'Losing an Empire and Winning Friends': Sandhurst and British Decolonization," in *The British End of the British Empire* (Cambridge: Cambridge University Press, 2018), 268.
 2. Richard Bitzinger, "Chinese Arms Production and Sales to the Third World" (Santa Monica, CA, 1991), vi.
 3. Eric Grove, "The Falklands War and British Defence Policy," *Defense and Strategy Analysis* 18, no. 4 (2010): 307–317; Secretary of State for Defence, *The Falklands Campaign: The Lessons* (London: HMSO, 1983), 35.
 4. Skype interview with Major General Colin Shortis, 11 October 2013.
 5. Interview with Curt Harig, 5 August 2013.
 6. T. P. Toyne-Sewell, "Zimbabwe and the British Military Advisory and Training Team," *Army Quarterly and Defence Journal* 121 (January 1991): 53–60.
 7. Paul Moorcraft, *Mugabe's War Machine: Saving or Savaging Zimbabwe?* (Barnsley, UK: Pen & Sword Military, 2011), 131.
 8. "Zimbabwe 'Cannot Afford' Congo War," *BBC News*, 31 August 2000, http://news.bbc.co.uk/2/hi/africa/904534.stm.
 9. Claude Welch, *Soldier and State in Africa: A Comparative Analysis of Military Intervention and Political Change* (Evanston, IL: Northwestern University Press, 1970), 7; Samuel Huntington, *The Soldier and the State: The Theory and Politics of Civil-Military Relations* (Cambridge, MA: Harvard University Press, 1957).
10. Blessing-Miles Tendi, "The Motivations and Dynamics of Zimbabwe's 2017 Military Coup," *African Affairs* 119, no. 474 (24 January 2020): 39–67.
11. Tendi, 39.
12. Herbert Howe, *Ambiguous Order: Military Forces in African States* (Boulder, CO: Lynne Rienner, 2001), 35.
13. Howe, 37.

14. Skype interview with Major General Colin Shortis, 21 October 2013.
15. Toyne-Sewell, "Zimbabwe and the British Military Advisory and Training Team."
16. Hanania Lungu and Naison Ngoma, "The Zambian Military—Trials, Tribulations and Hope," in *Evolutions and Revolutions: A Contemporary History of Militaries in Southern Africa*, ed. Martin Rupiya (Pretoria: Institute for Security Studies, 2005), 313–330.
17. "Increasing Training Capabilities for the British Army Training Unit Kenya—Inside DIO," accessed 14 April 2021, https://insideDIO.blog.gov.uk/2021/03/03/increasing-training-capabilities-for-the-british-army-training-unit-kenya/.
18. Eric Evans, *Thatcher and Thatcherism* (New York: Routledge, 2004), 87.
19. Gebru Tareke, *The Ethiopian Revolution: War in the Horn of Africa* (New Haven, CT: Yale University Press, 2009).
20. "The Price of Silence," *Panorama*, BBC1, 10 March 2002.
21. Reagan Library: European and Soviet Directorate NSC (Thatcher Visit—Dec 84 [4] Box 90902).
22. ZNA Public Relations Directorate, "People's Militia a Strong Base for Defence," *Zimbabwe National Army Magazine*, January 1986, 4.
23. ZNA Public Relations Directorate, 4.
24. Claire Taylor, *A Brief Guide to Previous British Defence Reviews* (London: House of Commons Library, 2010), 8.
25. A. W. Dennis, "The Integration of Guerrilla Armies into Conventional Forces: Lessons Learnt from BMATT in Africa," *South African Defence Review* 5 (1992): 4.

BIBLIOGRAPHY

UNPUBLISHED PRIMARY SOURCES
Admiralty Papers, Operational Reports (The National Archives, London, UK)
Cabinet Papers (The National Archives, London, UK)
Colonial Office Papers (The National Archives, London, UK)
Dominion Office Papers (The National Archives, London, UK)
Foreign and Commonwealth Office Papers (The National Archives, London, UK)
Imperial War Museum Interview Archive (London, UK)
Margaret Thatcher Papers (The Churchill Archive, UK)
Ministry of Defence Papers (The National Archives, London, UK)
National Security Council Papers (Reagan Library, Simi Valley, CA, USA)
Office of National Assessments Papers (The National Archives of Australia)
US State Department FOIA Archive (US State Department, Washington, DC)
War Office Papers (The National Archives, London, UK)
William Dimoline Papers (Liddell Hart Centre for Military Archives, UK)

NEWSPAPERS
Bulawayo Chronicle
Herald (formerly the *Rhodesian Herald*)
Independent (UK)
New York Times
Telegraph (UK)
The Times (UK)
Zimbabwe News
Zimbabwe Review

PUBLISHED PRIMARY SOURCES
The Africa Fund. *Don't Feed the Wild Geese*. New York: American Committee on
    Africa, 1978.
———. *Rhodesia to Zimbabwe: No Middle Ground in Africa*. New York: American
    Committee on Africa, 1969.
———. *Zimbabwe: Battleground for Freedom*. New York: American Committee
    on Africa, 1976.
"Announcement of Unilateral Declaration of Independence." *East Africa and Rho-
    desia*, 18 November 1965, 204–205.
Anti-Apartheid Movement. *Fire Force Exposed: The Rhodesian Security Forces and
    Their Role in Defending White Supremacy*. Anti-Apartheid Movement Collec-
    tion. Anti-Apartheid Movement, November 1979. Bodleian Library, University
    of Oxford.
———. "Memorandum to the Secretary of State for Foreign and Commonwealth
    Affairs: Oil Sanctions in Rhodesia." London: Anti-Apartheid Movement, 1978.

Barnes, Robert. "Vigilante! Anti–Stock Theft Force on a Rhodesian Ranch." *Soldier of Fortune*, April 1979, 54–59.

Bartlett, Hubert Moyse. *The King's African Rifles: A Study in the Military History of East and Central Africa 1890–1945*. Aldershot: Gale & Polden, 1956.

Bax, Timothy. *Three Sips of Gin: Dominating the Battlespace with Rhodesia's Elite Selous Scouts*. London: Helion, 2013.

Belfiglio, Valentine. "A Case for Rhodesia." *African Affairs* 77 (April 1978): 197–213.

Bitzinger, Richard. "Chinese Arms Production and Sales to the Third World." Santa Monica, CA: RAND Corporation, 1991.

Blake, Robert. *A History of Rhodesia*. New York: Alfred A. Knopf, 1977.

Bopela, Thula, and Daluxolo Luthuli. *Umkhonto we Sizwe: Fighting for a Divided People*. Alberton, South Africa: Galago Books, 2005.

Boys, R. A. "BMATT Zimbabwe." *Journal of the Royal Artillery* 109 (1982): 21–24.

Brelsford, W. V., ed. *The Story of the Northern Rhodesia Regiment*. Lusaka, Northern Rhodesia: Government Printer, 1954.

Brides, Lord Saint. "The Lessons of Zimbabwe-Rhodesia." *International Security* 4 (1980): 177–184.

Butcher, Tim. "Britain Will Pull Military Trainers Out of Zimbabwe." *Telegraph*, 20 February 2001.

Campbell, Guy. *The Charging Buffalo: A History of the Kenya Regiment, 1937–1963*. London: Leo Cooper, 1986.

Carrington, Peter. *Reflect on Things Past: The Memoirs of Lord Carrington*. London: Collins, 1988.

Catholic Commission for Justice and Peace inside Rhodesia. *Rhodesia: The Propaganda War*. New York: Africa Fund, 1977.

Catholic Commission for Justice and Peace inside Zimbabwe. *Gukurahundi in Zimbabwe: A Report on the Disturbances in Matabeleland and the Midlands 1980–1988*. New York: Columbia University Press, 2008.

Cawthra, Gavin. *Brutal Force: The Apartheid War Machine*. London: International Defence & Aid Fund for Southern Africa, 1986.

Charlton, Les. "Defence of Nation." *Horizon: The Magazine of the Rhodesian Selection Trust Group of Companies*, 1965.

Cilliers, J. K. *Counter-insurgency in Rhodesia*. London: Croom Helm, 1985.

Director of Security Manpower. *National Service Information Sheet*. Salisbury: Director of Security Manpower, 1977.

Enloe, Cynthia. *Ethnic Soldiers: State Security in Divided Societies*. Athens: University of Georgia Press, 1980.

Federation of Rhodesia and Nyasaland. *Annual Report of the Secretary for Defence and the Chief of General Staff and of the Chief of Air Staff for the Year Ended 31st December, 1960*. Salisbury: Government Printer, 1961.

———. *Debates of the Federal Assembly, Second Session, Second Parliament, 28th March to 19th July 1960*. Salisbury: Parliamentary Printer, 1961.

———. *Debates of the Federal Assembly, Second Session, Third Parliament*. Salisbury: Parliamentary Printer, 1963.

———. *Debates of the Federal Assembly, Third Session, First Parliament, 25th June, 1956 to 16th August, 1956*. Salisbury: Parliamentary Printer, 1957.

"First African Padre." *Assegai: The Magazine of the Rhodesian Army*, February 1979, 13.

Flower, Ken. *Serving Secretly: An Intelligence Chief on Record, Rhodesia into Zimbabwe, 1964 to 1981*. London: John Murray, 1987.

Fuller, Alexandra. *Don't Let's Go to the Dogs Tonight*. New York: Random House, 2003.

———. *Scribbling the Cat Travels with an African Soldier*. New York: Penguin Books, 2004.

Galbraith, John S. *Crown and Charter: The Early Years of the British South Africa Company*. Berkeley: University of California Press, 1974.

Gill, Leonard. *Remembering the Regiment*. Victoria, BC: Trafford, 2004.

Godwin, Peter. *Mukiwa: A White Boy in Africa*. New York: Grove Press, 1996.

Godwin, Peter, and Ian Hancock. *"Rhodesians Never Die": The Impact of War and Political Change on White Rhodesia, 1970–1980*. Oxford: Oxford University Press, 1993.

Gray, D. "Commissioning of African Officers at the School of Infantry, Gwelo." *Assegai: The Magazine of the Rhodesian Army*, July 1977, 19–20.

Great Britain, Colonial Office. *Colonial Office Annual Report on the East Africa High Commission, 1959*. London: HMSO, 1960.

———. *Colonial Office Report on the Colony and Protectorate of Kenya for the Year 1951*. London: HMSO, 1952.

———. *Colonial Office Report on the Colony and Protectorate of Kenya for the Year 1956*. London: HMSO, 1957.

———. *Colonial Office Report on the Colony and Protectorate of Kenya for the Year 1957*. London: HMSO, 1958.

———. *Colonial Office Report on the Colony and Protectorate of Kenya for the Year 1958*. London: HMSO, 1959.

———. *Colonial Office Report on the Colony and Protectorate of Kenya for the Year 1959*. London: HMSO, 1960.

———. *Colonial Office Report on the Colony and Protectorate of Kenya for the Year 1962*. London: HMSO, 1964.

———. *Colonial Reports: Northern Rhodesia, 1957*. Lusaka, Northern Rhodesia: Government Printer, 1958.

———. *Rhodesia, Report of the Commission on Rhodesian Opinion under the Chairmanship of the Right Honorable Lord Pearce, Presented to Parliament by the Secretary of State for Foreign and Commonwealth Affairs by Command of Her Majesty, May 1972*. London: HMSO, 1972.

"Grey's Scouts Ride Again." *Soldier of Fortune*, March 1978.

Hardinge, Arthur. *A Diplomat in the East*. London: Jonathan Cape, 1928.

Hutson, H. P. W. *Rhodesia: Ending an Era*. London: Springwood Books, 1978.

Information Service, Zambia. "Marshal of Zambia." *Zambia*, November 1966, 21.

———. "Wings Awarded to First Zambian Pilots." *Zambia*, December 1966, 21.

———. "Zambian Army Trainees." *Zambia*, February 1968, 19.

"Intake 183." *Assegai: The Magazine of the Rhodesian Army*, February 1979, 12–13.

"Integrated Training at Depot, Rhodesia Regiment." *Assegai: The Magazine of the Rhodesian Army*, December 1977, 17–18.

International Institute for Strategic Studies. "Part III: Non-aligned Countries." *Military Balance* 65, no. 1 (January 1965): 34–39.

"Interview with Rhodesian Army Recruiting Officer." *Soldier of Fortune*, Spring 1977, 14–16.

Itote, Waruhiu. *"Mau Mau" General*. Nairobi: East African Publishing House, 1967.

Keegan, John. *World Armies*. New York: Facts on File, 1979.

Kenya. *Kenya National Assembly Official Record (Hansard)*. Vol. 90. Nairobi, 1962.

———. *Kenya National Assembly Official Record (Hansard)*. Series 4, vol. 10. Nairobi, 1966.

Kinloch, Graham. "Problems of Community Development in Rhodesia." *Community Development Journal* 7 (October 1972): 189–193.

———. *Racial Conflict in Rhodesia: A Social-historical Study*. Washington DC: University Press of America, 1978.

———. "Social Types and Race Relations in the Colonial Setting: A Case Study of Rhodesia." *Phylon* 33 (1972): 276–289.

Kraus, Jon. "The Men in Charge." *Africa Report* 11 (April 1966): 16–20.

Lee, John. *African Armies and Civil Order*. New York: Praeger, 1969.

Leonard, Richard. *South Africa at War: White Crisis in Southern Africa*. Westport, CT: Lawrence Hill, 1983.

Liberation Support Movement. *Zimbabwe: The Final Advance, Documents on the Zimbabwe Liberation Movement*. Oakland, CA: Liberation Support Movement Press, 1978.

Llewellin, Lord. "Some Facts about the Federation of Rhodesia and Nyasaland." *African Affairs* 55 (October 1956): 266–272.

Luckham, A. R. "Institutional Transfer and Breakdown in a New Nation: The Nigerian Military." *Administrative Science Quarterly* 16, no. 4 (1971): 387–406.

Martin, Faan. *James and the Duck: Tales of the Rhodesian Bush War (1964–1980)*. Bloomington, IN: Authorhouse, 2007.

McAleese, Peter. *No Mean Soldier: The Autobiography of a Professional Fighting Man*. London: Orion, 1993.

McLaglen, Andrew V., dir. *The Wild Geese*. Varius, 1978.

McLaughlin, P. "Collaborators, Mercenaries or Patriots? The 'Problem' of African Troops in Southern Rhodesia during the First and Second World Wars." *Zimbabwean History* 10 (1979): 21–50.

———. "Victims as Defenders: African Troops in the Rhodesian Defence System 1890–1980." *Small Wars and Insurgencies* 2 (1991): 240–275.

Moorcraft, Paul, and Peter McLaughlin. *The Rhodesian War: A Military History*. Johannesburg: Jonathan Ball, 2008.

Moore, Robin. *Major Mike: As Told to Robin Moore*. New York: Charter, 1978.

Moore-King, Bruce. *White Man Black War*. London: Penguin Books, 1988.

Nkomo, Joshua. *Nkomo: The Story of My Life*. London: Methuen, 1984.

"Officers Commissioned at Inkomo Garrison." *Assegai: The Magazine of the Rhodesian Army*, March 1978, 17–20.

Pettman, Jan. *Zambia: Security and Conflict*. New York: St. Martin's Press, 1974.

"Presentation of Kim Rule's Sword." *Assegai: The Magazine of the Rhodesian Army*, September 1977, 19–20.

"The Price of Silence." *Panorama*. BBC1, 10 March 2002.

Ranger, Terence. "Conflict in Rhodesia: A Question of Evidence." *African Affairs* 77 (January 1978): 3–5.

Rhodesia, House of Assembly. *Parliamentary Debates, House of Assembly, Fourth Session, Thirteenth Parliament Comprising Period from 21st June, 1977 to 15th July 1977*. Salisbury: Government Printer, 1977.

Rhodesia, Ministry of Defence. *Pfumo Revanhu*. Salisbury: Government Printer, 1978.

Rhodesia, Ministry of Information. *Aggression: A Rhodesian Viewpoint*. Salisbury: Rhodesian Ministry of Information, 1977.

———. *Anatomy of Terror*. Salisbury: Rhodesian Ministry of Information, 1974.

———. *Background Briefing: Terrorists, Missionaries and the West*. Salisbury: Rhodesian Ministry of Information, 1977.

———. *The South African Rhodesian: A Special Breed*. Salisbury: Lin Mehmel Associates, 1977.

Rhodesia, Northern. *Report of the Commission Appointed to Review the Salaries and Conditions of Service of the Northern Rhodesia Public and Teaching Services and of the Northern Rhodesia Army and Air Force*. Lusaka, Northern Rhodesia: Government Printer, 1964.

Rhodesia, Southern. *Report of the Commander Military Forces for the Year Ended 31st December, 1950*. Salisbury: Government Printer, 1951.

Rhodesia and Nyasaland Army. *Ceremonial Parade: Farewell to the Federal Prime Minister the Right Honorable Sir Roy Welensky, KCMG, MP*. Salisbury: Government Printer, 1963.

———. *Dissolution of the Federation of Rhodesia and Nyasaland: Options Available to Officers and European Members*. Salisbury: Government Printer, 1963.

Rhodesian Army. "Terrorism Stops Here!" Poster, 1972. https://www.iwm.org.uk /collections/item/object/41832.

Rhodesian Information Office. *The New Environment*. Salisbury: Rhodesian Ministry of Information, 1973.

Rotberg, Robert I. *The Rise of Nationalism in Central Africa: The Making of Malawi and Zambia, 1873–1946*. Cambridge, MA: Harvard University Press, 1965.

Rupiah, Martin. "Demobilisation and Integration: 'Operation Merger' and the Zimbabwe National Defence Forces, 1980–1987." *African Security Review* 4 (1994): 52–64.

Secretary of State for Defence. *The Falklands Campaign: The Lessons*. London: HMSO, 1983.

Sibamba, Francis Gershom. *The Zambia Army and I: Autobiography of a Former Army Commander*. Ndola, Zambia: Mission Press, 2010.

Smith, Ian. *The Great Betrayal: The Memoirs of Ian Douglas Smith*. London: Blake Publishing, 1997.

———. "Southern Rhodesia and Its Future." *African Affairs* 63 (January 1964): 13–22.

South Africa, Truth and Reconciliation Commission. *Truth and Reconciliation Commission of South Africa Report*. Cape Town: Truth and Reconciliation Commission, 1999.

Spencer, Ian. "Settler Dominance, Agricultural Production and the Second World War in Kenya." *Journal of African History* 21 (1980): 497–514.

Stiff, Peter, and Ron Reid-Daly. *Selous Scouts: Top Secret War.* Alberton, South Africa: Galago Books, 1982.

Thatcher, Margaret. *The Downing Street Years.* New York: HarperCollins, 1993.

Towsey, Kenneth. "U.S. Rhodesian Policy." *Congressional Digest* 52 (February 1973): 56–62.

Toyne-Sewell, T. P. "Zimbabwe and the British Military Advisory and Training Team." *Army Quarterly and Defence Journal* 121 (January 1991): 53–60.

Turner, Arthur Campbell. "Independent Rhodesia." *Current History* 58 (March 1970): 129–134.

Weinrich, A. K. H. *Soldier and State in Africa: A Comparative Analysis of Military Intervention and Political Change.* Evanston, IL: Northwestern University Press, 1970.

———. "Strategic Resettlement in Rhodesia." *Journal of Southern African Studies* 3 (April 1977): 207–229.

Wheeler, Douglas. "African Elements in Portugal's Armies in Africa (1961–1974)." *Armed Forces and Society* 2 (February 1976): 233–250.

Wilkinson, Anthony. *Insurgency in Rhodesia, 1957–1973: An Account and Assessment.* London: International Institute for Strategic Studies, 1973.

Windrich, Elaine. *Britain and the Politics of Rhodesian Independence.* London: Croom Helm, 1978.

———. *The Rhodesian Problem: A Documentary History 1923–1973.* London: Routledge & Kegan Paul, 1975.

Winfrey, Carey. "Texan in the Rhodesian Army Says He Fights for Love, Not Money." *New York Times,* 2 September 1979, 10.

Woodmansee, John. "Mao's Protracted War: Theory vs. Practice." *Parameters* 3 (1973): 30–45.

Wylie, Dan. *Dead Leaves: Two Years in the Rhodesian War.* Pietermaritzburg: University of Natal Press, 2002.

Zambia. *Report of the Commission Appointed to Review the Grading Structure of the Civil Service, the Salary Scales of the Civil Service, the Teaching Service, the Zambian Police and the Prison Service. The Salary Scales and Wages of Non–Civil Service (Industrial) Employees of the Government and the Pay Scales and Conditions of Service of the Zambia Defence Forces.* Lusaka, Zambia: Government Printer, 1966.

ZNA Public Relations Directorate. "People's Militia a Strong Base for Defence." *Zimbabwe National Army Magazine,* January 1986, 4.

SECONDARY SOURCES

Albright, David. "South Africa's Nuclear Weapons Program." MIT Security Studies Program. March 2001. http://web.mit.edu/ssp/seminars/wed_archives01spring/albright.htm.

Anderson, David. *Histories of the Hanged: The Dirty War in Kenya and the End of Empire.* New York: W. W. Norton, 2005.

Ashford, Nicholas. "Creation of Zimbabwe Army Held Up." *The Times.* 6 June 1980.

———. "Missile Brought Down Rhodesian Airliner." *The Times*, 8 September 1978, 1.

———. "Zimbabwe to Disarm Both Guerrilla Factions." *The Times*, 18 February 1981, 7.

Balesi, Charles J. *From Adversaries to Comrades-in-Arms: West Africans and the French Military, 1885–1918*. Waltham, MA: Crossroads Press, 1979.

Beach, Hugh. "Carver, (Richard) Michael Power, Baron Carver (1915–2001)." In *Oxford Dictionary of National Biography*, edited by Lawrence Goldman. Oxford: Oxford University Press. Accessed 24 July 2013. http://www.oxforddnb.com.libezproxy.tamu.edu:2048/view/article/76553.

Bennett, Huw C. *Fighting the Mau Mau: The British Army and Counter-insurgency in the Kenya Emergency*. London: Cambridge University Press, 2012.

Binda, Alexandre. *Masodja: The History of the Rhodesian African Rifles and Its Forerunner the Rhodesian Native Regiment*. Johannesburg: 30 Degrees South Publishers, 2007.

Branch, Daniel. *Defeating Mau Mau, Creating Kenya: Counterinsurgency, Civil War and Decolonization*. London: Cambridge University Press, 2009.

Brands, Hal. "Wartime Recruiting Practices, Martial Identity and Post–World War II Demobilization in Colonial Kenya." *Journal of African History* 46 (2005): 103–125.

Brent, Winston. *Rhodesian Air Force: A Brief History 1947–1980*. Kwambonambi, South Africa: Freeworld Publications, 1987.

Burke, Edward. *An Army of Tribes: British Army Cohesion, Deviancy, and Murder in Northern Ireland*. Liverpool: Liverpool University Press, 2018.

Butler, L. J. "The Central African Federation and Britain's Post-war Nuclear Programme: Reconsidering the Connections." *Journal of Imperial and Commonwealth History* 36 (September 2008): 509–525.

"Cabinet Faces Crisis on Zambia Troops." *The Times*, 27 November 1965, 8.

Cain, P. J., and A. G. Hopkins. *British Imperialism, 1688–2000*. London: Longman, 2002.

Cameron, Hazel. "The Matabeleland Massacres: Britain's Wilful Blindness." *International History Review* 40 (2017): 1–16.

"Camp Fighting Caught RSM by Surprise." *Herald*, 6 March 1981, 3.

Cann, John. *Counterinsurgency in Africa: The Portuguese Way of War 1961–1974*. London: Greenwood Press, 1997.

Chan, Stephen. *Robert Mugabe: A Life of Power and Violence*. Ann Arbor: University of Michigan Press, 2003.

Clayton, Anthony. *The British Officer: Leading the Army from 1660 to the Present*. Harlow, UK: Pearson Longman, 2006.

———. *Counter-insurgency in Kenya: A Study of Military Operations against Mau Mau*. London: Frank Cass, 1976.

———. *France, Soldiers and Africa*. London: Brassey's Defence Publishers, 1988.

———. *Frontiersmen: Warfare in Africa since 1950*. London: University College London Press, 1999.

Clayton, Anthony, and David Killingray. *Khaki and Blue: Military and Police in British Colonial Africa*. Athens: Ohio University Center for International Studies, 1989.

Compagnon, Daniel. *A Predictable Tragedy: Robert Mugabe and the Collapse of Zimbabwe*. Philadelphia: University of Pennsylvania Press, 2011.

Cowderoy, Dudley, and Roy Nesbit. *War in the Air: Rhodesian Air Force, 1935–1980*. Alberton, South Africa: Galago Books, 1987.

Davidow, Jeffrey. *Peace in Southern Africa: The Lancaster House Conference on Rhodesia, 1979*. Boulder, CO: Westview Press, 1984.

Dennis, A. W. "The Integration of Guerrilla Armies into Conventional Forces: Lessons Learnt from BMATT in Africa." *South African Defence Review* 5 (1992). http://www.iss.org.za/Pubs/ASR/SADR5/Dennis.html.

DeRoche, Andrew. "'You Can't Fight Guns with Knives': National Security and Zambian Responses to UDI, 1965–1973." In *One Zambia, Many Histories: Towards a History of Post-colonial Zambia*, edited by Jan-Bart Gewald and Marja Hinfelaar, 77–97. Boston: Brill, 2008.

"Detective Helps SA Spy Escape." *Herald*, 19 November 1981, 1.

De Waal, D. C. *With Rhodes in Mashonaland*. Bulawayo: Books of Rhodesia, 1974.

Echenberg, Myron. *Colonial Conscripts: The Tirailleurs Senegalais in French West Africa, 1857–1960*. Portsmouth, NH: Heinemann, 1990.

Edgerton, Robert B. *Africa's Armies from Honor to Infamy: A History from 1791 to the Present*. Cambridge, MA: Westview Press, 2002.

Elkins, Caroline. *Imperial Reckoning: The Untold Story of Britain's Gulag in Kenya*. New York: Henry Holt, 2005.

Ellert, H. *The Rhodesian Front War*. Harare: Mambo Press, 1989.

Emizet, Kisangani. "Explaining the Rise and Fall of Military Regimes: Civil-Military Relations in the Congo." *Armed Forces and Society* 26 (Winter 2000): 203–227.

Evans, Eric. *Thatcher and Thatcherism*. New York: Routledge, 2004.

Evans, Michael. "Making an African Army: The Case of Zimbabwe, 1980–87." In *Peace, Politics and Violence in the New South Africa*, edited by Norman Etherington, 231–253. London: Hans Zell Publishers, 1992.

Farwell, Byron. *Armies of the Raj: From the Great Indian Mutiny to Independence, 1858–1947*. New York: Norton, 1989.

Fitzgibbon, Benjamin Grob. *Imperial Endgame: Britain's Dirty Wars and the End of Empire*. New York: Palgrave Macmillan, 2011.

Gibbs, Peter, Hugh Phillips, and Nick Russell. *Blue and Old Gold: The History of the British South Africa Police 1889–1980*. Johannesburg: 30 Degrees South, 2009.

Gordon, David F. *Decolonization and the State in Kenya*. London: Westview Press, 1986.

Grove, Eric. "The Falklands War and British Defence Policy." *Defense and Strategy Analysis* 18, no. 4 (2010): 307–317.

Grundy, Kenneth. *Soldiers without Politics: Blacks in the South African Armed Forces*. Berkeley: University of California Press, 1983.

Hemming, Philip E. "Macmillan and the End of the British Empire in Africa." In *Harold Macmillan and Britain's World Role*, edited by Richard Aldous and Sabine Lee, 97–122. London: Macmillan, 1996.

Hennessy, Peter, and Anthony Seldon. "The Attlee Government, 1945–1951." In *Ruling Performance: British Governments from Attlee to Thatcher*, edited by Peter Hennessy and Anthony Seldon, 28–62. Oxford: Blackwell, 1987.

Holland, R. F. *European Decolonization 1918–1981: An Introductory Survey*. New York: St. Martin's Press, 1985.

Horne, Gerald. *From the Barrel of a Gun: The United States and the War against Zimbabwe, 1965–1980*. Chapel Hill: University of North Carolina Press, 2001.

Hornsby, Charles. *Kenya: A History since Independence*. London: I. B. Tauris, 2012.

Howe, Herbert. *Ambiguous Order: Military Forces in African States*. Boulder, CO: Lynne Rienner, 2001.

Hubbard, Douglas H., Jr. *Bound for Africa: Cold War Fight along the Zambezi*. Annapolis, MD: Naval Institute Press, 2008.

Huntington, Samuel. *The Soldier and the State: The Theory and Politics of Civil-Military Relations*. Cambridge, MA: Harvard University Press, 1957.

"Increasing Training Capabilities for the British Army Training Unit Kenya—Inside DIO." Accessed 14 April 2021. https://insideDIO.blog.gov.uk/2021/03/03 /increasing-training-capabilities-for-the-british-army-training-unit-kenya/.

Jackson, Ashley. "British-African Defence and Security Concerns." *Defence Studies* 6 (September 2006): 351–376.

Jacob, Abel. "Israel's Military Aid to Africa, 1960–66." *Journal of Modern African Studies* 9, no. 2 (1971): 165–187.

Kent, John. *British Imperial Strategy and the Origins of the Cold War 1944–49*. Leicester, UK: Leicester University Press, 1993.

Keppel-Jones, Arthur. *Rhodes and Rhodesia: The White Conquest of Zimbabwe 1884–1902*. Kingston, ON: McGill-Queen's University Press, 1983.

"Killer Bomb at ZANU(PF) Headquarters." *Herald*, 19 December 1981, 1.

Killingray, David, and David Omissi. "Military Power in German Colonial Policy: The Schultztruppen and Their Leaders in East and South West Africa 1888–1918." In *Guardians of Empire: The Armed Forces of the Colonial Powers c. 1700–1964*, edited by David Killingray and David Omissi, 91–113. Manchester: Manchester University Press, 1999.

King, Anthony. *Frontline: Combat and Cohesion in the Twenty-First Century*. Oxford: Oxford University Press, 2015.

Kriger, Norma. *Guerrilla Veterans in Post-war Zimbabwe: Symbolic and Violent Politics, 1980–1987*. Cambridge: Cambridge University Press, 2003.

Kyle, Keith. *The Politics of the Independence of Kenya*. New York: St. Martin's Press, 1999.

Lamb, Richard. *The Macmillan Years, 1957–1963: The Emerging Truth*. London: John Murray, 1995.

Lawler, Nancy. *Soldiers of Misfortune: Ivoirien Tirailleurs of World War II*. Athens: Ohio University Press, 1992.

Learmont, J. H. "Reflections from Rhodesia." *RUSI: Royal United Services Institute for Defense Studies, Journal* 125 (December 1980): 47–55.

Leaver, John David. "Multiracialism and Nationisms: A Political Retrospective on 1950s Southern Rhodesia." *Journal of Third World Studies* 23 (2006): 167–188.

Legum, Colin. *The Battlefronts of Southern Africa*. New York: Africana Publishing, 1988.

Louis, Wm. Roger. "Britannia's Mau Mau." In *Penultimate Adventures with Britannia: Personalities, Politics and Culture in Britain*, edited by Wm. Roger Louis, 259–274. London: I. B. Tauris, 2008.

Louis, Wm. Roger, and Roger Owens, eds. *Suez 1956: The Crisis and Its Consequences.* Oxford: Clarendon Paperbacks, 1989.

Lowry, Donal. "The Impact of Anti-communism on White Rhodesian Political Culture ca. 1920s–1980." *Cold War History* 7 (May 2007): 169–194.

———. *Oxford Dictionary of National Biography—Welensky, Sir Ronald [Roy] (1907–1991), Prime Minister of the Federation of Rhodesia and Nyasaland.* November 2004. http://www.oxforddnb.com/view/printable/50688.

"Loyalty Is All, PM Tells Army." *Herald,* 31 October 1981, 1.

Lungu, Hanania, and Naison Ngoma. "The Zambian Military: Trials, Tribulations and Hope." In *Evolutions and Revolutions: A Contemporary History of Militaries in Southern Africa,* edited by Martin Rupiya, 313–330. Pretoria: Institute for Security Studies, 2005.

Luscombe, Stephen. "The Kenya Police: A Living History Written by Those Who Served: Volumes 1, 2 and 3." Accessed 26 January 2021. https://www.britishempire.co.uk/library/kenyapolice.htm.

MacKenzie, John. *Propaganda and Empire: The Manipulation of British Public Opinion, 1880–1960.* Manchester: Manchester University Press, 1984.

MacQueen, Norrie. *The Decolonization of Portuguese Africa: Metropolitan Revolution and the Dissolution of Empire.* New York: Longman, 1997.

Mandaza, Ibbo Day Joseph. "White Settler Ideology, African Nationalism and the 'Coloured' Question in Southern Africa: Southern Rhodesia/Zimbabwe, Northern Rhodesia/Zambia, and Nyasaland/Malawi, 1900–1976." PhD diss., University of York, 1979.

Melson, Charles. "Top Secret War: Rhodesian Special Operations." *Small Wars and Insurgencies* 16 (March 2005): 57–82.

Meredith, Martin. *The Fate of Africa from the Hopes of Freedom to the Heart of Despair: A History of 50 Years of Independence.* New York: Public Affairs, 2005.

Metcalf, Thomas R. *Imperial Connections: India in the Indian Ocean Arena, 1860–1920.* Berkeley: University of California Press, 2007.

"Military Teams from Britain and Korea Here to Stay." *Herald,* 13 November 1981.

Mills, Greg. "BMATT and Military Integration in Southern Africa." *South African Defence Review* 2 (1992): 1–10.

Minnich, James. *The North Korean People's Army: Origins and Current Tactics.* Annapolis, MD: Naval Institute Press, 2005.

Minter, William, and Elizabeth Schmidt. "When Sanctions Worked: The Case of Rhodesia Reexamined." *African Affairs* 87, no. 347 (1988): 207–237.

Mockaitis, Thomas. *British Counterinsurgency, 1919–1960.* London: Macmillan, 1990.

Moorcraft, Paul. *Mugabe's War Machine: Saving or Savaging Zimbabwe?* Barnsley, UK: Pen & Sword Military, 2011.

Moorcraft, Paul, and Peter McLaughlin. *The Rhodesian War: A Military History.* Johannesburg: Jonathan Ball, 2008.

"Mr. Kaunda to Build Up Forces Swiftly." *The Times,* 10 December 1965, 10.

Munene, Njagi. "The Colonial Legacy in Kenya-British Military Relations: 1963–2005," PhD diss., Kenyatta University, 2013.

Mungazi, Dickson. *The Last Defenders of the Laager: Ian Smith and F. W. de Klerk.* London: Praeger, 1998.

Newsinger, John. *British Counter-insurgency: From Palestine to Northern Ireland.* New York: Palgrave, 2002.

"No Blueprint for Success." *Herald,* 6 October 1981.

Parsons, Timothy. *The African Rank-and-File: Social Implications of Colonial Military Service in the King's African Rifles, 1902–1964.* Portsmouth, NH: Heinemann, 1999.

———. *The 1964 Army Mutinies and the Making of Modern East Africa.* Westport, CT: Praeger, 2003.

———. "'Wakamba Warriors Are Soldiers of the Queen': The Evolution of the Kamba as a Martial Race, 1890–1970." *Ethnohistory* 46 (1999): 671–701.

Percox, David. *Britain, Kenya and the Cold War: Imperial Defence, Colonial Security and Decolonisation.* New York: Tauris Academic Studies, 2004.

———. "Mau Mau and the Arming of the State." In *Mau Mau and Nationhood: Arms, Authority and Narration,* edited by E. S. Atieno Odhiambo and John Lonsdale, 121–155. Oxford: James Currey, 2003.

Phiri, Bizeck Jube. *A Political History of Zambia: From Colonial Rule to the Third Republic, 1890–2001.* Trenton, NJ: Africa World Press, 2006.

Pilossof, Rory. *The Unbearable Whiteness of Being: Farmers' Voices from Zimbabwe.* Harare: Weaver, 2012.

Raftopoulos, Brian, and Alois Mlambo, eds. *Becoming Zimbabwe.* Harare: Weaver, 2009.

Ranger, Terence. "Violence Variously Remembered: The Killing of Pieter Oberholzer in July 1964." *History in Africa* 24 (1997): 273–286.

Ranger, Terence, and Ngwabi Bhebe. *Soldiers in Zimbabwe's Liberation War.* Harare: University of Zimbabwe Publications, 1995.

Reese, Roger. *Red Commanders: A Social History of the Soviet Army Officer Corps, 1918–1991.* Lawrence: University Press of Kansas, 2005.

Reid, Richard J. *Warfare in African History.* Cambridge: Cambridge University Press, 2012.

———. *War in Pre-colonial Eastern Africa: The Patterns and Meanings of State Level Conflict in the 19th Century.* Athens: Ohio University Press, 2007.

"Rhodesia Discussions Break Down." *The Times,* 9 October 1965, 10.

Roberts, Brian. *Cecil Rhodes: Flawed Colossus.* New York: W. W. Norton, 1987.

Rupiah, Martin. "The 'Expanding Torrent': British Military Assistance to the Southern African Region." *African Security Review* 5 (1996): 51–59.

Sadomba, Zvakanyorwa Wilbert. *War Veterans in Zimbabwe's Revolution: Challenging Neo-colonialism and Settler and International Capital.* Suffolk: James Currey, 2011.

Seegers, Annette. "Revolutionary Armies of Africa: Mozambique and Zimbabwe." In *Military Power and Politics in Black Africa,* edited by Simon Baynham, 129–165. London: Croom Helm, 1986.

Seirlis, J. K. "Undoing the United Front? Coloured Soldiers in Rhodesia 1939–1980." *African Studies* 63 (July 2004): 73–94.

Shovelton, Patrick. "Sir Laurence Pumphrey: Diplomat Decorated for Wartime Bravery who Later Served as Ambassador to Pakistan." *The Independent,* 4 February 2010.

Shubin, Vladimir. *The Hot "Cold War": The USSR in Southern Africa.* Scottsville, South Africa: University of KwaZulu-Natal Press, 2008.

———. "Unsung Heroes: The Soviet Military and the Liberation of Southern Africa." *Cold War History* 7, no. 2 (May 2007): 251–262.

Shutt, Allison. "The Natives Are Getting Out of Hand: Legislating Manners, Insolence and Contemptuous Behavior in Southern Rhodesia, c. 1910–1963." *Journal of Southern African Studies* 33 (September 2007): 653–672.

Sibanda, Eliakim. *The Zimbabwe African People's Union, 1961–87: A Political History of Insurgency in Southern Rhodesia.* Trenton, NJ: Africa World Press, 2005.

Smyth, Rosaleen. "War Propaganda during the Second World War in Northern Rhodesia." *African Affairs* 83 (July 1984): 345–358.

"Soldiers Harass Tourists Near Inyanga." *Herald,* 12 December 1981.

"South Africa Invasion Threat Must Be Countered." *Herald,* 29 January 1981.

Stapleton, Timothy. *African Police and Soldiers in Colonial Zimbabwe, 1923–80.* Rochester, NY: University of Rochester Press, 2011.

———. "'Bad Boys': Infiltration and Sedition in the African Military Units of the Central African Federation (Malawi, Zambia and Zimbabwe) 1953–63." *Journal of Military History* 73 (October 2009): 1167–1193.

———. *A Military History of South Africa: From the Dutch-Khoi Wars to the End of Apartheid.* Santa Barbara, CA: Praeger, 2010.

———. *No Insignificant Part: The Rhodesian Native Regiment and the East Africa Campaign of the First World War.* Waterloo, ON: Wilfrid Laurier University Press, 2006.

Stedman, Stephen. *Peacemaking in Civil War: International Mediation in Zimbabwe, 1974–1980.* Boulder, CO: Lynne Rienner Publishers, 1991.

Stockwell, Sarah. "'Losing an Empire and Winning Friends': Sandhurst and British Decolonization." In *The British End of the British Empire,* 234–285. Cambridge: Cambridge University Press, 2018.

Strachan, Hew. "Training, Morale and Modern War." *Journal of Contemporary History* 41, no. 2 (April 2006): 211–227. https://doi.org/10.1177/0022009406062054.

Streak, Brian. "Farewell to the RLI." *Cheetah: The Magazine of the RLI Association,* October 1980, 1–2.

Streets, Heather. *Martial Races: The Military, Race and Masculinity in British Imperial Culture, 1857–1914.* Manchester: Manchester University Press, 2005.

Stubbs, Thomas. "Ethnopolitics and the Military in Kenya." In *Forging Military Identity in Culturally Pluralistic Societies: Quasi-Ethnicity,* edited by D. Zirker, 69–88. Lanham, MD: Lexington Books, 2015.

"Survivors Tell of Slaughter by Zimbabwe Army." *The Times,* 26 February 1983, 24.

Tareke, Gebru. *The Ethiopian Revolution: War in the Horn of Africa.* New Haven, CT: Yale University Press, 2009.

Taylor, Claire. *A Brief Guide to Previous British Defence Reviews.* London: House of Commons Library, 2010.

Taylor, Stephen. "British Hope to Keep Up the Good Work in Zimbabwe." *The Times*, 25 July 1981.
———. "British Team Reinforced in Zimbabwe." *The Times*, 27 October 1982, 8.
———. "Mr. Nkomo Takes On New Cabinet Tasks in Salisbury Compromise." *The Times*, 28 January 1981.
———. "Mugabe Slashes His Army," *The Times*, 27 November 1981.
———. "Nkomo Men Take Stock of Mugabe Snub." *The Times*, 12 January 1981, 4.
———. "White Officer to Lead Zimbabwe Forces." *The Times*, 8 August 1981, 4.
———. "Zimbabwe Jets Destroyed." *The Times*, 26 July 1982, 1.
———. "Zimbabwe Youth March to Back One-Party State." *The Times*, 22 September 1981, 2.
"Technical College on Non-racial Lines." *Kenya Daily Mail*, 1 March 1946.
Tendi, Blessing-Miles. "The Motivations and Dynamics of Zimbabwe's 2017 Military Coup." *African Affairs* 119, no. 474 (24 January 2020): 39–67.
"Thatcher Pledge on Aid to Zimbabwe." *The Times*, 20 May 1982, 8.
"Three White Security Men Arrested in Zimbabwe." *The Times*, 8 January 1982, 4.
Throup, D. W. "Renison, Sir Patrick Muir (1911–1965)." In *Oxford Dictionary of National Biography*, edited by Lawrence Goldman. Oxford: Oxford University Press. Accessed 3 April 2020. http://www.oxforddnb.com.lib-ezproxy.tamu.edu:2048/view/article/38476.
"Uneasy Calm Established in Bulawayo." *Herald*, 13 February 1981, 1.
Vinen, Richard. *National Service: Conscription in Britain, 1945–1963*. New York: Allen Lane, 2014.
Watts, Carl. "Killing Kith and Kin: The Viability of British Military Intervention in Rhodesia, 1964–5." *Twentieth Century British History* 16 (2005): 382–415.
Weitzer, Ronald. *Transforming Settler States: Communal Conflict and Internal Security in Northern Ireland and Zimbabwe*. Berkeley: University of California Press, 1990.
Welch, Claude E. "Civil-Military Relations in Newer Commonwealth States: The Transfer and Transformation of British Models." *Journal of Developing Areas* 12, no. 2 (1978): 153–170.
———. "Praetorianism in Commonwealth West Africa." *Journal of Modern African Studies* 10 (July 1972): 203–222.
———. *Soldier and State in Africa: A Comparative Analysis of Military Intervention and Political Change*. Evanston, IL: Northwestern University Press, 1970.
"Western Democracy May Not Be the Answer." *Herald*, 7 April 1981, 1.
White, Luise. "Civic Virtue, Young Men, and the Family: Conscription in Rhodesia, 1974–1980." *International Journal of African Historical Studies* 37 (2004): 103–121.
———. "'Heading for the Gun': Skills and Sophistication in an African Guerrilla War." *Comparative Studies in Society and History* 51 (2009): 236–259.
———. "'Whoever Saw a Country with Four Armies?': The Battle of Bulawayo Revisited." *Journal of Southern African Studies* 33 (September 2007): 619–631.
Whitehead, Phillip. "The Labour Governments, 1974–1979." In *Ruling Performance:*

British Governments from Attlee to Thatcher, edited by Peter Hennessy and Anthony Seldon, 241–273. Oxford: Basil Blackwell, 1989.

Whiting, Richard. "The Empire in British Politics." In *Britain's Experience of Empire in the Twentieth Century*, edited by Andrew S. Thompson, 161–210. Oxford: Oxford University Press, 2012.

Young, Benjamin. *Guns, Guerillas, and the Great Leader: North Korea and the Third World*. Stanford, CA: Stanford University Press, 2021.

Young, Eric. "Chefs and Worried Soldiers: Authority and Power in the Zimbabwe National Army." *Armed Forces and Society* 24 (1997).

"Zimbabwe Fears Backlash by Nkomo's Men." *The Times*, 18 February 1982, 6.

"Zimbabwe: Operation Glossary—A Guide to Zimbabwe's Internal Campaigns." *IRIN Humanitarian News and Analysis*, 1 May 2008. http://www.irinnews.org/report/78003/zimbabwe-operation-glossary-a-guide-to-zimbabwe-s-internal-campaigns.

Zimudzi, Tapiwa. "Spies and Informers on Campus: Vetting, Surveillance and Deportation of Expatriate University Lecturers in Colonial Zimbabwe, 1954–1963." *Journal of Southern African Studies* 33 (March 2007): 193–208.